D1520930

VARRO

ON THE LATIN LANGUAGE

II

LCL 334

VARRO

ON THE LATIN LANGUAGE
BOOKS VIII–X; FRAGMENTS

WITH AN ENGLISH TRANSLATION BY
RONALD G. KENT

HARVARD UNIVERSITY PRESS
CAMBRIDGE, MASSACHUSETTS
LONDON, ENGLAND

First published 1938
Revised and reprinted 1951
Reprinted 1958, 1967, 1979, 1993, 1999, 2006

LOEB CLASSICAL LIBRARY® is a registered trademark
of the President and Fellows of Harvard College

ISBN 0-674-99368-3

Printed on acid-free paper and bound by
Edwards Brothers, Ann Arbor, Michigan

CONTENTS

VARRO

M. TERENTI VARRONIS
DE LINGUA LATINA

LIBER VII EXPLICIT ; INCIPIT

LIBER VIII

QUAE DICANTUR CUR NON SIT ANALOGIA LIBER I

I. 1. Quom oratio natura tripertita esset, ut su-
perioribus libris ostendi, cuius prima pars, quemadmodum vocabula rebus essent imposita, secunda, quo
pacto de his declinata in discrimina ierint,[1] tertia, ut
ea inter se ratione coniuncta sententiam efferant,
prima parte exposita de secunda incipiam hinc. Ut
propago omnis natura secunda, quod prius illud
rectum, unde ea, sic declinata : itaque declinatur in
verbis : rectum homo, obliquum hominis, quod declinatum a recto.

§ 1. [1] *Sciop., for* ierunt.

---

§ 1. [a] That is, bent aside and downward, from the vertical.
The Greeks conceived the paradigm of the noun as the upper
right quadrant of a circle : the nominative was the vertical
radius, and the other cases were radii which ' declined ' to
the right, and were therefore called πτώσεις ' fallings,' which
the Romans translated literally by *casus*. The *casus rectus*
is therefore a contradiction in itself. The Latin verb *de-*

370

MARCUS TERENTIUS VARRO'S ON THE LATIN LANGUAGE

BOOK VII ENDS HERE, AND HERE BEGINS

BOOK VIII

ONE BOOK OF ARGUMENTS WHICH ARE AD-
VANCED AGAINST THE EXISTENCE OF THE
PRINCIPLE OF ANALOGY

I. 1. SPEECH is naturally divided into three parts,
as I have shown in the previous books : its first part
is how names were imposed upon things ; its second,
in what way the derivatives of these names have
arrived at their differences ; its third. how the words,
when united with one another reasoningly, express an
idea. Having set forth the first part, I shall from
here begin upon the second. As every offshoot is
secondary by nature, because that vertical trunk from
which it comes is primary, and it is therefore
declined [a] : so there is declension in words : *homo*
' man ' is the vertical, *hominis* ' man's ' is the oblique,
because it is declined from the vertical.

---

clinare is used in the meanings ' to decline (a noun),' ' to
conjugate (a verb),' and ' to derive ' in general, as well as
' to bend aside and down ' in a literal physical sense : it
therefore offers great difficulties in translating.

2.   De huiusce⟨modi⟩[1] multiplici natura discriminum ⟨ca⟩usae[2] sunt hae, cur et quo et quemadmodum
in loquendo declinata sunt verba.   De quibus duo
prima duabus causis percurram breviter, quod et tum,
cum de copia verborum scribam, erit retractandum et
quod de tribus tertium quod est habet suas permultas
ac magnas partes.

II. 3.   Declinatio inducta in sermones non solum
Latinos, sed omnium hominum utili et necessaria de
causa : nisi enim ita esset factum, neque di⟨s⟩cere[1]
tantum numerum verborum possemus (infinitae enim
sunt naturae in quas ea declinantur) neque quae
didicissemus, ex his, quae inter se rerum cognatio
esset, appareret.   At nunc ideo videmus, quod simile
est, quod propagatum : legi ⟨c⟩um ⟨de lego⟩[2] declinatum est, duo simul apparent, quodam modo
eadem dici et non eodem tempore factum ; at[3] si
verbi gratia alterum horum diceretur Priamus, alterum
Hecuba, nullam unitatem adsignificaret, quae apparet in lego et legi et in Priamus Priamo.

4.   Ut in hominibus quaedam sunt agnationes ac[1]
gentilitates, sic in verbis : ut enim ab Aemilio homines
orti Aemilii ac gentiles, sic ab Aemilii nomine de-
clinatae voces in gentilitate nominali : ab eo enim,

---

§ 2.   [1] *Added by L. Sp.*   [2] *L. Sp., for* orae.
§ 3.   [1] *Mue., for* dicere ; *cf.* § 5.   [2] *GS., for* legium *F ;
cf.* declinatum est ab lego *Aug. from B, and last sentence of
this section.*   [3] *Mue., for* ut.
§ 4.   [1] *L. Sp., for* ad.

---

§ 2.   [a] *Cf.* viii. 9 *in* quas.   [b] That is, the collective
vocabulary.
§ 3.   [a] The term ' inflection ' will be convenient oftentimes
to express *declinatio*, including both declension of nouns and
conjugation of verbs.

2. From the manifold nature of this sort there are these causes of the differences : for what reason, and to what product,[a] and in what way, in speaking, the words are declined. The first two of these I shall pass over briefly, for two reasons : because there will have to be a rehandling of the topics when I write of the stock of words,[b] and because the third of them has numerous and extensive subdivisions of its own.

II. 3. Inflection [a] has been introduced not only into Latin speech, but into the speech of all men, because it is useful and necessary ; for if this system had not developed, we could not learn such a great number of words as we have learned—for the possible forms into which they are inflected are numerically unlimited—nor from those which we should have learned would it be clear what relationship existed between them so far as their meanings were concerned. But as it is, we do see, for the reason that that which is the offshoot bears a similarity to the original : when *legi* ' I have gathered ' is inflected from *lego* ' I gather,' two things are clear at the same time, namely that in some fashion the acts are said to be the same, and yet that their doing did not take place at the same time. But if, for the sake of a word, one of these two related ideas was called *Priamus* and the other *Hecuba*, there would be no indication of the unity of idea which is clear in *lego* and *legi*, and in nominative *Priamus*, dative *Priamo*.

4. As among men there are certain kinships, some through the males, others through the clan, so there are among words. For as from an Aemilius were sprung the men named Aemilius, and the clan-members of the name, so from the name of *Aemilius* were inflected the words in the noun-clan : for from that

373

quod est impositum recto casu *A*emilius, orta *A*emilii,
*A*emilium, *A*emilios, *A*emiliorum et sic reliquae eiusdem quae sunt stirpis.

5. Duo igitur omnino verborum principia, impositio ⟨et declinatio⟩,[1] alterum ut fons, alterum ut
rivus. Imposticia nomina esse voluerunt quam
paucissima, quo citius ediscere possent, declinata
quam plurima, quo facilius omnes quibus ad usum
opus esset[2] dicerent.[3]

6. Ad illud genus, quod prius, historia opus est :
nisi *di*scendo[1] enim aliter id *non*[2] pervenit ad nos ; ad
reliquum genus, quod posterius, ars : ad quam opus
est paucis praeceptis quae sunt brevia. Qua enim
ratione in uno vocabulo declinare didiceris, in infinito
numero nominum uti possis : itaque novis nominibus
allatis[3] ⟨in⟩[4] consuetudinem sine dubitatione eorum
declinatus statim omnis dicit populus ; etiam novicii
servi empti in magna familia cito omnium conser-
vorum ⟨n⟩om⟨i⟩na[5] recto casu accepto in reliquos
obliquos declinant.

7. Qui s⟨i⟩[1] non numquam offendunt, non est
mirum : et enim ill*i*[2] qui primi nomina imposuerunt
rebus fortasse an in quibusdam sint lapsi : voluis⟨se⟩
enim putant⟨ur⟩[3] singularis res notare, ut ex his in
multitudine⟨m⟩[4] declinaretur, ab homine homines ;

§ 5. [1] *Added by L. Sp., V, p.* [2] *Canal, for* essent.
[3] *Ed. Veneta, for* dicerentur.
§ 6. [1] *Stephanus, for* descendendo. [2] *For* idum.
[3] *For* allatius. [4] *Added by Aug.* [5] *Aug., for* omnes.
§ 7. [1] *Aldus, for* quid. [2] *Aldus, for* illa. [3] *Ellis,
for* putant. [4] -dinem *H, for* -dine *F and other codd.*

§ 7. [a] That is, in the singular.

name which was imposed in the nominative case as *Aemilius* were made *Aemilii, Aemilium, Aemilios, Aemiliorum*, and in this way also all the other words which are of this same line.

5. The origins of words are therefore two in number, and no more : imposition and inflection ; the one is as it were the spring, the other the brook. Men have wished that imposed nouns should be as few as possible, that they might be able to learn them more quickly ; but derivative nouns they have wished to be as numerous as possible, that all might the more easily say those nouns which they needed to use.

6. In connexion with the first class, a historical narrative is necessary, for except by outright learning such words do not reach us ; for the other class, the second, a grammatical treatment is necessary, and for this there is need of a few brief maxims. For the scheme by which you have learned to inflect in the instance of one noun, you can employ in a countless number of nouns : therefore when new nouns have been brought into common use, the whole people at once utters their declined forms without any hesitation. Moreover, those who have freshly become slaves and on purchase become members of a large household, quickly inflect the names of all their fellow-slaves in the oblique cases, provided only they have heard the nominative.

7. If they sometimes make mistakes, it is not astonishing. Even those who first imposed names upon things perhaps made some slips in some instances : for they are supposed to have desired to designate things individually,[a] that from these inflection might be made to indicate plurality, as *homines* ' men ' from *homo* ' man.' They are supposed to have

sic mares liberos voluisse notari, ut ex his feminae
declinarentur, ut est ab Terentio Terentia ; sic in
recto casu quas imponerent voces, ut illinc essent
futurae quo declinarentur : sed haec in omnibus
tenere nequisse, quod et una⟨e⟩ et ⟨binae⟩[5] dicuntur
scopae, et mas et femina aquila, et recto et obliquo
vocabulo vis.

8. Cur haec non tam si⟨n⟩t[1] in culpa quam putant,
pleraque solvere non difficile, sed nunc non necesse :
non enim qui potuerint adsequi sed qui voluerint, ad
hoc quod propositum refert, quod nihilo minus[2] declinari potest ab eo quod imposuerunt[3] scopae scopa-
⟨rum⟩,[4] quam si imposuissent scopa, ab eo scopae, sic
alia.

III. 9. Causa, inquam, cur eas[1] ab impositis
nominibus declinarint, quam ostendi ; sequitur, in
quas voluerint[2] declinari aut noluerint, ut generatim
ac summatim item informem. Duo enim genera
verborum, unum fecundum,[3] quod declinando multas
ex se parit disparilis formas, ut est lego legi[4] legam,

[5] *Mette ;* unae et duae *A. Sp. ;* unae *Mue. ; for* una et.
  § 8. [1] *Aug., with B, for* sit.   [2] *For* nichilominus.
[3] *For* imposiuerunt.   [4] *Reitzenstein, for* scopa.
  § 9. [1] *Laetus, M, for* eam.   [2] *Laetus deleted* declinarint
after voluerint.   [3] *Rhol., for* ferundum.   [4] *L. Sp., for*
legis *: cf.* § 3 *end.*

[b] The genitive.

desired that male children be designated in such a
way that from these the females might be indicated
by inflection, as the feminine *Terentia* from the
masculine *Terentius* ; and that similarly from the
names which they set in the nominative case, there
might be other forms to which they could arrive by
inflection. But they are supposed to have been
unable to hold fast to these principles in every-
thing, because the plural form *scopae* denotes either
one or two brooms, and *aquila* ' eagle ' denotes both
the male and the female, and *vis* ' force ' is used
for the nominative and for an oblique case [b] of
the word.

8. Why such words are not so much at fault as
men think, it is in most instances not hard to explain,
but it is not necessary to do so at this time ; for it is
not how they have been able to arrive at the words,
but how they wished to express themselves, that is of
import for the subject which is before us : inasmuch
as genitive *scoparum* can be no less easily derived from
the plural *scopae* which they did impose on the object
as its name, than if they had given it the name *scopa*
in the singular, and made the genitive *scopae* from
this—and other words likewise.

III. 9. The reason, I say, why they made these
inflected forms [a] from the names which they had set
upon things, is that which I have shown ; the next
point is for me to sketch by classes, but briefly, the
forms [a] at which they have wished to arrive by inflection, or have not wished to arrive. For there are two
classes of words, one fruitful, which by inflection produces from itself many different forms, as for example
lego ' I gather,' *legi* ' I have gathered,' *legam* ' I shall

§ 9.   [a] Understand *voces* with *eas* and with *quas.*

sic alia, alterum genus sterile, quod ex se parit nihil,[5]
ut est et iam[6] vix *cras*[7] magis cur.

10. Quarum rerum usus erat simplex, ⟨simplex⟩[1]
ibi etiam vocabuli declinatus, ut in qua domo unus
servus, uno servili op*u*st[2] nomine, in qua[3] multi, pluribus. Igitur et in his rebus qu*ae*[4] sunt nomina, quod
discrimina vocis plura, propagines plures, et in his
rebus quae copulae sunt ac iungunt[5] verba, quod non
opus fuit declinari in plura, fere singula sunt : uno
enim loro alligare possis vel hominem vel equum vel
aliud quod, quicquid est quod cum altero potest
colligari. Sic quod dicimus in loquendo " Consul fuit
Tullius et Antonius," eodem illo ' et ' omnis binos
consules collig*a*re[6] possumus, vel dicam amplius,
omnia nomina, atque *a*deo[7] etiam omnia verba, cum
fulmentu*m*[8] ex una syllaba illud ' et ' maneat unum.
Quare duce natura ⟨factum⟩*st*,[9] quae imposita essent
vocabula rebus, ne ab omnibus his declina*t*us[10] puta-
re*mus*.[11]

IV. 11. Quorum[1] generum declinationes oriantur,
partes orationis sunt duae, ⟨ni⟩si[2] item ut D*i*on in
tris diviserimus partes res quae verbis significantur :

---

[5] *For* nichil.   [6] *GS., for* etiam.   [7] *L. Sp., for* vixerat;
cf. vix magis cras *Aug., with B.*
 § 10. [1] *Added by Sciop.*   [2] servili *L. Sp.*, opust *Sciop.,
for* seruilio post.   [3] *B, for* quam.   [4] *L. Sp., for* quorum.
[5] *Mue., for* iunguntur.   [6] *Aug., for* colligere.   [7] *Sciop.,
for* ideo.   [8] *Mue., for* fulmen tunc.   [9] *L. Sp., for* si.
[10] *Laetus, for* declinandus.   [11] *Fay, for* putarent.
 § 11. [1] *Laetus, for* quarum.   [2] *Roehrscheidt, for* si.

---

[b] The invariable and indeclinable words.
 § 10. [a] *Cf.* the *Marcipor* ' Marcus' boy,' of earlier times.
[b] In 63 B.C. ; the example compliments Cicero, to whom the
work is addressed.   [c] That is, we should expect some words
to be invariable and uninflected.

gather,' and similarly other words ; and a second class which is barren,[b] which produces nothing from itself, as for example *et* ' and,' *iam* ' now,' *vix* ' hardly,' *cras* ' to-morrow,' *magis* ' more,' *cur* 'why.'

10. In those things whose use was simple, the inflection of the name also was simple ; just as in a house where there is only one slave there is need of only one slave-name,[a] but in a house where there are many slaves there is need of many such names. Therefore also in those things which are names, because the differentiations of the word are several, there are more offshoots, and in those things which are connectives and join words, because there was no need for them to be inflected into several forms, the words generally have but one form : for with one and the same thong you can fasten a man or a horse or anything else, whatever it is, which can be fastened to something else. Thus, for example, we say in our talking, " Tullius *et* ' and ' Antonius were consuls " [b] : with that same *et* we can link together any set of two consuls, or—to put it more strongly—any and all names, and even all words, while all the time that one-syllabled prop-word *et* remains unchanged. Therefore under nature's guidance it has come about that we should not think that there are inflected forms from all these names which have been set upon things.[c]

IV. 11. In the word-classes in which inflections may develop, the parts of speech are two, unless, following Dion,[a] we divide into three divisions the ideas which are indicated by words : one division

§ 11. [a] An Academic philosopher of Alexandria, who headed an embassy to Rome in 56 to seek help against the exiled king Ptolemy Auletes, and was there poisoned by the king's agents.

VARRO

un*am*[3] quae adsignificat ca*s*us,[4] alter*am*[5] quae tempora, tertia⟨m⟩[6] quae neutrum. De his Aristoteles orationis duas partes esse dicit : vocabula et verba, ut homo et equus, et legit et currit.

12. Utriusque generis, et vocabuli et verbi, quaedam priora, quaedam posteriora ; priora ut homo, scribit, posteriora ut doctus et docte : dicitur enim homo doctus et scribit docte. Haec sequitur locus et tempus, quod neque homo nec scribi⟨t⟩[1] potest sine loco et tempore esse, ita ut magis sit locus homini coniunctus, tempus scriptioni.

13. Cum de his nomen sit primum (prius enim nomen est quam verbum temporale et reliqua posterius quam nomen et verbum), prima igitur nomina : quare de eorum declinatione quam de verborum ante dicam.

V. 14. Nomina declinantur aut in earum rerum discrimina, quarum nomina sunt, ut ab Terentius Terenti⟨a⟩,[1] aut in ea⟨s⟩[2] res extrinsecus, quarum ea nomina non sunt, ut ab equo equiso. In sua discrimina declinantur aut propter ipsius rei naturam de

---

[3] *B, for* unum.   [4] *Laetus, for* capus.   [5] *Laetus, B, for* alterum.   [6] *Mue., for* tertia.
§ 12.   [1] *B, H, Laetus, for* scribi.
§ 14.   [1] *Reitzenstein, for* Terenti ; *cf.* ix. 55, 59.   [2] *V, p, Laetus, for* ea.

---

[b] A division into nouns, verbs, and *convinctiones* went back to Aristotle, according to Quintilian, *Inst. Orat.* i. 4. 18 (*cf.* also Priscian, ii. 54. 5 Keil) ; but more detailed classifications of the parts of speech had also been made before Varro's time.   [c] *Rhet.* iii. 2 ; but *cf.* preceding note.
§ 12.   [a] That is, grammatically subordinate in the phrase.
§ 13.   [a] Since *verbum* means both ' word ' in general, and

which indicates also case, a second which indicates also time, a third which indicates neither.[b] Of these, Aristotle[c] says that there are two parts of speech ; nouns, like *homo* ' man ' and *equus* ' horse,' and verbs, like *legit* ' gathers ' and *currit* ' runs.'

12. Of the two kinds, noun and verb, certain words are primary and certain are secondary[a] : primary like *homo* ' man ' and *scribit* ' writes,' and secondary like *doctus* ' learned ' and *docte* ' learnedly,' for we say *homo doctus* ' a learned man ' and *scribit docte* ' writes learnedly.' These ideas are attended by those of place and time, because neither *homo* nor *scribit* can be asserted without the presupposition of place and of time—yet in such a way that place is more closely associated with the idea of the noun *homo*, and time more closely with the act of writing.

13. Since among these the noun is first—for the noun comes ahead of the verb,[a] and the other words stand later relatively to the noun and the verb—the nouns are accordingly first. Therefore I shall speak of the form-variations[b] of nouns before I take up those of verbs.

V. 14. Nouns are varied in form either to show differences in those things of which they are the names, as the woman's name *Terentia* from the man's name *Terentius*, or to denote those things outside, of which they are not the names, as *equiso* ' stable-boy ' from *equus* ' horse.' To show differences in themselves they are varied in form either on account of the nature of the thing itself about which mention is

---

' verb ' specifically, Varro here writes *verbum temporale* to avoid any ambiguity.   [b] *Declinatio* denotes not only declension, but conjugation of verbs, derivation by prefixes and suffixes, and composition.

qu*a*[3] dicitur aut propter illius ⟨usum⟩[4] qui dicit.
Propter ipsius rei discrimina, aut ab toto ⟨aut a parte.
Quae a toto, declinata sunt aut propter multitudinem
aut propter exiguitatem.   Propter exiguitatem⟩,[5] ut
ab homine homunculus, ab capite capitulum ; propter
multitudinem, ut ab homine homines ; ab eo ⟨abeo⟩[6]
quod alii dicunt cervices et id *H*ortensius in poematis
cervix.

15.   Quae a p*a*rte[1] declinata, aut a corpore, ut a
mamma mammosae, a manu manubria, aut ab animo,
ut a prudentia pruden⟨te⟩s,[2] ab ingenio ingeniosi.
Haec sine agitationibus ; at ubi motus maiores, item
ab animo ⟨aut a corpore⟩,[3] ut ab strenuitate et nobili-
tate strenui et nobiles, sic a pugnando et currendo
pugiles et cursores.   Ut aliae declinationes ab animo,
aliae a corpore, sic aliae quae extra hominem, ut
pecuniosi, agrarii, quod foris pecunia et ager.

VI. 16.   Propter eorum qui dicunt usum[1] declinati
casus, uti is qui de altero diceret, distinguere posset,

---

[3] *Vertranius, for* quo.   [4] *Added by GS., following Reitzenstein, who added it after* dicit.   [5] *Added by Reitzenstein ;*
aut a parte.   ab toto *added by L. Sp., after Aug., who
added* aut a parte.   a toto, *suggested to him by B* aut a parte
aut ab animo.   a toto.   [6] *Added by Fay.*
§ 15.   [1] *For* aperte.   [2] *L. Sp., for* prudens.   [3] *Added
by L. Sp.*
§ 16.   [1] *Vertranius, for* dicuntur sum.

---

§ 14.   [a] That is, syntactical variations, indicated by the
case-forms.   [b] Other categories resulting in variations
might have been listed.   [c] *Frag. Poet. Lat.*, page 91 Morel.
[d] As did also Ennius and Pacuvius, before Hortensius ; the
plural was the only regularly used form, outside the poets.
§ 15.   [a] We expect rather a plural adjective meaning ' big-
handed.'   [b] The long abstract nouns are of course derived
from the adjectives.   [c] Or perhaps in the original meaning
' farmers.'

made, or on account of the use to which the speaker puts the word.[a] On account of differences in the thing itself, the variation is made either with reference to the whole thing, or with reference to a part of it. Those forms which concern the whole are derived either on account of plurality or on account of small-ness.[b] On account of smallness, *homunculus* ' mani-kin ' is formed from *homo* ' man,' and *capitulum* ' little head ' from *caput* ' head.' On account of plurality, *homines* ' men ' is made from *homo* ' man ' ; I pass by the fact that others use *cervices* ' muscles of the neck and shoulders ' in the plural, and Hortensius [c] in his poems uses it in the singular *cervix*.[d]

15. Those which are derived from a part, come either from the body, as *mammosae* ' big-breasted women ' from *mamma* ' breast ' and *manubria* [a] ' handles ' from *manus* ' hand,' or from the mind, as *prudentes* ' prudent men ' from *prudentia* ' prudence ' and *ingeniosi* ' men of talent ' from *ingenium* ' innate ability.' The preceding are quite apart from move-ments ; but where there are important motions, the derivatives are similarly from the mind or from the body, as *strenui* ' the quick ' and *nobiles* ' the noble,' from *strenuitas* ' quickness ' and *nobilitas* ' nobility,' [b] and in this way also *pugiles* ' boxers ' and *cursores* ' runners ' from *pugnare* ' to fight ' and *currere* ' to run.' As some derivations are from the mind and others from the body, so also there are others which refer to external things, as *pecuniosi* ' moneyed men ' and *agrarii* [c] ' advocates of agrarian laws,' because *pecunia* ' money ' and *ager* ' field-land ' are exterior to the men to whom the derivatives are applied.

VI. 16. It was for the use of the speakers that the case-forms were derived, that he who spoke of another

383

VARRO

cum vocaret, cum daret, cum accusaret, sic alia eiusdem ⟨modi⟩[2] discrimina, quae nos et Graecos ad declinandum duxerunt. Sine[3] controversia ⟨sunt obliqui, qui nascuntur a recto : unde rectus an sit casus⟩[4] sunt qui quae⟨rant. Nos vero sex habemus, Graeci quinque⟩ [4] : quis vocetur, ut *Hercules* ; quemadmodum vocetur, ut *Hercule* ; quo vocetur, ut ad *Herculem* ; a quo vocetur, ut ab *Hercule* ; cui vocetur, ut *Herculi* ; cuius vocetur, ut *Herculis*.

VII. 17. Propter ea verba quae erant proinde ac cognomina, ut prudens, candidus, strenuus, quod in his praeterea sunt discrimina propter incrementum, quod maius aut minus in his esse potest, accessit declinationum genus, ut a candido candidius candidissimum sic a longo, divite, id genus aliis ut fieret.

18. Quae in eas res quae extrinsecus declinantur, sunt ab equo equile, ab ovibus ovile, sic alia : haec contraria illis quae supra dicta, ut a pecunia pecunio-

---

[2] *Added by Mue.*   [3] *For* sinae.   [4] *Added by Schoell apud GS. ; cf. note b.*

§ 16.   [a] Vocative, dative, accusative cases ; the accusative was in Latin a poorly named case, through a mistranslation of its Greek name.   [b] The only controversy was whether or not the nominative was to be called a case, and the text must be expanded to conform to this basic fact ; *cf.* Charisius, i. 154. 6-8 Keil, Priscian, ii. 185. 12-14 Keil, etc. *Cf.* viii. 1 note *a*, above.   [c] The Greeks had no ablative case.

§ 17.   [a] Nowhere recorded as a cognomen, despite Varro.   [b] Recorded as a cognomen in the Claudian and the Julian gentes, and in several others.   [c] Not recorded as a cognomen.   [d] Namely, comparison of adjectives.   [e] For such cognomina, *cf. Fulvius Nobilior* and *Fabius Maximus.* [f] *i.e.*, adjectives.

384

might be able to make a distinction when he was
calling, when he was giving, when he was accusing,[a]
and other differences of this same sort, which led us as
well as the Greeks to the declension of nouns. The
oblique forms which develop from the nominative are
without dispute to be called cases ; but there are
those who question whether the nominative is properly
a case.[b] At any rate, we have six forms, and the
Greeks five [c] : he who is called, as (nominative) *Hercules* ; how the calling is done, as (vocative) *Hercule* ;
whither there is a calling, as to (accusative) *Herculem* ;
by whom the calling is done, as by (ablative) *Hercule* ;
to or for whom there is a calling, as to or for (dative)
Herculi ; of whom the calling or called object is, as of
(genitive) *Herculis*.

VII. 17. There are certain words which are like
added family names, such as *Prudens* [a] ' prudent,'
Candidus [b] ' frank,' *Strenuus* [c] ' brisk,' and in them
differences may be shown by a suffix, since the quality
may be present in them to a greater or a smaller
degree : therefore to these words a kind of inflection [d]
is attached, so that from *candidum* ' shining white '
comes the comparative *candidius* and the superlative
candidissimum,[e] formed in the same way as similar
forms from *longum* ' long,' *dives* ' rich,' and other
words of this kind.[f]

18. The terms which are derived for application
to exterior objects, are for example *equile* ' horse-
stable ' from *equus* ' horse,' *ovile* ' sheepfold ' from
oves ' sheep,' and others in this same way ; these are
the opposite of those which I mentioned above,[a] such

§ 18. [a] Here, objects named by derivation from living
beings ; in § 15, living beings named by derivation from
inanimate objects.

sus, ab urbe urbanus, ab atro atratus : ut nonnunquam ab homine locus, ab eo loco homo, ut ab Romulo Roma, ab Roma Romanus.

19. Aliquot modis declinata ea quae foris : nam aliter qui a maioribus suis, Laton⟨i⟩us[1] et Priamidae, aliter quae ⟨a⟩[2] facto, ut a praedando praeda, a merendo merces ; sic alia sunt, quae circum ire non difficile ; sed quod genus iam videtur et alia urgent, omitto.

VIII. 20. In verborum genere quae tempora adsignificant, quod ea erant tria, praeteritum, praesens, futurum, declinatio facienda fuit triplex, ut ab saluto salutabam, salutabo ; cum item personarum natura triplex esset, qui loqueretur, ⟨ad quem⟩,[1] de quo, haec ab eodem verbo declinata, quae in copia verborum explicabuntur.

IX. 21. Quoniam dictum de duobus, declinatio[1] cur et in qua⟨s⟩[2] sit facta,[3] tertium quod relinquitur,

§ 19.   [1] p, Laetus, for latonus F.   [2] Added by Aug., with B.
§ 20.   [1] Added by Laetus after de quo, and transferred to this position by Mue.
§ 21.   [1] Mue., for duabus declinationibus.   [2] Kent, for qua ; cf. in quas viii. 9.   [3] A. Sp., for fama.

---

[b] Romulus is derived from Roma, not the reverse, as Varro has it.
§ 19.   [a] Apollo : but oftener Latonia (fem.), Diana.
[b] Especially Hector, Paris, Helenus, Deiphobus.   [c] Cf. v. 44.
§ 20.   [a] That is, verbs.

as *pecuniosus* ' moneyed man ' from *pecunia* ' money,'
urbanus ' city man ' from *urbs* ' city,' *atratus* ' clad in
mourning ' from *atrum* ' black.' Thus sometimes a
place is named from a man, and then a man from this
place, as Rome from Romulus [b] and then Roman
from Rome.

19. The nouns which relate to exterior objects are
derived in sundry ways : those like *Latonius* ' Latona's
child ' [a] and *Priamidae* ' Priam's sons,' [b] which are
derived from the names of their progenitors, are
formed in one way, and those which come from an
action are made in another way, such as *praeda*
' booty ' from *praedari* ' to pillage ' and *merces* ' wages ' [c]
from *mereri* ' to earn.' In the same way there are
still others, which can be enumerated without difficulty ; but because this category of words is now
clear to the understanding and other matters press
for attention, I pass them by.

VIII. 20. Inasmuch as in the class of words which
indicate also time-ideas [a] there were these three
time-ideas, past, present, and future, there had to be
three sets of derived forms, as from the present *saluto*
' I salute ' there are the past *salutabam* and the future
salutabo. Since the persons of the verb were likewise
of three natures, the one who was speaking, the one
to whom the speaking was done, and the one about
whom the speaking took place, there are these derivative forms of each and every verb ; and these forms
will be expounded in the account of the stock of verbs
which is in use.

IX. 21. Since two points have been discussed, why
derivation exists and to what products it eventuates,
the remaining third point shall now be spoken of,
namely, how and in what manner derivation takes

quemadmodum, nunc dicetur.[4] Declinationum genera
sunt duo, voluntarium et naturale ; voluntarium est,
quo ut cuiusque tulit voluntas declinavit. Sic tres
cum emerunt Ephesi singulos servos, nonnunquam
alius declinat nomen ab eo qui vendit Artemidorus,
atque Artemam appellat, alius a regione quod ibi
emit, ab Ion⟨i⟩a[5] Iona,[6] alius quod Ephesi Ephesium,
sic alius ab alia aliqua re, ut visum est.

22. Contra naturalem declinationem dico, quae
non a singulorum oritur voluntate, sed a com⟨m⟩uni
consensu. Itaque omnes impositis nominibus eorum
item declinant casus atque eodem modo dicunt huius
Artemidori[1] et huius Ionis et huius Ephesi,[2] sic in
casibus aliis.

23. Cum utrumque nonnunquam accidat, et ut in
voluntaria declinatione animadvertatur natura et in
naturali voluntas, quae, cuiusmodi sint, aperientur
infra ; quod utraque declinatione alia fiunt similia,
alia dissimilia, de eo Graeci Latinique libros fecerunt
multos, partim cum alii putarent in loquendo ea verba
sequi oportere, quae ab similibus similiter essent
declinata, quas appellarunt ἀναλογίας,[1] alii cum id

---

[4] *Aug., for* dicitur.   [5] *Laetus, for* Iona.   [6] *Mue., for*
Ionam.

§ 22.   [1] *Apparently Varro's own slip for* Artemae.
[2] *Rhol., for* Ephesis.

§ 23.   [1] *For* analogiias.

---

§ 21.   [a] This term includes both word-formation and word-
inflection.   [b] Practically equal to subjective and objective.
[c] A common type of hypocoristic or nickname, *cf. Demas*
from *Democritus* and similar names, *Hippias* from *Hip-
parchus*, etc.

§ 22.   [a] This is inflection.   [b] Specifically, declension.
§ 23.   [a] *Cf.* viii. 15-16, 51.   [b] *Cf.* page 118 Funaioli.

place. There are two kinds of derivation,[a] voluntary and natural.[b] Voluntary derivation is that which is the product of the individual person's volition, directing itself apart from control by others. So, when three men have bought a slave apiece at Ephesus, sometimes one derives his slave's name from that of the seller Artemidorus and calls him *Artemas*[c]; another names his slave *Ion*, from Ionia the district, because he has bought him there; the third calls his slave *Ephesius*, because he has bought him at Ephesus. In this way each derives the name from a different source, as he preferred.

22. On the other hand I call that derivation natural, which is based not on the volition of individuals acting singly, but on general agreement.[a] So, when the names have been fixed, they derive the case-forms of them in like fashion,[b] and in one and the same way they all say in the genitive case *Artemidori*, *Ionis*, *Ephesi*; and so on in the other cases.

23. Sometimes both are found together, and in such a way that in the voluntary derivation the processes of nature are noted, and in the natural derivation the effects of volition; of what sort these are, will be recounted below.[a] Since in the two kinds of derivation some things approach likeness and others become unlike, the Greeks and the Latins[b] have written many books on the subject: in some of them certain writers express the idea that in speaking men ought to follow those words and forms which are derived in similar fashion from like starting-points— which they called the products of Analogy[c]; and

---

[c] The regularizing principle which tends to eliminate irregular forms of less frequent occurrence, still called Analogy, by scientific linguists.

389

neglegendum putarent ac potius sequendam ⟨dis⟩-
similitudinem,² quae in consuetudine est, quam
vocarunt³ ἀ⟨ν⟩ωμαλίαν ,⁴ cum, ut ego arbitror, utrumque sit nobis sequendum, quod ⟨in⟩⁵ declinatione
voluntaria sit anomalia, in naturali magis analogia.

24. De quibus utriusque generis declinationibus
libros faciam bis ternos, prioris tris de earum declinationum disciplina, posteriores *de*¹ eius disciplinae
propaginibus. De prioribus primus erit hic, quae
contra similitudinem declinationum dicantur, secundus, quae contra dissimilitudinem, tertius de similitudinum forma ; de quibus quae expe*diero*² singulis
tribus, tum de alteris totidem scribere ac dividere³
incipiam.

X. 25. Quod huiusce¹ libri est dicere contra eos
qui similitudinem sequuntur, quae est ut in aetate
puer ad senem, ⟨puella⟩² ad anum, in verbis ut est
scribo scribam,³ dicam prius contra universam analogiam, dein tum de singulis partibus. A natura
sermo⟨nis⟩⁴ incipiam.

XI. 26. Omnis oratio cum debeat dirigi ad utilitatem, ad quam tum denique pervenit, si est aperta

---

² *Aug., with B, for* similitudinem.   ³ *For* vocarum.
⁴ *Aldus, for* ΛωΜΑϵΝΑΝ.   ⁵ *Added by Aug.*
§ 24. ¹ *L. Sp., for* ex.   ² *Mue. ;* expedierint *Aug. ; for*
experiero.   ³ *L. Sp. deleted* incipimus *after* dividere.
§ 25. ¹ *For* huiuscae.   ² *Added by Aldus.*   ³ *L. Sp.
deleted* dico *after* scribam.   ⁴ *Aug., for* sermo.

---

d The irregularities summed up in this term are the products
of the regular working of ' phonetic law,' unrestrained by the
operation of Analogy ; the term Anomaly names it from
the product rather than from the working process.   *e* It
seems better henceforth to translate *analogia* by Regularity
or the like, rather than to keep the word Analogy.

others are of opinion that this should be disregarded and rather men should follow the dissimilar and irregular, which is found in ordinary habitual speech —which they called the product of Anomaly.[d] But in my opinion we ought to follow both, because in voluntary derivation there is Anomaly, and in the natural derivation there is even more strikingly Regularity.[e]

24. About these two kinds of derivation I shall write two sets of three books each : the first three about the principles of these derivations, and the latter set about the products of these principles. In the former set the first book will contain the views which may be offered against likeness in derivation and declension ; the second will contain the arguments against unlikeness ; the third will be about the shape and manner of the likenesses. What I have set in order on these topics, I shall write in the three separate books ; then on the second set of topics I shall begin to write, with due division into the same number of books.

X. 25. Inasmuch as it is the task of this book to speak against those who follow likeness [a]—which is like the relation of boy to old man in the matter of human life, and like that of girl to old woman, and in verbs is the relation of *scribo* ' I write ' and *scribam* ' I shall write '—I shall speak first against Regularity in general, and then thereafter concerning its several subdivisions. I shall begin with the nature of human speech.

XI. 26. All speaking ought to be aimed at practical utility, and it attains this only if it is clear

§ 25. [a] That is, regularity of paradigms resulting from the process of Analogy.

et brevis, quae petimus, quod obscurus[1] et longi⟨or⟩[2] orator est odio; et cum efficiat aperta, ut intellegatur, brevis, ut[3] cito intellegatur, et aperta⟨m⟩[4] consuetudo, brevem temperantia loquentis, et utrumque fieri possit sine analogia, nihil[5] ea opus est. Neque enim, utrum Herculi an Herculis clavam dici oporteat, si doceat analogia, cum utrumque sit in consuetudine, non neglegendum,[6] quod aeque sunt et brevi⟨a⟩ et aperta.

XII. 27. Praeterea quoius[1] utilitatis causa quaeque res sit inventa, si ex ea quis id sit consecutus, amplius ea⟨m⟩[2] scrutari cum sit nimium otiosi, et cum utilitatis causa verba ideo sint imposita rebus ut ea⟨s⟩[3] significent, si id consequimur una consuetudine, nihil[4] prodest analogia.

XIII. 28. Accedit[1] quod quaecumque usus causa ad vitam sint assumpta, in his no⟨strumst⟩[2] utilitatem quaerere, non similitudinem : itaque in vestitu cum dissimillima sit virilis toga tunica⟨e⟩,[3] muliebri⟨s⟩[4] stola pallio, tamen inaequabilitatem hanc sequimur[5] nihilo[6] minus.

XIV. 29. In aedificiis, quom[1] non videamus habere

<hr>

§ 26. [1] *Aldus, for* obscurum. [2] *GS., for* longi (*Aldus* longus). [3] *Aldus, for* et. [4] *Aug., for* aperta. [5] *For* nichil. [6] *Aug. deleted* sunt *after* neglegendum.

§ 27. [1] *Mue., for* quod ius. [2] *Aug., for* ea. [3] *Vertranius, for* ea. [4] *For* nichil.

§ 28. [1] *Aldus, for* accidit. [2] *Fay, for* non. [3] *Laetus, for* tunica. [4] *Cuper, for* muliebri. [5] *Aug., with B, for* sequitur. [6] *For* nichilo.

§ 29. [1] *Mue.;* quod quom *L. Sp.; for* quod.

and brief : characteristics which we seek, because
an obscure and longish speaker is disliked. And
since clear speaking causes the utterance to be
understood, and brief speaking causes it to be understood quickly, and since also habitual use makes the
utterance clear and the speaker's self-restraint makes
it brief, and both these can be present without Regularity, there is no need of this Regularity. For if
Regularity should instruct us whether we ought to
say *Herculi* [a] or *Herculis* for the genitive, as in the
phrase ' the club of Hercules,' we must not fail to
disregard its teaching, since both are in habitual use,
and both forms are equally short and clear.

XII. 27. Besides, if from a thing one has secured
that useful service for which it was invented, it is the
act of a person with a great deal of idle time, to
examine it further ; and since the useful service for
which names are set upon things is that the names
should designate the things, then if we secure this
result by habitual use alone, Regularity adds no gain.

XIII. 28. There is the additional fact that in
those things which are taken into our daily life for
use, it is our practice to seek utility and not to seek
resemblance ; thus in the matter of clothing, although
a man's *toga* [a] is very unlike his tunic,[b] and a woman's
stola [c] is very unlike a *pallium*,[d] we make no objection
to the difference.

XIV. 29. In the case of buildings, although we do

§ 26. [a] This form occurs in Plautus, *Persa* 2, *Rudens* 822,
and in other authors.
§ 28. [a] The formal outer garment of a Roman man.
[b] A shirt or undergarment.   [c] The dress of a Roman
matron.   [d] The long outer garment of the Greeks, properly
a man's garb only, but worn also by prostitutes both in
Greece and in Italy as a sign of their livelihood.

⟨ad⟩[2] atrium περίστυλον[3] similitudinem et cubiculum
ad equile,[4] tamen propter utilitatem in his dissimilitudines potius quam similitudines sequimur[5] : itaque
et hiberna triclinia et aestiva non item valvata ac
fenestrata facimus.

XV. 30.   Quare cum, ut[1] in vestitu aedificiis, sic in
supellectile cibo ceterisque omnibus quae usus ⟨causa⟩[2]
ad vitam sunt assumpta dominetur inaequabilitas, in
sermone quoque, qui est usus causa constitutus, ea
non repudianda.

XVI. 31.   Quod si quis duplicem putat esse summam, ad quas metas[1] naturae sit perveniendum in usu,
utilitatis et elegantiae, quod non solum vestiti esse
volumus ut vitemus frigus, sed etiam ut videamur vestiti
esse honeste, non domum habere ut simus in tecto et
tuto solum, quo[2] necessitas contruserit, sed etiam ubi
voluptas retineri possit, non solum vasa ad victum
habilia, sed etiam figura bella atque ab artifice ⟨ficta⟩,[3]
quod aliud homini, aliud humanitati satis est ; quod-
vis sitienti homini poculum idoneum, humanitati
⟨ni⟩si[4] bellum parum ; sed cum discessum e⟨s⟩t[5] ab
utilitate ad voluptatem, tamen in eo ex dissimilitudine
plus voluptatis quam ex similitudine saepe capitur.

32.   Quo nomine et gemina conclavia dissimiliter

<hr/>

[2] *Added by L. Sp.*   [3] *For* ΠεΡΗCΤhΛΟΝ.   [4] *Mue.
deleted* quod *after* equile.   [5] *V, p, Mue., for* sequamur.
§ 30.   [1] *Stephanus, for* et.   [2] *Added by L. Sp.*
§ 31.   [1] *For* maetas.   [2] *Aug. (quoting a friend), for*
quod.   [3] *Fay ;* facta *L. Sp. ; to fill a blank space in F of
about 4 letters.*   [4] *Aldus, for* si.   [5] *Aug., with B, for* et.

<hr/>

§ 29.   [a] The garden in the rear part of the house, surrounded
by colonnaded porticos.   [b] The main hall in the front of
the house, with a central opening to the sky under which
there was a rectangular water-basin built in the floor.

not see the persistyle [a] bearing resemblance to the atrium [b] nor the sleeping-room bearing resemblance to the horse-stable, still, on account of the utility in them we seek for unlikenesses rather than likenesses ; so also we provide winter dining-rooms and summer dining-rooms with a different equipment of doors and windows.

XV. 30. Therefore, since difference prevails not only in clothing and in buildings, but also in furniture, in food, and in all the other things which have been taken into our daily life for use, the principle of difference should not be rejected in human speech either, which has been framed for the purpose of use.

XVI. 31. But if one should think that the sum of those natural goals to which we ought to attain in actual use consists of two items, that of utility and that of refinement, because we wish to be clothed not only to avoid cold but also to appear to be decently clothed ; and we wish to have a house not merely that we may be under a roof and in a safe place into which necessity has crowded us together, but also that we may be where we may continue to experience the pleasures of life ; and we wish to have table-vessels that are not merely suitable to hold our food, but also beautiful in form and shaped by an artist—for one thing is enough for the human animal, and quite another thing satisfies human refinement : any cup at all is satisfactory to a man parched with thirst, but any cup is inferior to the demands of refinement unless it is artistically beautiful :—but as we have digressed from the matter of utility to that of pleasure, it is a fact that in such a case greater pleasure is often got from difference of appearance than from likeness.

32. On this account, identical rooms are often

poli*u*nt[1] et lectos non omnis paris magnitudine ac
figura faciunt. Quod ⟨si⟩[2] esset[3] analogia petenda
supellectili, omnis lectos haberemus domi ad unam
formam et aut cum fulcro aut sine eo, nec cum ad
tricliniarem gradum, non item ad cubicularem ; neque
potius delectaremur supellectile distincta quae esset
ex ebore ⟨aliisve⟩[4] rebus disparibus figuris quam
grabatis,[5] qui ἀνὰ λόγον[6] ad similem formam plerumque eadem materia fiunt. Quare aut negandum
nobis disparia esse iucunda aut, quoniam necesse est
confiteri, dicendum verborum dissimilitudine⟨m⟩,
quae sit in consuetudine,[7] non esse vitandam.

XVII. 33.   Quod si analogia sequenda est nobis,
aut ea observanda est quae est in consuetudine aut
quae non est. Si ea quae est sequenda est, praeceptis nihil[1] opus est, quod, cum consuetudinem
sequemur, ea nos sequetur ; si quae non est in consuetudine, qu*a*eremus : ut quisque duo verba in
quattuor formis finxer*i*t[2] similiter, quamvis haec
nolemus, tamen erunt sequenda, ut Iuppit⟨r⟩i,[3]
Marspitrem ? Quas si quis servet analogias, pro
insano sit reprehendendus. Non ergo ea est sequenda.

§ 32.   [1] *Koeler, for* pollent.   [2] *Added by Laetus.*
[3] *Laetus, for* essent.   [4] *Fay ;* aliisque *Laetus ; to fill a
blank space of about 4 letters in F ; cf.* ix. 47.   [5] *For*
grabattis.   [6] *Mue., for* analogon *; cf.* x. 2.   [7] *For*
consuetudinem.
§ 33.   [1] *For* nichil.   [2] *Vertranius, for* finxerunt.   [3] *L.
Sp., for* Iuppiti.

§ 33.   [a] Namely, genitive, dative, accusative, ablative,
from the nominative as starting-point.   [b] Such forms,
retaining and inflecting the *pater* which forms the second

ornamented in unlike manner, and couches are not all made the same in size and shape. But if Regularity were to be sought in furniture, we should have all the couches in the house made in one fashion, and either with posts or without them, and when we had a couch suited for use beside the dining-table, we should not fail to have just the same for bedroom use ; nor should we rather be delighted with furniture which was decorated with varying figures of ivory or other materials, any more than in camp-beds, which with regularity are almost always made of the same material and in the same shape. Therefore either we must deny that differences give pleasure, or, since we must admit that they do, we must say that the un-likeness in words which is found in habitual usage, is not something to be avoided.

XVII. 33. But if we must follow Regularity, either we must observe that Regularity which is present in ordinary usage, or we must observe also that which is not found there. If we must follow that which is present, there is no need of rules, because when we follow usage, Regularity attends us. But if we ought to follow the Regularity which is not present in ordinary usage, then we shall ask, When any one has made two words in four forms [a] according to the same pattern, must we employ them just the same, even though we do not wish to—as for example a dative *Iuppitri* and an accusative *Marspitrem* ? [b] If any one should persist in using such ' regular forms,' he ought to be rebuked as crazy. This kind of Regularity, therefore, is not to be followed.

part of *Iuppiter* and *Marspiter*, are quite abnormal, and are found chiefly in the grammarians as examples of forms which are not to be used.

VARRO

XVIII. 34.   Quod si oportet id es⟨se⟩,[1] ut a similibus similiter omnia declinentur verba, sequitur, ut ab
dissimilibus[2] dissimilia debeant fingi, quod non fit :
nam et ⟨ab⟩[3] similibus alia fiunt similia, alia dissimilia, et ab dissimilibus partim similia partim dissimilia.   Ab similibus similia, ut a bono et malo
bonum malum ; ab similibus dissimilia, ut ab lupus
lepus lupo lepori.   Contra[4] ab dissimilibus dissimilia,
ut Priamus Paris, Priamo Pari ; ab dissimilibus
similia, ut Iupiter ovis, Iovi ovi.

35.   Eo iam magis analogias ⟨esse negandum,[1]
quod non modo ab similibus⟩[2] dissimilia finguntur, sed
etiam ab isdem[3] vocabulis dissimilia neque a dissimilibus similia, sed etiam eadem.   Ab isdem[4] vocabulis dissimilia fingi apparet, quod, cum duae sint
Albae, ab una dicuntur Albani, ab altera Albenses ;
cum trinae fuerint Athenae, ab una dicti Athenae⟨i⟩,[5]
ab altera Athenaiis, a tertia Athenaeopolitae.

36.   Sic ex diversis verbis multa facta in declinando
inveniuntur eadem, ut cum dico ab Saturni Lua Luam,

§ 34.   [1] id esse *Canal ;* ita esse *Mue., for* id est.   [2] *L.
Sp., for* his similibus.   [3] *Added by L. Sp. ;* a *Aug., with B.*
[4] *Aug., for* contraria.
§ 35.   [1] *Added by L. Sp.*   [2] *Added by Christ, who has*
non solum a, *for which Groth, citing L. Sp., gives* non modo
ab.   [3] *Mue. ;* iisdem *Laetus ; for* hisdem.   [4] *For*
hisdem.   [5] *Laetus, for* Athenae.

§ 34.   [a] Or accusative masculine.
§ 35.   [a] Inhabitants of *Alba Longa.*   [b] Inhabitants of
Alba Fucens or *Fucentia,* among the *Aequi* on the borders of
the Marsi.   [c] There were several cities named Athens,
only that in Attica being important ; the forms of the names
are uncertain, especially that of the second, which may
however stand for Ἀθηναιεῖς like *Aeolis* v. 25 for Αἰολεῖς.
There were many ethnics in -ευς, plural -εῖς.

398

XVIII. 34. But if the proper thing is that all words that start from similar forms should be inflected similarly, it follows that from dissimilar starting forms dissimilar forms should be made by inflection ; and this is not what is found. For from like forms some like forms are made, and other unlike forms, and from unlike forms also come some like forms and some unlike forms. For instance, from likes come likes, as from *bonus* ' good ' and *malus* ' bad ' come the neuter [a] forms *bonum* and *malum* ; also from likes come unlikes, as from *lupus* ' wolf ' and *lepus* ' hare ' come the unlike datives *lupo* and *lepori*. On the other hand, from unlikes there are unlikes, as from the nominatives *Priamus* and *Paris* come the datives *Priamo* and *Pari* ; also from unlikes there are likes, as nominatives *Iupiter* ' Jupiter,' *ovis* ' sheep,' and datives *Iovi* and *ovi*.

35. So much the more now must it be denied that Regularities exist, because not only are unlikes made from likes, but also from identical words unlikes are made, and not merely likes, but identicals are made from unlikes. From identical names unlikes, it is clear, are made, because while there are two towns named *Alba*, the people of the one are called *Albani* [a] and those of the other are called *Albenses* [b] ; while there are three cities named Athens, the people of the one are called *Athenaei*, those of the second are *Athenaiis*, those of the third *Athenaeopolitae*. [c]

36. Similarly, many words made in derivation from different words are found to be identical, as when I say accusative *Luam* from Saturn's *Lua*, [a] and

§ 36. [a] An old Italic goddess who expiated the blood shed in battle ; her formulaic connexion with Saturn is uncertain.

VARRO

et ab solvendo luo[1] luam.[2] Omnia[3] fere nostra
⟨n⟩omina[4] *virilia*[5] et muliebria multitudinis cum recto
casu fiunt dissimilia, *ea*⟨de⟩m ⟨in⟩[6] dand⟨i⟩[7] : dissimilia, ut mares Terentiei, feminae Terentia⟨e⟩,[8]
eadem in dandi, vireis Terentieis et mulieribus
Terentieis. Dissimile Plautus et Plautius, ⟨Marcus et
Marcius⟩[9] ; et co⟨m⟩mune, ut huius Plauti et Marci.

XIX. 37. Denique si est analogia, quod in multis
verbis e⟨s⟩t[1] similitudo verborum, sequitur, quod in
pluribus est dissimilitudo, ut non sit in sermone
sequenda analogia.

XX. 38. Postremo, si est in oratione, aut in
omnibus eius partibus est aut in aliqua[1] : at[2] in omnibus non est, in aliqua esse parum est, ut album esse
Aethiopa[3] non satis est quod habet candidos dentes :
non est ergo analogia.

XXI. 39. Cum ab similibus verbis quae declinantur similia fore polliceantur qui analogias esse dicunt,
et cum simile tum[1] denique dicant esse[2] verbo verbum, ex eodem si[3] genere eadem figura transitum de
cassu in cassum similiter ostendi possit, qui haec
dicunt utrumque ignorant, et in quo loco similitudo
debeat esse, et quemadmodum spectari soleat, simile

§ 36. [1] *Suerdsioeus, for* abluo.   [2] *Aug., for* abluam.
[3] *For* omina.   [4] *L. Sp., for* omina.   [5] *Scaliger, for* libe-
ralia.   [6] *L. Sp., for* eum.   [7] *Laetus, for* dant.   [8] *Laetus,
for* femina ē terentia.   [9] *Added by Groth.*

§ 37. [1] *Aug., for* et.

§ 38. [1] *Aug., with B, deleted* esse parum *after* aliqua.
[2] *Canal, for* et.   [3] *Mue., for* ethiopam.

§ 39. [1] *Aug., with B, for* simili laetum.   [2] *L. Sp., for*
dicantes se.   [3] *L. Sp., for* sit.

---

[b] *Solvendo* is here attached to *luo* as a gloss, just as *Saturni* is
attached to *Lua.*   [c] The older spelling -EI, historically
correct in these forms, was normal after I until the end of the

400

also *luam* as future of *luo* ' loosing.' [b] Almost all our names of men and women are unlike in the nominative case of the plural, but are identical in the dative : unlike, as the men *Terentii*,[c] the women *Terentiae*, but identical in the dative, men *Terentiis* [c] and women *Terentiis*.[c] Unlike are *Plautus* and *Plautius*, *Marcus* and *Marcius* ; and yet there is a form common to both, namely the genitive *Plauti* and *Marci*.[d]

XIX. 37. Finally, if Regularity does exist for the reason that in many words there is a likeness of the word-forms, it follows that because there is unlikeness in a greater number of words the principle of Regularity ought not to be followed in actual talking.

XX. 38. In the last place, if Regularity does exist in speech, it exists either in all its parts or in some one part ; but it does not exist in all, and it is not enough that it exists in some one part, just as the fact that an Ethiopian has white teeth is not enough to justify us in saying that an Ethiopian is white : therefore Regularity does not exist.

XXI. 39. Since those who declare that Regularities exist, promise that the inflected forms from like words will be alike, and since they then say that a word is like another word only if it can be shown that starting from the same gender and the same inflectional form it passes in like fashion from case to case, those who make these assertions show their ignorance both of that in which the likeness must be found and of how the presence or absence of the like-

Republic, and was therefore Varro's regular orthography. In the translation the standardized Latin forms are used. [d] The contracted form ending in -I was practically the exclusive form used as genitive of nouns ending in -IUS in the nominative, until the end of the Republic.

sit necne. Quae cum ignorant, sequitur ut, cum
⟨de⟩ analogia[4] dicere non possint, sequi ⟨non⟩[5] debeamus.

40. Quaero enim, verbum utrum dicant vocem
quae ex syllabis est ficta, eam quam audimus, an quod
ea significat, quam intellegimus, an utrumque. Si
vox voci esse debet similis, nihil[1] refert, quod significat
mas an femina sit, et utrum nomen an vocabulum sit.
quod illi[2] interesse dicunt.

41. Sin illud quod significatur debet esse simile,
Diona et Theona quos dicunt esse paene ipsi gemini,
inveniuntur esse dissimiles, si alter erit puer, alter
senex, aut unus albus et alter Aethiops, item aliqua
re alia dissimile⟨s⟩.[1] Sin ex[2] utraque parte debet
verbum esse simile, non cito invenietur qui⟨n⟩[3] in
altera utra re claudicet, nec Perpenna et Alfen⟨a⟩[4]
erit simile, quod alterum nomen virum, alterum
mulierem significat. Quare quoniam ubi similitudo
esse debeat nequeunt ostendere, impudentes sunt qui
dicunt esse analogias.

XXII. 42. Alterum illud quod dixi, quemadmodum simile ⟨s⟩pectari[1] oporteret, ignorare apparet
ex eorum praecepto, quod dicunt, cum transierit e

[4] GS., for analogiam ; cf. viii. 43.   [5] Added by Vertranius.
   § 40.   [1] For nichil.   [2] Laetus, for illae.
   § 41.   [1] Aug., for dissimile.   [2] For ex ex.   [3] Ed.
Veneta, for qui.   [4] GS.; Alphena L. Sp.; Alphaena
Rhol.; Alfaena Laetus ; for Alfaen.
   § 42.   [1] Victorius, for expectari.

   § 41.   [a] These names were often used by the philosophers
as a typical pair in their discussions ; the accusatives Diona
and Theona in the text, instead of the nominative, are assimil-

ness is wont to be recognized. Since they are ignorant of these matters, it follows that we ought not to follow them, inasmuch as they are unable to pronounce with authority on the subject of Regularity.

40. For I ask whether by a ' word ' they mean the spoken word which consists of syllables, that word which we hear, or that which the spoken word indicates, which we understand, or both. If the spoken word must be like another spoken word, it makes no difference whether what it indicates is male or female, and whether it is a proper name or a common noun ; and yet the supporters of Regularity say that these factors do make a difference.

41. But if that which is denoted by like words ought to be like, then *Dion* and *Theon*,[a] which they themselves say are almost identical, are found to be unlike, if the one is a boy and the other an old man, or one is white and the other an Ethiopian [b] ; and likewise if they are unlike in some other respect. But if the word must be like in both directions, there will not quickly be found one that is not defective in one respect or the other, nor will *Perpenna* and *Alfena* prove to be alike, because the one name denotes a man and the other a woman. Therefore, since they are unable to show wherein the likeness must exist, those who assert that Regularities exist are utterly shameless.

XXII. 42. The other matter that I have mentioned, how the likeness is to be recognized, they clearly fail to appreciate in that they set up a precept that only when the passage is made from the nomina-

ated to the immediately following relative. [b] For the same contrast, *cf.* Juvenal, 2. 23 : *Loripedem rectus derideat, Aethiopem albus* ; *cf.* also ix. 42, below.

nominandi casibus in eos quos appellant vocandi, tum
denique posse dici rectos esse similis aut dissimilis :
esset enim ut si quis, Menaechmos[2] geminos cum
videat, dicat non posse iudicare similesne sint, nisi
qui ex his sint nati considerarit num discrep*ent*[3]
inter se.

43. Nihil,[1] inquam, quo magis minusve sit simile
quod conferas cum altero, ad iudicandum extrinsecus
oportet sumi. Quare cum ignorent,[2] quemadmodum
similitudo debeat sumi, de analogia dicere non possunt.
Haec apertius dixissem, nisi brevius eo nunc mallem,
quod infra sunt planius usurpanda. Quare quod ad
universam naturam verborum attinet, haec attigisse
modo satis est.

XXIII. 44. Quod ad partis singulas orationis,
deinceps dicam. Quoius quoniam sunt divisiones
plures, nunc ponam potissimum *eam*[1] qua dividitur
oratio secund*um*[2] naturam in quattuor partis : in
eam[3] quae habet casus et quae habet ⟨tempora et
quae habet⟩[4] neutrum et in qua est utrumque. Has
vocant quid*am*[5] appellandi, dicendi, adminiculandi,
iungendi. Appellandi dicitur ut homo et Nestor,

---

[2] *Aldus, for* Me hech mos.   [3] *Aug., for* nunc discrepat.
§ 43.   [1] *For* nichil.   [2] *Rhol., for* ignorarent.
§ 44.   [1] *Lachmann, for* iam.   [2] *Lachmann, for* secunda
ut.   [3] *Mue., with a, for* iam.   [4] *Added from* H *and* G.
[5] *Laetus, for* quidem.

---

§ 42.   [a] Thus *lupus* and *lepus*, though alike in the nominative, are not alike because their other case-forms are not alike
in their endings ; *cf.* § 34.   But *lupus* and *campus* are judged
to be likes, when the other case-forms are found to be alike
in their endings.   [b] In Plautus's play, the *Menaechmi* ; in
Varro's comparison, the Menaechmus twins are the nominatives with like endings, and the children of the Menaechmi
are the derivative case-forms.

§ 43.   [a] x. §§ 3 ff., 10 ff.

tives to the vocative forms can it be said whether the nominatives are like or unlike [a] ; for this would be as if a man, on seeing the Menaechmus twins,[b] should say that he could not decide whether or not they were alike, unless he should scrutinize their children, to see if they showed any differences from one another.

43. Nothing, I say, whereby that which you are comparing with the other may be made more like it or less like it, ought to be brought in from outside, for the purpose of aiding the decision. Therefore, since they do not know in what way the likeness ought to be drawn, they are incompetent to speak about Regularity. I should have said this more plainly, if I were not wishing now to speak more briefly because later on [a] these matters are to be treated at greater length. Accordingly it is sufficient now to have touched upon them as far as is connected with the general nature of words.

XXIII. 44. I shall next speak of what concerns the individual parts of speech. Since there are several methods of division thereof, I shall now take by preference that by which speech is according to its nature divided into four parts : that which has case-forms, that which has time-forms, that which has neither, that in which both case and time are indicated.[a] Some grammarians call these the parts respectively of naming, saying, supporting, joining [b] : the part of naming is said to be such words as *homo* ' man ' and *Nestor*,

§ 44. [a] Participles. [b] The part of ' supporting ' includes the adverbs, as indeclinable modifiers ; that of ' joining ' includes participles, which are so called because they join in the same word the indication of case and that of time, or else because they unite in themselves the syntactical functions of adjective and verb (*cf.* Greek μετοχή ' sharing,' as name of the participle).

dicendi ut scribo et lego, iungendi ut[6] ⟨scribens et legens⟩,[7] adminiculandi ut docte et commode.

45. Appellandi partes sunt quattuor, e quis dicta a quibusdam provocabula quae sunt ut quis, quae[1]; ⟨vocabula⟩[2] ut scutum,[3] gladium; nomina ut Romulus, Remus; pronomina ut hic, haec. Duo media dicuntur nominatus; prima et extrema articuli. Primum genus est infinitum, secundum ut infinitum, tertium ut finitum,[4] quartum finitum.

46. Haec singulatim triplicia esse debent quod ⟨ad⟩[1] sexum, multitudinem, casum: sexum, utrum virile an muliebre an neutrum sit, ut doctus docta doctum; multitudinem, unum an plura significet, ut hic hi, haec ⟨hae⟩[2]; casum, utrum recto sit ut Marcus, an obliquo ut Marco, an com⟨m⟩uni ut ovis.[3]

XXIV. 47. His di⟨s⟩cretis[1] partibus singulas perspice, quo facilius nusquam esse analogias quas sequi debeamus videas. Nempe esse oportebat vocis formas ternas, ut in hoc humanus humana humanum, sed habent quaedam binas, ut cervus cerva,

---

[6] *Zippmann deleted* que *after* ut.   [7] *Added by Zippmann;* cf. x. 17.

§ 45.   [1] *Aug., for* que.   [2] *Added by Laetus, cf.* viii. 52, *and* x. 19.   [3] *Bentinus deleted* ut *after* scutum.   [4] *Aug., for* effinitum.

§ 46.   [1] quod ad *L. Sp.:* quoad *Aug.; for* quod.   [2] *Added by Mue.*   [3] *L. Sp., for* iouis; *cf.* viii. 49, *but also* viii. 74.

§ 47.   [1] *Aug., for* decretis.

---

[c] The third and the fourth items are here reversed in order from the previous listing.

§ 45.   [a] The neuter form of this word is quoted by Nonius Marcellus, 208. 12 M., from Lucilius (1187 Marx), though it

that of saying such as *scribo* ' I write ' and *lego* ' I read,' that of joining *^c* such as *scribens* ' writing ' and *legens* ' reading,' that of supporting such as *docte* ' learnedly ' and *commode* ' suitably.'

45. The kinds of naming are four, of which the words which are like (masc.) *quis*, (fem.) *quae* ' which ' have by certain grammarians been called Provocables; those like *scutum* ' shield ' and *gladium ^a* ' sword ' have been called Vocables : those like *Romulus* and *Remus* have been called Proper Nouns ; those like (masc.) *hic*, (fem.) *haec* ' this ' have been called Pronouns.*^b* The two middle kinds are called Denominations ; the first and last are called Articles. The first class is indefinite, the second is almost indefinite, the third is almost definite, the fourth is definite.

46. Each of these ought to be threefold in nature, as concerns gender, number, and case : gender, whether it is masculine or feminine or neuter, as masc. *doctus*, fem. *docta*, neut. *doctum* ' learned ' ; number, whether it denotes one or more, as masc. sing. *hic*, pl. *hi* ' these,' and fem. sing. *haec*, pl. *hae* ; case, whether it is in the nominative, as *Marcus*, or in an oblique case, as *Marco*, or in a non-distinctive case-form, as *ovis* ' sheep.'

XXIV. 47. Now that these divisions have been made, examine them one by one, that you may the more easily see that there are nowhere any Regularities which we ought to follow. To be sure some words had to have three several forms, as in this example : masc. *humanus*, fem. *humana*, neut. *humanum* ' human ' ; but some have only two apiece, like

is condemned by Quintilian, *Inst. Orat.* i. 5. 16.   *^b* Varro distinguishes two kinds of pronouns : *provocabula*, which subordinate, and *pronomina*, which do not.

VARRO

quaedam singulas, ut aper, et sic multa. Non ergo est in huiuscemodi generibus analogia.

XXV. 48. Et in multitudine ut unum significat pater, plures patres, sic omnia debuerunt[1] esse bina. Sed et singularia solum sunt multa, ut cicer, siser : nemo enim dicit cicera, sisera ; et multitudinis sunt, ut salinae ⟨balneae⟩[2] : non enim ab his singulari specie dicitur salina et balnea. Neque ab eo quod dicunt balneum habet multitudinis consuetudo : nam quod est ut praedium balneum, debuerunt esse plura, ut praedia balnea, quod non est : non est ergo in his quoque analogia.

XXVI. 49. Alia casus[1] habent et rectos et obliquos, alia rectos solum, alia modo obliquos habent : utrosque ut Iuno, Iunonis, rectos modo ut Iupiter, Maspiter, obliquos solum ut Iovis, Iovem : non ergo in his est analogia.

XXVII. 50. Nunc videamus in illa quadripertita. Primum si esset analogia[1] in infiniteis[2] articulis, ut est quis[3] quoius,[4] sic diceretur quae quaius[5] ; et ut est quis quoi,[6] sic diceretur qua quae : nam est proportione simile : ut deae bonae quae, sic[7] dea bona qua[8]

§ 48.   ¹ *Aug., with B, for* debuerint.   ² *Added by L. Sp.*
§ 49.   ¹ Alia casus *is repeated in F.*
§ 50.   ¹ *L. Sp. deleted* ut *after* analogia.   ² *For* infeineiteis.   ³ *L. Sp. deleted* quem *after* quis.   ⁴ *Aug., H, for* cuius.   ⁵ quaius *L. Sp.;* quam quaius *Aug.; for* quamuis.   ⁶ quis quoi *Aug., for* a quiuis cui.   ⁷ *L. Sp., for* sit.   ⁸ *Sciop., for* quae.

§ 48.   ª *Cf.* ix. 68.
§ 49.   ª The oblique cases lack the affixed -*piter* = *pater* of the nom.-voc. form, and have the appearance therefore of not coming from the same word.
§ 50.   ª This form is nowhere found in use.   ᵇ Gen.
408

cervus ' stag,' *cerva* ' hind,' and certain others have but one, like *aper* ' boar ' ; and so on with many others. Therefore Regularity simply does not exist in classes of this sort.

XXV. 48. In number also, as *pater* ' father ' denotes one and *patres* ' fathers ' denotes more than one, all ought in this fashion to have two forms. But many are singulars only, like *cicer* ' chickpea ' and *siser* ' skirret '—for nobody says *cicera* and *sisera* in the plural ; and there are words that are plurals only, such as *salinae* ' saltworks ' and *balneae* ' public baths ' : for from these there are no singulars *salina* and *balnea* in use. Nor from the singular *balneum* does general usage make a plural : for because *balneum* ' bath ' [a] is like *praedium* ' farm estate,' there ought to be plurals, *balnea* as well as *praedia*, but this is not the case. Therefore in these also there is no Regularity.

XXVI. 49. Some have both nominatives and oblique cases, others have nominatives only, others oblique cases only : both, as in nom. *Iuno*, gen. *Iunonis* ; nominatives only, as in *Iupiter*, *Maspiter* [a] ; oblique cases only, as in gen. *Iovis*, dat. *Iovi*. Therefore in these Regularity does not exist.

XXVII. 50. Now let us look into those of the fourfold division. First, if there were Regularity in the indefinite articles, the proper forms would be feminine *quae*, gen. *quaius*,[a] like masculine *quis*, gen. *quoius* [b] ; and as *quoi* is dative to masculine *quis*, so *quae* [c] would be used as dative to feminine *qua*. For it is similar by proportion : *dea bona qua* ' a good goddess who ' is like *deae bonae quae* ' to a good goddess to whom.'

quoius and dat. *quoi* were the regular forms down to the end of the Republic.   [c] The writing *quai* for the dat. sing. fem. is found on one inscription, *Corp. Insc. Lat.* ii. 89.

est ; et ut est quem quis, sic quos ques. Quare quod nunc dicitur qui homines, dici oportuit ques.

XXVIII. 51.   Praeterea ut est ab is[1] ⟨ei⟩,[2] sic ab ea eae diceretur, quod nunc dicitur ei, ⟨et⟩[3] pronuntiaretur ut in i⟨e⟩is[4] viris, sic e⟨ai⟩s[5] mulieribus ; et ut est in rectis casibus ⟨is⟩[6] ea,[7] in obliquis esset eius eaius ; nunc non modo in virili sicut in muliebri dicitur eius, sed etiam in neutris articulis, ut eius viri, eius mulieris, eius pabuli, cum discriminentur in rectis casibus is ea id.   De hoc genere parcius tetigi, quod librarios haec sp⟨i⟩*nosiora*[8] ind*ilig*entius[9] elaturos putavi.

XXIX. 52.   De nominat*ibus*[1] qui[2] accedunt proxime ad ⟨in⟩finitam[3] naturam articulorum atque appellantur vocabula, ut homo equus, eorum declinationum genera sunt quattuor : unum nominandi, ut ab equo equile, alterum casuale, ut ab equo equum,

---

§ 51.   [1] *Laetus, for* his.   [2] *Added by Laetus.*   [3] *Added by C. F. W. Mueller.*   [4] *Aug., with B, for* his.   [5] *A. Sp.;* ceis *Mue.;* eaeis *Aug.; for* es.   [6] *Added by Aug.*   [7] *Mue.* deleted id *after* ea.   [8] *Victorius, for* sponsiora.   [9] *Sciop., for* indulgentius.

§ 52.   [1] *L. Sp., for* nominatiuis.   [2] *L. Sp., with H, for* quae.   [3] *Aug., for* finitam ; *cf.* viii. 45.

---

[d] This form is well attested for old Latin ; *cf.* Charisius, i. 91 and 133 Keil, who cites it from Pacuvius (*R.O.L.* ii. 252-253 Warmington) and Cato, and Festus, 261 a 23 M.

§ 51.   [a] Found in Plautus, *Miles* 348, Cato, *Agr.* 46. 1 and 142 ; but out of use in Varro's time.   [b] This form, with the older orthography, must here be restored in Varro's text, to make clear the logic of his argument ; but to restore -*eis* for all the dative-ablative plurals in -*is* would confuse rather than help the reader, though Varro certainly used the -*eis* spelling after a preceding -*i*-, and probably elsewhere.   [c] Or *eaes*, with Fay ; the logic does not make clear precisely what form Varro would consider to have been a ' regular ' formation.

Similarly, the nom. masc. *ques* stands in the same relation to acc. *quos*, as the sing. masc. *quis* to the acc. *quem* ; therefore for the *qui homines* ' which men ' which is now used in the nominative, we ought to say *ques*.[d]

XXVIII. 51. Besides, as from masc. *is* ' this ' there is dat. *ei*, so from fem. *ea* there would be spoken a dat. *eae*,[a] which is now actually spoken as *ei* ; and like the dat. pl. in *ieis* [b] *viris* ' to these men,' there would be pronounced a dat. pl. fem. *eais* [c] *mulieribus* ' to these women.' And as in the nominatives there are masc. *is*, fem. *ea*, in the oblique forms there would be masc. *eius*, fem. *eaius* [d] ; but now *eius* is said for the genitive not only in the masculine and the feminine alike, but even in the neuter articles, as *eius viri* ' of this man,' *eius mulieris* ' of this woman,' *eius pabuli* ' of this fodder,' although masc. *is*, fem. *ea*, neut. *id* are distinguished in the nominative. I have touched upon this classification more sparingly, because I am of opinion [e] that the copyists will not take proper care in transferring these quite confusing matters.

XXIX. 52. From the appellations which come nearest to the indefinite nature of the articles and are called common nouns, such as *homo* ' man ' and *equus* ' horse,' there are four kinds of derivation [a] : one of name-giving, as *equile* ' horse-stable ' from *equus* ' horse ' ; the second that of the cases, as accusative *equum* from *equus* ; the third that of augmentation, as

---

[d] Nowhere found.   [e] The condition of the manuscripts shows that Varro was right.

§ 52.   [a] We should call these four respectively derivation by suffixes, declension, comparison of adjectives, derivation by a suffix denoting diminution ; the fourth is a division of the first, and so also, in the broad sense, is the third, though it has a more specialized function.

tertium augendi, ut ab albo albius, quartum minuendi,
ut ⟨a⟩[4] cista cistula.

53. Primum genus, ut dixi, id est, cum ⟨ab⟩[1]
aliqua parte orationis declinata sunt recto casu vocabul*a*,[2] ut a balneis balneator. Hoc fere triplices
habet radices, quod et a vocabulo oritur, ut a venatore
venabulum, et a nomine, ut a Tibure[3] Tiburs, e*t*[4] a
verbo, *ut*[5] a currendo cursor. In nullo horum analogiam servar*i*[6] videbis.

XXX. 54. Primum cum dicatur ut ab ove et sue
ovile et suile, sic a bove bovile non dicitur ; et cum
simile sit avis et ovis, neque dicitur ut ab ave aviarium
⟨ab ove oviarium, neque ut⟩[1] ab ove ovile ab ave avile ;
et cum debuerit esse ut a cubatione cubiculum sic[2] a
sessione sediculum, non est.

55. Quoniam taberna, ubi ven*it*[1] vinum, a vino
vinaria, a creta cretaria, ab unguento unguentaria
dicitur, ἀνὰ λόγον[2] si essent vocabula, ubi caro venit,
carnaria, ubi pelles, pelliaria, ubi calcei, calcearia
diceretur, non laniena ac pellesuina et sutrina. Et

---

[4] *Added by Aldus.*

§ 53.   [1] *Added by L. Sp.*   [2] *Aldus, for* vocabulum.
[3] *Laetus, for* tibura.   [4] *Aug., with B, for* tibur Sed.
[5] *For* et.   [6] *Aug., a, for* servare.

§ 54.   [1] *Added by Mue., after Stephanus.*   [2] *Laetus,
for* sit.

§ 55.   [1] *For* uenet.   [2] *GS. ;* analogon *L. Sp. ; for*
analogion.

---

§ 53.   [a] That is, declinable stems, and not merely other
case-forms of the same stem.   [b] Properly, both from *venari*
' to hunt.'

§ 54.   [a] The correct form is *bubile* ; but Charisius, i. 104.
28 Keil, testifies that Cato used *bovile* at least once.
[b] Properly both from *sedere* ' to sit ' ; despite Varro, Festus,

albius ' whiter ' from *album* ' white ' ; the fourth that of diminution, as *cistula* ' little box ' from *cista* ' box.'

53. The first class, as I have said, is that in which words in the nominative *a* are derived from some part of speech, as *balneator* ' bath-keeper ' from *balneae* ' public baths.' This class has in general three sources, because it develops from a common noun, as *venabulum* *b* ' hunting spear ' from *venator* ' hunter,' and from a proper name, as *Tiburs* ' man of Tibur ' from *Tibur*, and from a verb, as *cursor* ' runner ' from *currere* ' to run.' In none of these will you see Regularity preserved.

XXX. 54. First, although from *ovis* ' sheep ' and *sus* ' swine ' there are said *ovile* ' sheepfold ' and *suile* ' hog-sty,' there is no *bovile* *a* from *bos* ' ox ' ; and although *avis* ' bird ' and *ovis* ' sheep ' are alike, we do not say *oviarium* from *ovis* as we say *aviarium* ' aviary ' from *avis*, nor do we say *avile* from *avis* as we say *ovile* ' sheepfold ' from *ovis* ; and although there ought to be a *sediculum* ' chair ' from *sessio* *b* ' sitting ' like *cubiculum* ' sleeping-room ' from *cubatio* *c* ' reclining,' there is not.

55. Since a shop where wine is sold is called *vinaria* from *vinum* ' wine,' and *cretaria* from *creta* ' chalk,' *a* *unguentaria* from *unguentum* ' perfume,' then if words went in regular fashion a shop where *caro* ' meat ' is sold would be called *carnaria*, one where *pelles* ' hides ' are sold would be called *pelliaria*, one where *calcei* ' shoes ' are sold would be called *calcearia*, instead of *laniena* ' butcher's shop,' *pellesuina* ' leather-shop,' *sutrina*

336. 6 M., quotes *sediculum* as occurring, but without mentioning where. *c* Properly both from *cubare* ' to recline.'
§ 55. *a* That is, ' Cretan (earth),' used at Rome for cleaning purposes.

413

sicut est ab uno uni, ab tribus trini, a quattuor quadrini, sic a duobus duini, non bini diceretur ; nec non
ut quadrigae trigae, sic potius duigae quam bigae.
Permulta sunt huiusce generis, quae quoniam admoni-
tus perspicere potest, omitto.

XXXI. 56.   Vocabula quae ab nominibus oriuntur,
si ab similibus nominibus similia esse debent, dicemus,
quoniam gemina sunt Parma[1] Roma, ⟨ut⟩ Parmenses
⟨sic Romenses⟩[2] ; aut quoniam est similis Roma Nola
Parma, dicemus ut Romani Nolani sic Parmani ; et a
Pergamo, ab Ilio similiter Pergamenus Ilienus ; aut
ut Ilius[3] et Ilia mas et femina, sic Pergamus et Pergama vir et mulier ; et quoniam similia nomina sunt
Asia Libya, dicemus Asiaticos et Libyaticos homines.

XXXII. 57.   Quae vocabula dicuntur a verbis,
fiunt ut a scribendo scriptor, a legendo lector, haec
quoque non servare similitudinem licet videre ex his :
cum similiter dicatur ut ab amando amator, ab salu-
tando salutator, ⟨non est⟩[1] a cantando cantator ; et

§ 56.   [1] *Sciop. deleted* Alba *after* Parma *; cf.* viii. 35.
[2] *After Fay's* ut Parmenses sic Albenses Romenses *;* ut
Parmenses Albenses Romenses *Mue. ;* Romenses et Albenses
ut Parmenses *Aug.* (*quoting a friend*)*; for* Parmenses.
[3] *Aug., with B, deleted* unus *after* Ilius.
§ 57.   [1] *Added by Canal* (*L. Sp. placed* non est *after* cantator *; Popma added* non *before* cantator).

---

[b] The plural of *unus* is used to modify nouns plural in
form but singular in meaning ; though not strictly a multi-
plicative (*singuli* means ' one apiece '), *uni* is quoted here
because its ending agrees with that of the higher multipli-
catives.   [c] Varro fails to realize that before a vowel *du-*
varied with *dw-*, and that *dw-* at the beginning of a Latin
word became *b-* ; so that *bini* and *bigae* are quite proper
in these series.

' cobbler's shop.' And just as from *unus* ' one '
comes the plural *uni* [b] ' one set of,' and from *tres*
' three ' comes *trini* ' three each,' from *quattuor* ' four '
quadrini ' four each,' so from *duo* ' two ' there should
be a *duini* and not a *bini* [c] ' two each '; also, after
quadrigae ' team of four ' and *trigae* ' team of three,'
there should be rather *duigae* than *bigae* ' team of
two.' There are a great many examples of this class,
but I pass them by, since he who has had his attention
called to them cannot fail to notice them.

XXXI. 56. If words which develop from proper
names ought to be alike if from like names, then since
Parma and *Roma* are identical we shall say *Romenses*,[a]
like *Parmenses* ; or since *Roma, Nola, Parma* are alike,
we shall say *Parmani*,[a] like *Romani* and *Nolani*. And
from *Pergamum* and *Ilium* we shall have not only
Pergamenus ' Pergamene,' but also *Ilienus* [a] ; or like
Ilius and *Ilia* ' Ilian ' male and female, we shall say
Pergamus [a] and *Pergama* [a] respectively for a man
and a woman of Pergamum. And since *Asia* and
Libya are like names, we shall call the people Asiatic
and Libyatic.[b]

XXXII. 57. The words which are made from
verbs are such as *scriptor* ' writer ' from *scribere* ' to
write ' and *lector* ' reader ' from *legere* ' to read ';
that those also do not preserve a likeness can be seen
from the following : although *amator* ' lover ' from
amare ' to love ' and *salutator* ' saluter ' from *salutare*
' to salute ' are formed in like manner, there is no
cantator [a] ' singer ' from *cantare* ' to sing '; and

§ 56. [a] Forms not in use, formed for purposes of argument. [b] Not *Libyatici*, but *Libyci* was the form in use.
§ 57. [a] Up to Varro's time, only *cantor* was used ; *cantator* is a later word.

cum dicatur lassus sum metendo ferendo, ex his vocabula non reddunt proportionem, quo⟨niam⟩² non fit
ut messor fertor. Multa sunt item in hac specie in
quibus potius consuetudinem sequimur quam rationem verborum.

58. Praeterea cum sint ab eadem origine verborum vocabula dissimilia superiorum, quod simul
habent casus et tempora, quo vocantur participia, et
multa sint contraria ut amo amor, *lego legor*,¹ ab amo
et eiusmodi omnibus verbis oriuntur praesens et
futurum *ut*² amans et amaturus,³ ab eis verbis tertium
quod debet fingi praeteriti, in lingua Latina reperiri
non potest : non ergo est analogia. Sic a*b* a*mor*⁴
legor et eiusmodi verbis⁵ vocabulum eius generis
praeteriti te⟨m⟩poris fit, ut amatus,⁶ neque praesentis
et futuri ab his fit.

59. Non est ergo analogia, praesertim cum tantus
numerus vocabulorum in eo genere interierit¹ quod
dicimus. In his verbis quae contraria non habent,
⟨ut⟩² loquor et venor, tamen dicimus loquens et
venans, locuturus ⟨et venaturus,³ locutus et venatus⟩,⁴
quod secundum analogias non est, quoniam dicimus

---

² *L. Sp., for* quo.
§ 58. ¹ *L. Sp., for* amor amo seco secor. ² *Bentinus, for* et.
³ *H, B, Laetus, for* ueta maturus. ⁴ *Aug., for* amabor.
⁵ *Aug., for* uerbi est. ⁶ *L. Sp., for* amaturus eram sum ero.
§ 59. ¹ *Laetus, for* inter orierit. ² *Added by L. Sp.*
³ *Added by Laetus.* ⁴ *Added by Fay.*

ᵇ The corresponding noun of agency is *lator.*
§ 58. ᵃ That is, active and passive voices. ᵇ Of the
active voice. ᶜ Of the passive voice. ᵈ Varro does not
consider the gerundive *amandus* to be a future passive participle.

though we say " I am tired with *metendo* ' reaping '
and *ferendo* ' carrying,' " the words from these do not
represent a like relation, since there is no *fertor* [b]
' carrier ' made like *messor* ' reaper.' There are likewise many others of this class in which we follow usage
rather than conformity to the verbs.

58. Besides these there are other words which
also originate from verbs but are unlike those of which
we have already spoken, because they have both cases
and tenses, whence they are called participles. And
as many verbs have opposite forms,[a] such as *amo* ' I
love,' *amor* ' I am loved,' *lego* ' I read,' *legor* ' I am
read,' from *amo* and all verbs of this kind [b] there
develop present and future participles, such as *amans*
' loving ' and *amaturus* ' about to love,' but from these
verbs the third form which ought to be made, namely
the past participle, cannot be found in the Latin
language : therefore there is no Regularity. So also
from *amor* ' I am loved,' *legor* ' I am read,' and verbs
of this kind [c] the word of this class is made for past
time, as *amatus* ' loved,' but from them none is made
for the present and the future.[d]

59. Therefore there is no Regularity, especially
since such a great number of words has perished [a] in
this class which we are mentioning. In these verbs
which have not both voices, such as *loquor* ' I speak '
and *venor* ' I hunt,' [b] we none the less say *loquens*
' speaking ' and *venans* ' hunting,' *locuturus* ' about
to speak ' and *venaturus* ' about to hunt,' *locutus*
' having spoken ' and *venatus* ' having hunted.' This
is not according to the Regularities, since we say

§ 59. [a] That is, many verbs lack a complete paradigm
that includes both active and passive forms.   [b] Deponent
verbs.

loquor et venor, ⟨non loquo et veno⟩,[5] unde [6] illa erant
superiora ; e⟨o⟩ minus[7] servantur, quod[8] ex his quae
contraria verba non habent[9] alia efficiunt terna, ut ea
quae dixi, alia bina, ut ea quae dicam : currens
ambulans, cursurus ambulaturus : tertia enim praeteriti non sunt, ut cursus sum, ambulatus sum.

60. Ne in his quidem, quae saepius quid fieri
ostendunt, servatur analogia : nam ut est a cantando
cantitans, ab amando amitans non est et sic multa.
Ut in his singularibus, sic in multitudinis : sicut enim
cantitantes seditantes[1] non dicuntur.

XXXIII. 61. Quoniam est vocabulorum genus
quod appellant compositicium et negant conferri id
oportere cum simplicibus de quibus adhuc dixi, de
compositis separatim dicam. Cum ab tibiis et canendo
tibicines dicantur, quaerunt, si analogias sequi oporteat, cur non a cithara et psalterio et pandura dicamus
citharicen et sic alia ; si ab aede et tuendo ⟨aeditumus

---

[5] *Added by L. Sp.*   [6] venor unde *Laetus, for* uenerunt
de.   [7] *L. Sp., for* eminus.   [8] *Mue. deleted* cum *after*
quod.   [9] *Aug., with B, for* habentur.
   § 60.   [1] *M, Laetus, for* sed ettitantes.

---

[c] That is, the deponent verbs, since they lack the active
forms otherwise, should not have the active participles
which actually they have.   [d] Deponent verbs.   [e] Intransitive verbs of active form, which naturally have
no passive, and consequently no passive participle.
[f] Varro's logic here deserts him, since the deponent verbs
have a perfect participle of passive form and active meaning, and there is no reason why intransitive verbs of active
form should not have a perfect participle passive in form
and active in meaning : in fact, such a participle is sometimes
found, like *adultus* ' grown up,' from *adolescere* ' to grow up.'

loquor and *venor*, not *loquo* and *veno*, whence came the forms given above.[c] The Regularities are the less preserved, because some of the verbs which have not both voices, make three participles each, like those which I have named,[d] and other make only two each,[e] such as those which I shall now name : *currens* ' running ' and *ambulans* ' walking,' *cursurus* ' about to run ' and *ambulaturus* ' about to walk ' ; for the third forms, those of the past, do not exist,[f] as in *cursus sum* ' I am run,' *ambulatus sum* ' I am walked.'

60. But Regularity is not preserved even in those which indicate that something is done with greater frequency ; for though there is a *cantitans* ' repeatedly singing ' from *cantare* ' to sing,' there is no *amitans* ' repeatedly loving ' from *amare* ' to love,' and similarly with many others. The situation is the same in the forms of the plural as in those of the singular : though the plural *cantitantes* is used, *seditantes*[a] ' sitting ' is not.

XXXIII. 61. Since there is a class of words which they call compositional, saying that they ought not to be grouped in the same category with the simple words of which I have so far spoken, I shall deal separately with these compounds. Since from *tibiae* ' pipes ' and *canere* ' to play ' the *tibicines* ' pipers ' are named, they ask, If we ought to follow the Regularities, why then from *cithara* ' lute ' and *psalterium* ' psaltery ' and *pandura* ' Pan's strings ' should we not say *citharicen*[a] ' lute-player ' and the rest in the same way ? If from *aedes* ' temple ' and *tueri* ' to guard ' the *aedi-*

§ 60. [a] The singular *seditans* also is not used, which is implied by Varro, but not stated.

§ 61. [a] *Citharista*, fem. *citharistria*, are used, both taken from Greek.

dicatur, cur non ab atrio et tuendo⟩[1] potius atritumus
sit quam atriensis ; si ab avibus capiendis auceps
dicatur, debuisse aiunt a piscibus capiendis ut aucu-
pem sic pisci⟨cu⟩pem[2] dici.

62. Ubi lavetur aes *a*erarias, non aerelavinas
nominari ; et ubi fodiatur argentum argentifodinas
dici, neque ⟨ubi⟩[1] fodiatur ferrum ferrifodinas ; qui
lapides *c*aedunt lapicidas, qui ligna, lignicidas non
dici ; neque ut aurificem sic argentificem ; non
doctum dici indoctum, non salsum insulsum. Sic ab
hoc quoque fonte quae profluant, ⟨analogiam non
servare⟩[2] animadvertere est facile.

XXXIV. 63. Reliquitur de casibus, in quo Aristarchei suos contendunt nervos. XXXV. Primum si
in his esset[1] analogia, dicunt d*e*bu*i*sse[2] omnis nominatus[3] et articulos habere totidem casus : nunc alios
habere unum solum, ut litteras singulas omnes, alios
tris, ut praedium praedii praedio, alios quattuor, ut

§ 61.   [1] *The omission in F (and all codd.) was filled by
Laetus with editus est cur ab atrio et tuendo ; Aldus inserted*
non *after* tuendo ; Mue. *wrote* aeditumus *and (with B) set*
non *after* cur ; A. Sp. *proposed* dicatur *for* sit.   [2] *Aug.,
with B, for* piscipem.
§ 62.   [1] *Added by Laetus.*   [2] *Added by Christ.*
§ 63.   [1] *For* essent.   [2] *Aldus, for* de risse.   [3] *L. Sp.,
for* nominatiuos.

b The regular word is *piscator* ; one inscription has *piscicapus.*
§ 62.   *a* Regularly *ferrariae* ' iron-mines.'   *b* Regularly
lignatores ' wood-cutters.'   *c* Regularly *argentarius* ' silversmith.'   *d* The difference here consists in the change of the
radical vowel of *salsus*, when it comes to stand in a medial
syllable ; the process is called Vowel Weakening.
§ 63.   *a* Aristarchus, of Samothrace, famous grammarian
of Alexandria, lived about 216–144 B.C. He wrote many
commentaries on Greek authors, and many works on gram-
mar, in which he defended the principle of Regularity.

tumus ' sacristan ' is named, why from *atrium* ' main hall ' and *tueri* ' to guard ' is it not *atritumus* ' butler ' rather than *atriensis* ? And if from *avis capere* ' to catch birds ' the *auceps* ' fowler ' is named, they say, from *piscis capere* ' to catch fish ' there ought to be a *pisciceps* [b] ' fisherman ' named like the *auceps*.

62. They remark also that establishments where *aes* ' copper ' *lavatur* ' is refined ' are called *aerariae* ' smelters ' and not *aerelavinae* ' copper-washery '; and places where *argentum* ' silver ' *foditur* ' is mined ' are called *argentifodinae* ' silver-mines,' but that places where *ferrum* ' iron ' is mined are not called *ferrifodinae* [a] ; that those who *caedunt* ' cut ' *lapides* ' stones ' are called *lapicidae* ' stone-cutters,' but that those who cut *ligna* ' firewood ' are not called *lignicidae* [b] ; that there is no term *argentifex* [c] ' silversmith ' like *aurifex* ' goldsmith '; that a person who is not *doctus* ' learned ' is called *indoctus*, but one who is not *salsus* ' witty ' is called *insulsus*.[d] Thus the words which come from this source also, it is easy to see, do not observe Regularity.

XXXIV. 63. It remains to consider the problem of the cases, on which the Aristarcheans [a] especially exert their energies. XXXV. First, if in these there were Regularity, they [b] say that all names and articles ought to have the same number of cases ; but that as things are some have one only,[c] like all individual letters, others have three,[d] like *praedium praedii*

Among his pupils were important scholars of the next generation.   [b] Those who do not believe in the principle of Regularity.   [c] These are the indeclinable nouns.   [d] Varro counts only different case-forms : where he finds three, the nom., acc., and voc. are identical, and the dat. and abl. are identical ; etc.

mel mellis melli melle, alios quinque, ut quintus
quinti quinto quintum quinte, alios sex, ut unus unius
uni unum une uno : non esse ergo in casibus analogias.

XXXVI. 64. Secundo quod *Crates*,[1] cur quae
singulos habent casus, ut litterae Graecae, non dicantur alpha alphati alphatos, si idem mihi respondebitur
quod *Crateti*,[2] non esse[3] vocabula nostra, sed penitus
barbara, qu*a*eram, cur idem nostra nomina et Persarum et ceterorum quos vocant barbaros cum casibus
dica⟨n⟩t.[4]

65. Quare si essent in analogia, aut ut Poenicum
et *A*egyptiorum vocabula singulis casibus dicerent,
aut pluribus ut Gallorum ac ceterorum ; nam dicunt
al*au*da alau*das*[1] et sic alia. Sin[2] quod scrib*u*nt[3] dicent,
quod Poenicum si⟨n⟩t,[4] singulis casibus ideo eas litteras Graecas nominari : sic Graeci nostra senis
casibus non quinis[5] dicere debebant ; quod cum non
faciunt, non est analogia.

XXXVII. 66. Quae si esset,[1] negant ullum casum
duobus modis debuisse dici ; quod fit contra. Nam
sine reprehensione vulgo alii dicunt in singulari hac

§ 64. [1] *Laetus, for* grates.   [2] *Laetus, for* grateti.
[3] *Aug., with B, for* essent.   [4] *Laetus, for* dicat.
§ 65. [1] *Scaliger, for* alacco alaucus.   [2] *Popma, for*
alias in.   [3] *Popma, M, for* scribent.   [4] *Rhol., for* sit.
[5] *Laetus transposed* quinis non.
§ 66. [1] *Laetus, for* essent.

§ 64. [a] Crates of Mallos, head of the Pergamene school of
scholarship, was a contemporary and opponent of Aristarchus, and championed the principle of Anomaly.
[b] Names of letters were indeclinable both in Greek and in
Latin.
§ 65. [a] Not the Carthaginians, but the Phoenicians.
[b] Varro knew that neither language had a case system.

praedio ' farm,' others four, like *mel mellis melli melle* ' honey,' others five, like *quintus quinti quinto quintum quinte* ' fifth,' others six, like *unus unius uni unum une uno* ' one '; therefore in cases there are no Regularities.

XXXVI. 64. Second, in reference to what Crates [a] said as to why those which have only one case-form each are not used in the forms *alpha*, dat. *alphati*, gen. *alphatos*, because they are Greek letters [b]—if the same answer is given to me as to Crates, that they are not our words at all, but utterly foreign words, then I shall ask why the same persons use a full set of case-forms not only for our own personal names, but also for those of the Persians and of the others whom they call barbarians.

65. Wherefore, if these proper names were in a state of Regularity, either they would use them with a single case-form each, like the words of the Phoenicians [a] and the Egyptians,[b] or with several, like those of the Gauls and of the rest : for they say nom. *alauda* [c] ' lark,' gen. *alaudas*, and similarly other words.   But if, as they write, they say that the Greek letters received names with but one case-form each for the reason that they really belong to the Phoenicians, then in this way the Greeks ought to speak our words in six cases [d] each, not in five : inasmuch as they do not do this, there is no Regularity.

XXXVII. 66. If Regularity existed, they say, no case ought to be used in two forms ; but the opposite is found to occur.   For without censure quite commonly some say in the ablative singular *ovi* ' sheep '

---

[c] The text is desperate here ; but at any rate *alauda* is Celtic.
[d] Greek had no form by which it might represent the Latin ablative.

ovi et avi, alii hac ove et ave ; in multitudinis hae
puppis restis et hae puppes restes ; item quod in
patrico[2] casu hoc genus dispariliter dicuntur civitatum
parentum et civitatium parentium, in accusandi hos
montes fontes et hos montis fontis.

XXXVIII. 67. Item cum, si sit analogia, debeant
ab similibus verbis similiter declinatis similia fieri et
id non fieri ostendi possit, despiciendam eam esse
rationem. Atqui ostenditur : nam qui potest similius
esse quam gens, mens,[1] dens ? Cum horum casus
patricus et accusativus in multitudine sint dispariles[2] :
nam a primo fit gentium et gentis, utrubique ut sit
⟨I⟩,[3] ab secundo mentium et mentes,[4] ut in priore solo
sit I, ab tertio dentum et dentes, ut in neutro sit.

68. Sic item quoniam simile est recto casu surus
lupus lepus, rogant, quor non dicatur proportione[1]
suro lupo lepo. Sin respondeatur similia non esse
quod ea vocemus dissimiliter sure lupe lepus (sic enim
respondere voluit Aristarchus Crateti : nam cum
scripsisset similia esse Philomedes Heraclides Melicertes, dixit non esse similia : in vocando enim cum
⟨E⟩[2] brevi dici Philomede⟨s⟩,[3] cum E longo Heraclide,

---

[2] *Laetus, for* patricos.
  § 67.   [1] *L. Sp. transposed* mens gens *of F.*   [2] *For* disparilis.   [3] *Added by Aug., with B.*   [4] *Laetus, for* mentis.
  § 68.   [1] *Aldus, for* proportionem.   [2] *Added by Laetus.*
[3] *Mue., for* philomede.

---

  § 66.   [a] The doublet forms originated from the amalgama-
tion, in Latin, of the declension of consonant-stems and that
of *i*-stems.
  § 67.   [a] Varro is alone in giving a gen. *dentum* ; all others
use *dentium*. In the accusative, the form in *-is* is historically

and *avi* ' bird,' others say *ove* and *ave* ; in the plural, the nominative is *puppis* ' ship's sterns ' and *restis* ' ropes,' also *puppes* and *restes* ; likewise there is the fact that in the genitive plural of words of this class there are used the variant forms *civitatum* ' of states,' *parentum* ' of parents,' and *civitatium, parentium*, and in the accusative plural *montes* ' mountains,' *fontes* ' springs,' and *montis, fontis.*[a]

XXXVIII. 67. Likewise they say that, if there is Regularity, like forms ought to be made from like words declined alike, and that this can be shown not to take place ; that therefore this theory is to be rejected. And yet this failure can be shown ; for how can anything be more alike than *gens* ' clan,' *mens* ' mind,' *dens* ' tooth ' ? Despite which their genitives and accusatives in the plural are unlike ; for from the first word are made *gentium* and *gentis*, with I in both, from the second come *mentium* and *mentes*, with I in the former only, from the third *dentum* and *dentes*,[a] with I in neither form.

68. So likewise since *surus* ' stake,' *lupus* ' wolf,' *lepus* ' hare ' are alike in the nominative, they ask why there is not said in like fashion [a] *suro, lupo, lepo*. But if the answer is given that they are not alike, because in the vocative we use the unlike forms *sure*, *lupe, lepus* (this to be sure is what Aristarchus wished to say in reply to Crates ; for when Crates had written that *Philomedes, Heraclides, Melicertes* were alike, he said that they were not alike, because in the vocative [b] *Philomedes* is said with a short E, *Heraclide*

correct in all three ; -*es* was transferred to them by the influence of consonant-stems.

§ 68. [a] Datives or ablatives ; *lepus* has dat. *lepori*, abl. *lepore*. [b] Greek names, with their Greek vocative forms.

cum ⟨A⟩[4] brevi Melicerta[5]), in hoc dicunt Aristar*ch*um non intellexisse quod qu*a*eretur s*e* non
solvere.[6]

69. Sic enim, ut quicque in obliquis casibus dis-
crepavit, dicere potuit propter eam rem rectos casus
no*n*[1] esse similis ; quom qu*a*eratur duo inter se
similia sint necne, non debere extrinsecus adsum⟨i⟩[2]
cur similia s*i*nt.[3]

70. Item si esset analogia, similiter ut dicunt
aves oves sues, dicerent item avium ovium suium. Si
analogia est, inquit, cur populus dicit Dei Penates,
Dei Consentes, cum sit ut hic reus fer⟨re⟩us deus,
sic hei re⟨e⟩i fer⟨re⟩ei de⟨e⟩i ?[1]

71. Item qu*a*erunt, si sit analogia, cur appellant
omnes aedem Deum Consentium et non Deorum
Consentium ? Item quor dicatur mille denarium, non
mille denariorum ? Est enim hoc vocabulum figura
ut Va*t*inius,[1] Manilius, denarius : debet igi*t*ur dici ut
Va*t*iniorum[2] Maniliorum denariorum ; et non equum

---

[4] *Added by Sciop.*   [5] *Sciop., for* Melicerte.   [6] *Groth,*
for si non solveret.
  § 69. [1] *Aug., with B, for* noti.   [2] *Laetus, for* adsum.
[3] *L. Sp., for* sunt.
  § 70. [1] *All additions by L. Sp.*
  § 71. [1] *Laetus, for* uarinius.   [2] *Laetus, for* uariniorum.

---

  § 69. [a] Aristarchus.   [b] Crates and his followers.
  § 70. [a] For the correct *suum*.   [b] Crates.   [c] With EI
graphic for long *i* ; but *cf.* note *e*.   [d] The twelve Great
Gods : Jupiter, Neptune, Vulcan, Mars, Mercury, Apollo,
Juno, Ceres, Vesta, Venus, Diana, Minerva. *Consentes*
' who are together,' rather than for *consentientes* ' who agree

with a long E, *Melicerta* with a short A), in this, they
say, Aristarchus did not realize that he was not giving
a solution of the question that was asked.

69. For in this way, whenever there was any
difference in the oblique cases, he [a] could say that for
this reason the nominatives were not alike ; but since
the question is whether the two nominatives are like
each other, or not, there should be nothing brought
in from outside, they say,[b] as to why they are alike or
different.

70. Likewise if there were Regularity, then just
as they say in like fashion the nominatives *aves* ' birds,'
oves ' sheep,' *sues* ' swine,' they would say in the genitive *suium* [a] just as they do *avium* and *ovium*. If there
is Regularity, he [b] says, why do the people say *dei* [c]
' gods ' in *Dei Penates* ' Household Gods ' and *Dei
Consentes* ' United Gods,' [d] although in the nominative
singular *deus* ' god ' is just like *reus* ' defendant,'
ferreus ' of iron,' and so the plurals should be *reei,*[e]
ferreei, deei ?

71. Likewise they ask, if Regularity exists, why
do people all say the Temple *Deum* [a] *Consentium* ' of
the United Gods ' and not *Deorum Consentium* ? Likewise, why do they say a thousand *denarium* [a] ' of
denarii ' and not a thousand *denariorum* ? For this
word *denarius* is in form exactly like *Vatinius* and
Manilius, and therefore *denariorum* ought to be used
as genitive, like *Vatiniorum* and *Maniliorum*. They

in council.'   [e] All with EI for long I ; unless we are to read
di above, and *rei, ferrei, dei* here. At any rate, the normal
plural of *deus* was monosyllabic, and was not made like the
plurals of the other words.

§ 71. [a] The genitive in -UM was an older form than that
in -ORUM, and was retained in many words pertaining to
religion and law, and in weights and measures.

427

puplicum mille assarium esse, sed mille assariorum:
ab uno enim assario multi assarii, ab eo assariorum.

72. Item secundum illorum rationem debemus
secundis syllabis longis Hectórem Nestórem : est enim
ut quaestor praetor Nestor quaestorem praetorem
Nestórem, quaestóris praetóris Nestóris ; et non
debuit dici quibus das, his[1] das : est enim ut hi[2] qui
his quis, a⟨u⟩t[3] sicut quibus hibus.

73. Cum dicatur da patri familias,[1] si analogias
sequi vellent, non debuerunt dicere hic pater familias,
quod est ut Atiniae Catiniae familiae, sic una Atinia
Catinia familia. Item plures patres familias dicere
non debuerunt, sed, ut Sisenna scribit, patres familiarum.

74. Neque oportebat consuetudinem natare[1] alios
dicere boum greges, alios boverum, et signa alios
Ioum, alios Ioverum, cum esset ut Iovis bovis struis et

§ 72. [1] *Mue.*, for quis.   [2] *L. Sp. ;* hei *Sciop. ; for* ei.
[3] *L. Sp., for* at.
§ 73. [1] *B, Ed. Veneta, for* familiai.
§ 74. [1] *Canal, for* notare.

---

[b] That of an *eques* in the Roman army ; *cf.* Pauly-Wissowa,
Realenc. d. cl. Altertumswiss. vi. 277.   [c] Probably *mille
assarium* is a single word, a compound adjective, in the
accusative singular, since the word *assarius* is not otherwise
known ; *cf.* F. Stolz, *Lateinische Grammatik*, ed. 5, page
212, revised by M. Leumann: *milleassarius* ' worth one
thousand *asses librales*.'
§ 72.   [a] These names are Greek, and have short *o* in the
oblique cases, in Greek ; the Roman writers usually imitated
the Greek quantities, even though it made them unlike the
native Latin words.   [b] *Quis, quibus*, and *his* are familiar
in the dat.-abl. plural ; but *hibus* is well attested only in
Plautus, *Curculio*, 506.
§ 73.   [a] A genitive of an older type.   [b] Varro seems to
think that in the nominative *pater familias*, the *familias* also
428

say also that a cavalryman's horse [b] is worth not a thousand *assarium* [c] ' of assarii,' but a thousand *assariorum* ; for from the singular *assarius* comes the plural *assarii*, and from that should come the genitive *assariorum*.

71. Likewise, according to their theory, it is with long second syllables that we should pronounce *Hectōrem* and *Nestōrem* [a] ; for the accusatives *quaestorem praetorem Nestōrem*, and the genitives *quaestōris praetōris Nestōris* correspond to the nominatives *quaestor praetor Nestor*. And we ought not to say *quibus das* ' to whom you give,' *his das* ' to these you give ' ; for it is dative *his* and *quis*, like nominative *hi* and *qui*, or else it is *hibus* like *quibus*.[b]

73. Although the dative *patri familias* [a] ' to the father of the household ' is used, still, if they wished to follow Regularities, they ought never to have said nominative *pater familias*, because the word is genitive *familiae*, like *Atiniae* and *Catiniae*, and therefore nominative *familia*,[b] like *Atinia* and *Catinia*. Likewise, they ought not to say *patres familias* [c] ' fathers of a household,' but as Sisenna [d] writes, they should say *patres familiarum* ' fathers of households.'

74. Nor ought usage to fluctuate, in that some said herds *boum* ' of cattle,' others *boverum*,[a] and others said statues *Ioum* ' of Jupiters,' others *Ioverum*,[a] since

---

is a nominative ; or else the text is too corrupt for restoration. [c] In favour of this form, see Charisius, i. 107 Keil. [d] Page 128 Funaioli ; L. Cornelius Sisenna, 119–67 B.C., orator and statesman, author of a history dealing chiefly with the times of Sulla.

§ 74. [a] It is doubtful if these forms had any real existence ; if so, *boverum* was formed after *iugerum*, and *Ioverum* after *Venerum*, to avoid the inconvenient forms *boum* and *Ioum*, which Varro would have pronounced *bovom* and *Iovom*.

VARRO

Iovem bovem struem Iovi bovi strui ; nec cum haec
convenirent in obliquis casibus, dubitare debuerunt in
rectis, in quibus[2] nunc in consuetudine aliter dicere,
pro Ious[3] Iupiter, pro b⟨o⟩us[4] bos, pro strus[5] strues.[6]

XXXIX. 75. Deinceps dicam de altero genere
vocabulorum, in quo contentiones fiunt, ut albu*m*[1]
albius albissumum, in quo it⟨em⟩[2] analogias non servari apparet : nam cum sit simile salsum caldum et
dicatur ab his salsius caldius, salsissimum caldissimum, debuit dici, quoniam simile est bonum malum,
ab his bonius et malius, bonissimum et malissimum.
Nonne dicitur bonum melius optimum, ⟨malum peius
pessimum⟩ ?[3]

76. In aliis verbis nihil[1] ⟨de⟩est,[2] ut dulcis dulcior
dulcissimus, in aliis primum, ut peium ⟨a⟩[3] peius
pessimum, in aliis medium, ut caesior ⟨a⟩[3] caesius
caesi⟨s⟩sumus, in aliis bina sunt quae ⟨de⟩sint[4] ab
eadem voce declinata, et ea ita ut alias desint secundum et tertium, ut in hoc mane manius manissime,
alias ut duo prima absint, ut ab optimum optius

[2] *L. Sp., for* propinquibus.   [3] *L. Sp., for* iouis.   [4] *L. Sp., for* bus.   [5] *L. Sp., for* struus.   [6] *L. Sp., for* struis.
§ 75. [1] *Rhol., for* albus.   [2] *Mue., for* id.   [3] *Added by Aug., with B.*
§ 76. [1] *For* nichil.   [2] *Aldus, for* est.   [3] *Added by A. Sp.*   [4] *Mue., for* sint.

[b] The reasoning demands hypothetical nominatives bearing
the same relation to the oblique forms, so that either *Ious,
bous, strus* or *Iovis, bovis, struis* must be posited as the
unused ' regular ' nominatives.
§ 75. [a] Adjectives and adverbs.   [b] Varro normally, but
not always, quotes adjectives in the neuter form.   [c] The
syncopated form of *calidum*, common in popular speech at
the time of Varro ; *cf.* Quintilian, *Inst. Orat.* i. 6. 19. For
430

like the genitive *Iovis bovis struis* were the accusative *Iovem bovem struem* and the dative *Iovi bovi strui* ; and since these agreed in the oblique cases, they ought not to have varied in the nominative forms, in which it is now customary to use different formations, *Iupiter* for *Ious*,[b] *bos* for *bous*,[b] *strues* ' heap of offering-cakes ' for *strus*.[b]

XXXIX. 75. Next I shall speak of a second [a] class of words, in which degrees of comparison are made, like *album* [b] ' white,' *albius* ' whiter,' *albissumum* ' whitest,' in which likewise it is clear that the Regularities are not preserved. For whereas *salsum* 'salty' and *caldum* [c] ' hot ' are alike, and from these are made the comparatives *salsius* and *caldius*, and the superlatives *salsissimum* and *caldissimum*, there should be made from *bonum* ' good ' and *malum* ' bad,' since these are alike, the comparatives *bonius* and *malius*, the superlatives *bonissimum* and *malissimum*. But are not the actual forms in use *bonum melius optimum*, and *malum peius pessimum* ?

76. In some words no form is lacking ; for example, *dulcis* ' sweet,' *dulcior*, *dulcissimus*. In others the first or positive degree is lacking, as *peium* from *peius* ' worse,' *pessimum* ' worst ' ; in others the second is lacking, as *caesior* from *caesius* ' blue-eyed,' superlative *caesissimum* [a] ; in still others two are lacking which are derived from the same word, and these in such a way that in some instances the second and the third are lacking, as *manius* and *manissime* in connexion with the adverb *mane* ' early in the morning ' ; that in others the first two are wanting, as *optum* and *optius*

metrical facility the poets normally used positive *calidus*, comparative (nom. sing.) *caldior*.

§ 76.   [a] This form is not otherwise attested.

optum, alias ut primum et tertium desit, ut a melius
melum[5] melissumum.

77. Praeterea si dicerentur similiter, cum similia
essent ⟨m⟩acer[1] tener et macerrimus[2] tenerrimus, non
discreparet in his macrior tenerior,[3] neque alia tri-
syllaba ⟨alia quadrisyllaba⟩[4] fierent ; et si in his
dominaretur similitudo, diceremus ut candidissimus
candidissima, pauperrumus pauperrima, sic candidus
candida, pauper paupera ; et ut dicimus doctus docta,
doctissimus doctissima, sic diceremus frugalissumus
frugalissima, frug⟨al⟩us et frug⟨al⟩a.[5]

78. Et si proportione[1] esse⟨nt⟩ verba, ut[2] uno
vocabulo dicimus virum et mulierem sapientem et
diligentem et sapientiorem et diligentiorem, sic diceremus item, cum pervenissemus ad summum, quod
nunc facimus aliter : nam virum dicimus sap⟨i⟩entis-
simum et diligentissimum, feminam sapientissimam
et diligentissimam. Quod ad vocabulorum huius
generis exempla pertinet, multa sunt reliqua ; sed ea

[5] *L. Sp., for* melummelius.
  § 77. [1] *Laetus, for* acer ; *L. Sp. deleted* sacer *after* macer ;
see note a. [2] *L. Sp. deleted* sacerrimus *after* macerrimus.
[3] *Aug., with B, for* tenerrimus. [4] *Added by Sciop.* [5] *L.
Sp., for* frugus et fruga.
  § 78. [1] *Laetus, for* proportionem. [2] *Aldus, for* et.

---

[b] The corresponding ideas were expressed by forms unrelated
etymologically, *cf.* § 75.
  § 77. [a] The mss. have *sacer* between *macer* and *tener*, and
sacerrimus between *macerrimus* and *tenerrimus* ; but the
word is out of place in this passage, as it has no comparative,
for which *sanctior* is regularly substituted. [b] *Pauper*

from *optimum* [b] ' best ' ; and that in others the first and the third are lacking, as *melum* and *melissumum* from *melius* ' better.'

77. Besides, if they were spoken in like manner, then since *macer* ' lean ' and *tener* ' tender ' [a] are alike, and their superlatives *macerrimus* and *tenerrimus*, there would be no difference in their comparatives *macrior* and *tenerior*, nor would some such words have three syllables and others four. And if likeness ruled in such words, then just as we say *candidissimus* ' most shining ' and fem. *candidissima*, *pauperrumus* ' poorest ' and fem. *pauperrima*, so we should say *candidus* ' shining ' and fem. *candida*, *pauper* ' poor ' and fem. *paupera*.[b] And as we say *doctus* ' learned ' and fem. *docta*, *doctissimus* ' most learned ' and fem. *doctissima*, so we should say *frugalissumus* ' most thrifty ' and fem. *frugalissima*, *frugalus* ' thrifty ' and fem. *frugala*.[c]

78. And if words were in regular relation to each other, as with one word [a] we call a man and a woman *sapiens* ' wise ' and *diligens* ' diligent,' *sapientior* ' wiser ' and *diligentior* ' more diligent,' so we should speak in the same way when we had come to the superlative—a thing which we now do quite otherwise [b] : for we call a man *sapientissimus* and *diligentissimus*, a woman *sapientissima* and *diligentissima*. As for examples of words of this class, there are many still remaining ; but those which have been mentioned

serves for all genders in the nominative, as it belongs to the third declension. [c] The form in actual use for the positive is the dative noun *frugi* : older Latin used *frugalis*.

§ 78. [a] These third declension adjectives use the same forms for masc. and fem. [b] All superlatives are of the second and first declensions, distinguishing the fem. from the masc. forms.

VARRO

quae dicta, ad iudicandum satis sunt, quo*r*[3] analogias
in collatione verborum sequi non debeamus.

XL. 79. Magnitudinis vocabula cum possint esse
terna, ut cista cistula cistella, in ⟨aliis⟩ media[1] non
sunt, ut in his macer macricolus macellus, niger nigricolus nigellus.   Item minima in quibusdam non sunt,
ut avis avicula av⟨i⟩cella,[2] caput capitulum capitellum.
In hoc genere vocabulorum quoniam multa desunt,
dicendum est non esse in eo potius sequendam quam
consuetudinem rationem.   Quod ad vocabulorum
genera quattuor pertinet, ut in hoc potius consuetudinem quam analogias dominari facile animadverti
possit, dictum est.

XLI. 80. Sequitur de nominibus, quae differunt a
vocabulis ideo quod sunt finita ac significant res pro-
prias, ut Paris *H*elena, cum vocabula sint infinita ac
res com⟨m⟩unis designent,[1] ut vir mulier ; e quibus
sunt alia nomina ab nominibus, ut Il*i*um ab Ilo et Il*i*a
ab Il*i*o,[2] alia a vocabulo, ut ab albo Albius, ab atro
Atrius.   In neutris servata est analogia : nam et cum
sit a Romulo Roma, proportione non est quod debuit
esse ⟨Romula, non Roma⟩.[3]

---

[3] *L. Sp., for* quod *F* (*corrected from* quorum).

§ 79.   [1] *Aug.* (*quoting a friend*), *for* in mediis.   [2] *For*
aucella.

§ 80.   [1] *Aug., with B, for* designentur.   [2] *Aug., with B,*
for illum ab illo et illa ab illo.   [3] *Added by Stephanus, cf.*
ix. 50 ; *but the lacuna is more serious, for it should show also*
irregularity in the derivation of proper names from common
nouns.

---

§ 79.   [a] That is, diminution in size.   [b] The forms *aucella*
and *avicella* do occur in later Latin.

are enough for the formation of a judgement why in the comparison of words we do not have to follow Regularities.

XL. 79. Whereas there can be a set of three words to indicate size,[a] like *cista* ' casket,' *cistula*, *cistella*, in some the middle terms do not exist, as in these : *macer* ' lean,' *macricolus*,[b] *macellus*, and *niger* ' black,' *nigricolus*,[b] *nigellus*. Likewise in certain words the terms for least size do not exist, such as *avis* ' bird,' *avicula*, *avicella*,[b] and *caput* ' head,' *capitulum*, *capitellum*.[b] Since in this class of words there are many forms lacking, we must say that in it theory must not be followed rather than usage.

As to the four classes of common nouns, I have said enough ; and it can easily be observed that here usage governs rather than Regularities.

XLI. 80. The matter of proper nouns now follows, which differ from common nouns in that they are definite and denote special things, like the names *Paris* and *Helen*, while common nouns are indefinite and indicate general ideas, like *vir* ' man ' and *mulier* ' woman.' Among these there are some proper names from proper names, like *Ilium* from *Ilus*,[a] and *Ilia* [b] from *Ilium* ; others are from a common noun, like *Albius* [c] from *album* [d] ' white,' *Atrius* from *atrum* ' black.' In neither set is Regularity preserved : for inasmuch as from *Romulus* comes the name *Roma*, there is not the form which should have come into existence by regular relation, namely, *Romula* and not *Roma*.

§ 80. [a] Grandfather of Priam. [b] Daughter of Numitor, and mother of Romulus and Remus. [c] Family name of Tibullus. [d] The word *vocabulum* ' common noun ' includes in Varro's terminology both substantive and adjective.

81. ⟨Item Perpenna debuit esse⟩[1] Perpenni filia, non Perpennae ⟨filius. Nam⟩[2] Perpenna mulieris nomen esse debuit et nata esse a Perpenno, quod est ut Arvernus[3] Percelnus Perpennus, Arverna[3] Percelna Perpenna. Quod si Marcus Perpenna virile est nomen et analogia sequenda, Lucius *A*elia et Quintus Mucia virilia nomina esse debebunt ; item quae dicunt ab Rhodo, Andro, Cyzico Rhodius, ⟨Andrius⟩,[4] Cyzicenus, similíter Cyzicius dici ⟨debebat⟩,[5] et civis unus quisque : no*n*[6] ut Athen*a*eus dicitur rhetor nomine, etsi non sit Atheniensis.

82. In hoc ipso analogia non est, quod alii nomina habent ab oppidis, alii aut non habent aut non ut debent habent.

83. Habent plerique libertini a municipio manumissi, in quo, ut societatum et fanorum servi, non servarunt proportione[1] rationem, et Romanorum liberti debuerunt dici ut a Faventia Faventinus, ab Reate Reatinus sic a Roma Romanus, ut nomin*e*ntur[2] libertini[3] orti ⟨a⟩[4] publicis servis Romani, qui manumissi ante quam sub magistratu⟨u⟩*m*[5] nomina, qui eos liberarunt, succedere c⟨o⟩eperunt.

---

§ 81. [1] item *added by Stephanus*, Perpenna *by Kent*, debuit esse by *L. Sp.*   [2] *Added by Kent.*   [3] *Mue., for* Arb-.   [4] *Added by Aldus.*   [5] *Added by Mue.*   [6] *Canal, for* nam.

§ 83. [1] *L. Sp., for* proportionem.   [2] *Vertranius, for* nominantur.   [3] *Vertranius, for* a libertinis.   [4] *Added by Mue.*   [5] *Sciop., for* magistratus.

---

§ 81. [a] A well-known Roman family name of Etruscan origin ; masculine, though of the first declension.   [b] Instead of the actual *Aelius* and *Mucius*.   [c] Of the second century

81. Likewise, *Perpenna* [a] ought to be the daughter of *Perpennus*, not the son of *Perpenna*. For *Perpenna* ought to be the name of a woman, and to mean a child of *Perpennus*; this is like masculine *Arvernus*, *Percelnus*, feminine *Arverna* and *Percelna*, so also *Perpennus* and *Perpenna*. But if *Marcus Perpenna* is a man's name and Regularity is to be followed, then *Lucius Aelia* and *Quintus Mucia* [b] will have to be men's names. Likewise the names which they use derived from *Rhodus* 'Rhodes,' *Andros*, and *Cyzicus*, are *Rhodius* 'Rhodian,' *Andrius* 'Andrian,' and *Cyzicenus* 'Cyzicene'; but if made in like manner the last ought to be *Cyzicius*, and each name ought to denote a citizen of the place: not as a certain rhetorician is called Athenaeus,[c] although he is not an Athenian by birth.

82. In this very matter, then, there is no Regularity, because some have names from the towns, others either have names from other sources or have names from towns from which they ought not to get them.

83. Most freedmen set free by a free town get their names from the town; in this matter, those who were slaves of guilds and temples have not observed the rule in the same way; and the freedmen of the Romans ought to have got the name *Romanus*,[a] like *Faventinus* from *Faventia* and *Reatinus* from *Reate*. In this way the freedmen whose parents were state slaves would be named *Romanus*, who had been set free before they began to take the names of the magistrates who set them free.

B.C.: not to be confused with the more celebrated Athenaeus of Naucratis, of the second century A.D., who wrote the *Deipnosophistae*.

§ 83. [a] Cf. Livy, iv. 61. 10.

84. Hinc quoque illa nomina Lesas, Ufenas, Carrinas, Maecenas, quae cum essent ab loco ut Urbinas, et tamen Urbin⟨i⟩us,[1] ab his debuerunt dici ad nostrorum nominum ⟨similitudinem[2] Lesius Ufenius Carrinius Maecenius⟩[3] . . . [4]

§ 84. [1] *GS.;* Urbinus *older editions; for* uerbinus. [2] *Added by Laetus.* [3] *Added by GS.* [4] *Here the rest of the line, and all the reverse of the folio, are left vacant in F; but the remaining material which was contained in the book would have occupied much more space. Probably an entire quaternion had been lost from the archetype of F.*

84. From this practice came also such names as *Lesas, Ufenas, Carrinas, Maecenas* [a] ; since these are from the place of origin, like *Urbinas,*[b] alongside *Urbinius,* there should from them have been formed, after the likeness of our names, the names *Lesius, Ufenius, Carrinius, Maecenius.*[c] . . .

§ 84. [a] Regularly formed cognomina ; *Lesas* is not otherwise known, but the other three are. *Maecenas* was the friend of Augustus and the patron of literary men. [b] From Urbinum in Umbria. [c] Inasmuch as Roman gentile names almost always ended in *-ius.*

⟨M. TERENTI VARRONIS
DE LINGUA LATINA

LIBER VIII EXPLICIT ; INCIPIT

LIBER VIIII⟩

I. 1. . . . ⟨Insignis eorum est error qui malunt
quae⟩[1] nesciunt docere quam discere quae ignorant :
in quo fuit Crates, nobilis grammaticus, qui fretus
Chrysippo, homine acutissimo qui reliquit περὶ ἀνω-
μαλίας *III* libros,[2] contra analogian atque Aristar-
c*hum*[3] est nixus, sed ita, ut script*a* indicant eius, ut
neutrius videatur pervidisse voluntatem, quod et
Chrysippus de inaequabilitate cum scribit sermon*is*,[4]
propositum habet ostendere similes res dissimilibus
verbis et dissimiles simil*ibus*[5] esse vocabulis notatas,
id quod est verum,[6] et *quod*[7] Aristarchus, de aequa-
bilitate *cum* scribit[8] ei⟨us⟩de⟨m⟩,[9] verborum similitudinem quandam[10] ⟨in⟩ inclinatione[11] sequi iubet,
quoad patiatur consuetudo.

§ 1.   [1] *The folio contains but 23 lines instead of the usual
39, and as traces of the heading were formerly visible, the
lost text was not very extensive. The subject-matter of the
first extant sentence also indicates that not much has been
lost ; the additions are by Boot.*   [2] *L. Sp., for* lei libri.
440

MARCUS TERENTIUS VARRO'S
ON THE LATIN LANGUAGE

BOOK VIII ENDS HERE, AND HERE BEGINS

BOOK IX

I. 1. . . . They are a prey to extraordinary error, who prefer to teach what they do not know, rather than to learn that of which they are ignorant. In this position was the famous grammarian Crates, who placed his reliance on Chrysippus, a man of great acumen who left three books *On Anomaly*, and contended against Regularity and Aristarchus, but in such a way—as his writings show—that he does not seem to have understood thoroughly the intent of either. For Chrysippus, when he writes about the Inconsistency of speech, has as his object the showing that like things are denoted by unlike words and that unlike things are denoted by like words, as is true; and Aristarchus, when he writes about the Consistency of the same, bids us follow a certain likeness of words in their derivation, as far as usage permits.

---

[3] *For* Aristharcum.   [4] *Stephanus, with B, for* sermones.
[5] dissimilis similibus *Wilmanns, for* dissimilibus similes.
[6] *Aldus, for* uerbum.   [7] *Mue., for* cum.   [8] *Mue., for* conscribit.   [9] *GS., for* et de.   [10] *Groth, for* quarundam.   [11] *A. Sp. ; in* declinatione *L. Sp. ; for* inclinationes.

441

VARRO

2. Sed ii qui in loquendo partim sequi iube⟨n⟩t[1]
nos consuetudinem partim rationem, non tam discrepant, quod consuetudo et analogia coniunctiores
sunt inter se quam iei credunt,

3. quod est nata ex quadam consuetudine analogia et ex hac ⟨consuetudine item anomalia.[1] Quare
quod[2]⟩ consuetudo ex dissimilibus et similibus verbis
eorumque[3] declinationibus constat, neque anomalia
neque analogia est repudianda, nisi si non est homo
ex anima, quod est[4] ex corpore et anima.

4. Sed ea quae dicam quo facilius pervideri possint,
prius de trinis copulis discernendum (nam[1] confusim
ex utraque parte pleraque dicuntur, quorum[2] alia ad
aliam referri debent summam) : primum de copulis
naturae et ⟨u⟩suis[3] : haec enim duo sunt quo deri-
gunt⟨ur⟩[4] diversa, quod aliud est dicere ⟨esse⟩[5] verborum analogias, aliud dicere uti oportere analogiis ;
secundum de copulis multitudinis ac finis, utrum
omnium verborum dicatur esse analogia⟨r⟩um[6] usus
an maioris partis ; tertium de copulis personarum,
qui eis debe⟨a⟩nt[7] uti, quae sunt plures.

5. Alia enim populi universi, alia singulorum, et de
ieis non eadem oratoris et poetae, quod eorum non

§ 2. [1] *Victorius, for* iubet.
§ 3. [1] *Added by Mue.*   [2] *Added by L. Sp.*   [3] *L. Sp.,
for* eorum quod.   [4] homo ex anima quod est *is repeated in*
F, *but was deleted by* A. Sp., *with* V, p *;* ex anima quod est
was deleted by Aug., with B.
§ 4. [1] *Aug. deleted* cum *after* nam.   [2] *Aldus, for*
quarum.   [3] *L. Sp., for* suis *; cf. Gellius,* iv.16. 1.   [4] *GS. ;*
quod derigunt *L. Sp. ; for* quod erigunt.   [5] *Added by L.
Sp. : cf.* § 6.   [6] *Mue., for* analogia an.   [7] *Kent, for*
debent.

§ 4. [a] Gellius, iv. 16 says that Varro always made the
442

2.   But those who give us advice in the matter of speaking, some saying to follow usage and others saying to follow theory, are not so much at variance, because usage and regularity are more closely connected with each other than those advisers think.

3.   For Regularity is sprung from a certain usage in speech, and from this usage likewise is sprung Anomaly.   Therefore, since usage consists of unlike and like words and their derivative forms, neither Anomaly nor Regularity is to be cast aside, unless man is not of soul because he is of body and of soul.

4.   But that what I am about to say may be more easily grasped, first there must be a clear distinction of three sets of relations ; for most things are said indiscriminately in two ways, and of them some ought to be referred to one principle and others to other principles.   First, the distinction of the relations of nature and use [a] ; for these are two factors which are diverse in the goals toward which they direct themselves, because it is one thing to say that Regularities exist in words, and another thing to say that we ought to follow the Regularities.   Second, the distinction of the relations of extension and limitation, whether the use of the Regularities should be said to be proper in all words, or only in a majority of them.   Third, the distinction in the relations of the speaking persons, how [b] the majority of persons ought to observe the Regularities.

5.   For some words and forms are the usage of the people as a whole, others belong to individual persons ; and of these, the words of the orator and those of the poet are not the same, because their

genitive of the fourth declension in -UIS.   [b] *Qui* is here the instrumental-ablatival adverb.

idem ius. Itaque populus universus debet in omnibus verbis uti analogia et, si perperam est consuetus, corrigere se ipsum, cum orator non debeat in omnibus uti, quod sine offensione non potest facere, cum poeta[1] transilire lineas impune possit.

6. Populus enim in sua potestate, singuli in illius : itaque ut suam quisque consuetudinem, si mala est, corrigere debet, sic populus suam. Ego populi consuetudinis non sum ut dominus, at ille meae est. Ut rationi optemperare debet gubernator, gubernatori unus quisque in navi, sic populus rationi, nos[1] singuli populo. Quare ad quamcumque summam in dicendo referam si animadvertes, intelleges, utrum dicatur analogia esse an uti oportere ⟨ea ; itemque intelleges si ad analogiam usum loquendi oportea⟩t redigere, tum dici id in populum aliter ac ⟨in singulos nec⟩ i⟨de⟩m de omnibus dici[2] in eum qui sit in populo.

II. 7. Nunc iam primum dicam pro universa analogia, cur non modo ⟨non⟩[1] videatur esse reprehendenda, sed etiam cur in usu quodammodo sequenda ; secundo de singulis criminibus, quibus rebus possint quae dicta sunt contra solvi, dicam ita ut generatim

§ 5. [1] *L. Sp., for* poetae.
§ 6. [1] *Laetus, B, for* non.   [2] *F has here* uti oporteret redigeretur dici id in populum aliter ac inde omnibus dici ; *Aug., with B, read* redigere *for* redigeretur ; *Mue. emended to* uti oportere ea ; et quom poscitur ut usus ad id quod oporteret redigeretur dici, *etc., deleting* inde omnibus dici *as a gloss ; Reiter proposed* uti oportere et redigere, tum dici, *with the same deletion ; GS. proposed that which is in the text, except that for their* usus loquendi oporteret redigeretur, *I have adopted* usum loquendi oporteat redigere tum, *taking* oporteat *from Fay* (ubi oporteat redigere tibi dici, *with the rest like Mueller's version), and* redigere tum *from Reiter.*
§ 7. [1] *Added by Stephanus.*

rights and limitations are not the same. Therefore the people as a whole ought in all words to use Regularity, and if it has a wrong practice, it ought to correct itself ; whereas the orator ought not to use Regularity in all words, because he cannot do so without giving offence, and on the other hand the poet can with impunity leap across all the bounds.

6. For the people has power over itself, but the individuals are in its power ; therefore as each one ought to correct his own usage if it is bad, so should the people correct its usage. I am not the master—so to speak—of the people's usage, but it is of mine. As a helmsman ought to obey reason, and each one in the ship ought to obey the helmsman, so the people ought to obey reason, and we individuals ought to obey the people. Therefore, if you will take notice of each principle on which I shall base my argument in the matter of speaking, you will appreciate whether Regularity is said merely to exist, or it is said that we ought to follow it ; and likewise you will appreciate that if the practice of speech ought to be reduced to Regularity, then this is meant for the people in a different sense from that in which it is meant for individuals, and that that which is taken from the entire body of speakers is not necessarily meant in the same form for him who is only an individual in the people.

II. 7. Now I shall speak first in support of Regularity as a whole, why, as it seems, it not only should not be censured, but even should in practice be followed in a certain measure ; and secondly, concerning the several charges against it, I shall give the arguments by which the objections can be refuted, arranging them in such a way that I shall include,

445

comprehenda*m*[2] et ea quae in priore libro sunt dicta
et ea quae possunt dici atque[3] illic praeterii.

III. 8. Primum quod aiunt, qui bene loqui velit
consuetudinem sequi oportere, non rationem similitudinum, quod, alter*am*[1] si neglegat, sine offensione
facere non possit, alter*am*[1] si sequatur, quod sine
reprehensione non sit futurum, e⟨r⟩ra⟨n⟩t,[2] quod qui
in loquendo consuetudinem qua oportet uti sequitur,
⟨eam sequitur⟩[3] non sine[4] ratione.

IV. 9. Nam vocabula ac verba quae declinamus
similiter, ea in consuetudine esse videmus et ad ea⟨m⟩[1]
conferimus et, si quid est erratum, non sine ea cor-
rigimus. Nam ut, qui triclinium constrarunt, si quem
lectum de tribus unum imparem posuerunt aut de
paribus nimium aut parum produxerunt, una cor-
rigimus et ad consuetudinem co⟨m⟩munem et ad
aliorum tricliniorum analogias, sic si quis in oratione
in pronuntiando ita declinat verba ut dicat disparia,
quod peccat redigere debemus ad ceterorum similium
verborum rationem.

V. 10. Cum duo peccati genera sint in declina-
tion*e*,[1] unum quod in consuetudinem perperam recep-
tum est, alterum quod nondum est et perperam dicatur,
unum dant non oportere dici, quod ⟨non⟩[2] sit in consuetudine, alterum non conceditur quin ita dicatur,

---

[2] *Aldus, for* compraehendant. [3] *For* atquae.
§ 8. [1] *L. Sp., for* alterum. [2] *Aug., for* erat. [3] *Added
by Mue., after L. Sp.* [4] *Mue. deleted* ea *after* sine.
§ 9. [1] *Aug., with B, for* ea.
§ 10. [1] *L. Sp., for* declinationum. [2] *Added by Aug.*

---

§ 9. [a] Or a set of dining-couches : the Romans placed
three couches on three sides of a square in the centre of which
446

item by item, those which have been narrated in the previous book and also those which can be presented but were passed over by me in that place.

III. 8. First, as to their alleging that he who wishes to speak well ought to observe usage and not the theory of likenesses, because if he disregards the former he cannot do so without giving offence, and if he follows the latter it will not be without incurring rebuke : they are mistaken, because he who in speaking follows the usage which he ought to employ, is following it also without disregard of the theory.

IV. 9. For we see that nouns and verbs which we inflect in similar ways are in general usage, and we compare others with this usage, and if there is any error we make the correction with the help of usage. For if those who have arranged the dining-room *a* have among the three couches set one that is of a different size, or among couches that match have brought one too far forward, or not far enough, we join in making the correction according to common usage and to the analogies of other dining-rooms ; in the same way, if in speech any one in his utterance should so inflect the words as to speak irregular forms, we ought to revise his mistake according to the model of other similar words.

V. 10. Now there are two kinds of wrong forms in inflection ; one, that which has been erroneously accepted into general usage ; the other, that which is not yet so accepted and may be called incorrect. The latter they grant ought not to be said, because it is not in usage, but as for the former they merely do not admit the propriety of saying it in this way ;

stood the dining-table.   The couches should be identical and symmetrically placed.

ut si⟨t⟩³ similiter, cum id faciant, ac, si quis puerorum
per delicias pedes male ponere atque imitari vatias
c⟨o⟩eperit, hos corrigi oportere si conceda⟨n⟩t,⁴ contra
si quis in consuetudine ambulandi iam factus sit vatia
aut conpernis, si eum corrigi non conceda⟨n⟩t.⁴

11. Non sequitur, ut stulte faciant qui pueris in
geniculis alligent serperastra, ut eorum depravata
corrigant crura ? Cum *ri*tuperandus¹ non sit medicus
qui e longinqua mala consuetudine aegrum in meliorem traducit, quare reprehendus sit qui orationem
minus valentem propter malam consuetudinem tradu-
cat in meliorem ?

VI. 12. Pictores Apelles,¹ Protogenes, sic alii
artufices egregii non reprehendundi, quod consuetudinem Miconos, Dioris,² Arimmae, etiam superiorum
non sunt secuti : Aristophanes improbandus, qui
potius in quibusdam veritatem³ quam consuetudinem
secutus ?

VII. 13. Quod si viri sapientissimi, et in re
militari et in aliis rebus multa contra veterem consuetudinem cum essent ⟨a⟩usi,¹ laudati, despiciendi
sunt qui potiorem dicunt oportere esse consuetudinem
ratione.

VIII. 14. An cum quis perperam consuerit quid
facere in civitate, non modo ⟨non⟩¹ patiemur, sed

³ *Laetus, for* si.   ⁴ *Aldus, for* concedat.
  § 11.   ¹ *G, H, Victorius, for* detuperandus.
  § 12.   ¹ *For* Appelles.   ² *Aug., with* B, *for* Dioros.
³ *p, Laetus, for* ueteritatem.
  § 13.   ¹ *Canal, for* usi.
  § 14.   ¹ *Added by Aug., with* B.

§ 11.   ᵃ The interrogation-mark was placed here by
Mueller ; the question is sarcastic.

so that when they do this it is just as if they should grant that the boys ought to be corrected in case any of them in wilfulness begins to manage his feet awkwardly and to imitate the bowlegged, but should refuse to grant that one should be corrected if he in his habit of walking has already become bowlegged or knock-kneed.

11.   Does it not follow that they act foolishly who fasten splints on the knees of children, to straighten their crooked leg-bones ? [a]   Since even that physician is not to be censured who makes a healthier man out of one who has been ill as a result of a long-continued bad habit, why should he be blamed who brings into better condition a way of speech which has been less effective on account of bad usage ?

VI. 12.   The painters Apelles [a] and Protogenes,[b] and other famous artists are not to be blamed because they did not follow the ways of Micon,[c] Diores,[d] Arimmas,[d] and even earlier craftsmen ; then must Aristophanes [e] be condemned because in some things he followed reality rather than usage ?

VII. 13.   But if the wisest men have been praised because both in warfare and in other things they had dared do much that was against old usage, then they must be despised who say that usage ought to be considered as better than good theory.

VIII. 14.   Or when a person has been accustomed to do something wrong in civil life, shall we not only

§ 12.   [a] Distinguished Greek painter of the time of Alexander the Great.   [b] Distinguished Greek painter, contemporary of Apelles.   [c] Sculptor and painter at Athens, middle of the fifth century B.C.   [d] Entirely unknown otherwise ; the names are perhaps corrupt, *cf.* Bergk in *Philol.* xxx. 682 (1870), and Georges in *Fleckeisen's Jahrbücher*, cxxxv. 768 (1887).   [e] See v. 9 note *a.*

etiam p⟨o⟩ena² afficiemus, idem si quis perperam consuerit dicere verbum, non corrigemus, cum id fiat
sine p⟨o⟩ena ?

IX. 15.   Et hi qui pueros in ludum mittunt, ut
discant quae nesciunt verba quemadmodum scribant,
idem barbatos qui ignorabunt verba quemadmodum
oporteat dici non docebimus, ut sciant qua ratione
conveniat dici ?

X. 16.   Sed ut nutrix pueros a lacte non subito
avellit a consuetudine, cum a cibo pristino in meliorem
traducit, sic maiores in¹ loquendo a minus² commodis
verbis ad ea quae sunt cum ratione modice traducere
oportet.   Cum sint ⟨in⟩³ consuetudine contra ratio-
ne⟨m⟩⁴ alia verba ita ut ea facile tolli possint, alia
ut videantur esse fixa, quae leviter haerent ac sine
offensione commutari possunt⁵ statim⁶ ad rationem
corrigi oportet, quae autem sunt ita ut in praesentia
corrigere nequeas quin ita dicas, his oportet, si possis,
non uti : sic enim obsolescent ac postea iam obliterata
facilius corrigi poterunt.

XI. 17.   Quas novas verbi declinationes ratione¹
introductas respuet forum, his boni poetae, maxime

---

² G, a, Laetus, for penam.
   § 16.   ¹ Mue., for in maioris.   ² Aug., for animus.
³ Added by Ed. Veneta.   ⁴ Laetus, for ratione.   ⁵ Aldus,
for possint.   ⁶ Mue., for si enim.
   § 17.   ¹ Laetus, for rationes.

---

   § 14.   ᵃ Representing idem, nom. sing. The whole sentence
is a double question, of which the first part is really a statement of fact as a basis for the real query, which comes at
the end.
   § 15.   ᵃ Hi, hanging nom., resumed by barbatos.   ᵇ Varro
refers to wrong forms and wrong pronunciations of the
words.

not tolerate him but even visit him with punishment
—and yet *a* if a person has the habit of saying a
word wrong, shall we not correct him, when this
may be done without actual punishment ?

IX. 15. And these men *a* who send their boys to
school to learn how to write words which they don't
know—shall we not likewise instruct these men,
bewhiskered adults as they are, who do not know
how the words ought to be spoken, that they may
know by what logical theory they may properly be
pronounced ? *b*

X. 16. But as the nurse does not with sudden-
ness tear her nurslings away from their wonted
method of feeding, when she changes them from their
first food to a better, so we ought to go gradually
and judiciously in matters of speech, in changing
older persons from less suitable words to those
which accord with logical theory. Since among the
illogical words which are in common usage there are
some which can easily be eliminated, and others of
such a sort that they seem firmly fixed,*a* it is proper
to correct at once in the direction of logic only those
which are lightly attached and can be changed
without giving offence ; but those which are such
that for the present you cannot make the correction
so as not to speak them thus, these you ought, if
possible, to refrain from using. For thus they will
become unwonted and afterward, when already
blurred to the memory, they can be more easily
corrected.

XI. 17. Such new inflectional forms as are introduced by logical theory but are rejected by the
speech of the forum, these the good poets, especially

§ 16.   *a Cf.* § 10.

scaenici, consuetudine subigere aures populi debent,
quod poetae multum possunt in hoc : propter eos
quaedam verba in declinatione melius, quaedam
deterius dicuntur. Consuetudo loquendi est in
motu : itaque sole⟨n⟩t[2] fieri et meliora[3] deteriora ⟨et
deteriora⟩[4] meliora ; verba perperam dicta[5] apud
antiquos aliquos propter poetas non modo nunc dicuntur recte, sed etiam quae ratione dicta sunt tum,
nun⟨c⟩[6] perperam dicuntur.

XII. 18. Quare qui ad consuetudinem nos vocant,
si ad rectam, sequemur : in eo quoque enim est
analogia ; si ad eam invitant quae est depravata,
nihilo[1] magis sequemur, nisi cum erit necesse, quam[2]
in ceteris rebus mala exempla : nam ea quoque, cum
aliqua vis urget, inviti sequemur. XIII. Neque enim
Lysippus artificum priorum potius ⟨secutus⟩[3] est
vitiosa quam artem ; sic populus facere debet, etiam
singuli, sine offensione quod fiat populi.

19. Qui amissa ⟨non⟩[1] modo quaerant, sed etiam
quod indicium dent, idem, ex sermone si quid
deperiit, non modo nihil[2] impendunt ut requirant, sed
etiam contra indices repugnant ne restituatur ?[3]

20. Verbum quod novum et ratione introductum

---

[2] *Canal, for* solet.   [3] *Canal, for* meliore.   [4] *Added by
Canal.*   [5] *For* dictam.   [6] *Aug., for* num.
§ 18. [1] *For* nichilo.   [2] *Canal, for* sequar.   [3] *Added
here by GS. ; after* vitiosa *by Laetus.*
§ 19. [1] *Added by Aug.*   [2] *For* nichil.   [3] *II, Ed.
Veneta, for* restituantur.

---

§ 18. [a] Of Sicyon, famous sculptor, contemporary of
Alexander the Great.

the dramatists, ought to force upon the ears of the people and accustom them to them. For the poets have great power in this sphere : they are responsible for the fact that certain words are now spoken with improved inflections, and others with worse. The usage of speech is always shifting its position : this is why words of the better sort are wont to become worse, and worse words better ; words spoken wrongly by some of the old-timers are on account of the poets' influence now spoken correctly, and on the other hand some that were then spoken according to logical theory, are now spoken wrongly.

XII. 18. Therefore those who summon us to obey usage, we shall follow, if it be to a correct usage. For in this also there is the principle of Regularity : if they invite us to that usage which is perverted and irregular, we shall not follow it unless it becomes necessary, any more than we follow bad examples in other things ; for we do follow them too, though against our inclinations, when some force bears down upon us. XIII. And in fact Lysippus [a] did not follow the defects of the artists who preceded him, but rather their artistry ; just so should the people do in their speech, and even the individuals, so far as it may be done without offence to the people as a whole.

19. There are some persons who not only hunt for lost articles, but even of their own initiative give any information which they may have : do the same persons, if something has been lost from speech, not only not exert themselves in hunting for it, but even fight against the informers, to keep it from being put back into its place ?

20. As for a word that is new and has been intro-

VARRO

quo minus[1] recipiamus, vitare non debemus. XIV.
Nam ad usum in vestimentis aedificiis supellectili[2]
novitati non impedit vetus consuetudo : quem enim
amor assuetudinis potius in pannis possessorem
retinet, quem ad nova vestimenta traducit ? XV. An
non saepe veteres leges abrogatae novis cedunt ?

XVI. 21. Nonne inusitatis formis vasorum re-
centibus e Graecia adlatis[1] obliteratae antiquae
consuetudinis sinorum et capularum[2] species ? His
formis vocabulorum incontaminati⟨s⟩[3] uti nolent
quas[4] docu⟨e⟩rit ratio[5] propter consuetudinem
veterem ? Et tantum inter duos sensus interesse
volunt, ut oculis semper aliquas figuras supellectilis novas conquirant, contra auris expertis
velint esse ?

XVII. 22. Quotus quisque iam servos[1] habet
priscis nominibus ? Quae mulier suum instrumentum
vestis atque auri veteribus vocabulis appellat ? Sed
indoctis[2] non tam irascendum quam huiusce pravitatis
patronis.

23. Si enim usquequaque non[1] esset analogia,
tum sequebatur, ut in verbis quoque non esset, non,
cum esset usquequaque, ut est, non esse in verbis.
XVIII. Quae enim est pars mundi quae non innumerabiles habeat analogias ? Caelum an mare an
terra, quae in his ?

24. Nonne in caelo ut ab aequinoctiali circulo ad

§ 20. [1] *Vertranius deleted* ut *after* minus.   [2] *Aug. ;*
suppelectili *B ;* supellectilis *Rhol. ; for* suppellectilis.
§ 21. [1] *Aug. ;* allatis *Laetus ; for* ablatis.   [2] *For* capul-
larum.   [3] *L. Sp. ;* ut contaminatis *Mue. ; for* incontami-
nati.   [4] *Stephanus, for* nollent quae.   [5] *Rhol., for*
oratio.
§ 22. [1] *Aldus, for* seruor.   [2] *Aug., for* inductis.
§ 23. [1] *Aug., with B, for* nomen.
454

duced according to logical theory, we ought not for this to shun giving it a hospitable welcome. XIV. For long-standing custom is not a hindrance to novelty in garments, buildings, and utensils, when it is a question of use ; what victim of a habit does the love of that habit rather keep in rags, when the love of novelty [a] is leading him toward new garments ? XV. Are not old laws often annulled and succeeded by new laws ?

XVI. 21. Have not the forms of the old-fashioned pots and cups been swept into oblivion by the unfamiliar shapes of the vessels recently brought from Greece ? Shall they then, on account of old-time habit, be unwilling to use these unsullied forms of words, which good reason has taught them ? And do they claim that there is such difference between the two senses, that for their eyes that are always seeking some new shapes of their furniture, but they wish their ears to have no share in similar novelties ?

XVII. 22. Out of how many slave-owners is there now one who has slaves bearing the ancient names ? What woman calls her outfit of clothing and jewelry by the old words ? But it is not so much at the unlearned that anger must be felt, as at the advocates of this perversity.

23. For if there were Regularity in no place at all, then it follows that there would be none in words either ; not that when it is everywhere present (as it is in fact), there is none in words. XVIII. For what part of the world is there which does not have countless Regularities ? Sky or sea or land, what Regularities are there in these ?

24. As in the sky there is a division from the

§ 20.   [a] Supply *amor novitatis* as subject of *traducit*.

solstitialem et hinc ad septemtrionalem divisum, sic
contra[1] paribus partibus idem a bruma versum contraria parte ?   Non quantum pol*u*⟨s⟩[2] superior abest[3]
a septemtrionali cir⟨culo et is a solstitiali, quem sol
cir⟩cumit cum i*t*[4] ad solstitium,[5] tantundem abest
inferior ab eo quem ἀνταρκτικὸν[6] vocant astrologi et
is a brumal*i* ?[7] Non, quemadmodum quodque signum exortum hoc anno,[8] quotquot annis eodem modo
exoritur ?

25.   Num aliter sol a bruma venit ad aequinoctium,
ac contra cum ad solstitium venit, ad aequinoctialem
circulum et inde ad brumam ?   Nonne luna, ut ab
sole discedit ad aquilonem et inde redit in eandem
viam, sic inde fertur ad austrum et regreditur inde ?
Sed quid plura de astris, ubi difficilius reperitur quid
sit aut fiat in motibus dissimiliter ?

XIX. 26.   At in mari, credo, motus non habent
similitudines[1] geminas, qui in XXIII⟨I⟩[2] horis luna-
ribus cotidie quater se mutant, ac cum sex horis
*a*estus creverunt, totidem decreverunt, rursus idem,
itemque ab his.   An hanc analogian ad diem servant,
ad mensem non item, alios motus sic item cum

---

§ 24. [1] *For* contra a.   [2] *Scaliger, for* polo.   [3] *Mue.
deleted* et abest et *after* abest.   [4] *Added and changed by
GS.* (a solstitiali *Kent, for* ad solstitialem *GS.*), *for* circumit
cum his.   [5] *For* solistitium.   [6] *B, for* arti articon.
[7] *Kent, for* ad brumalem.   [8] *Aldus deleted* quod *after*
anno.
§ 26. [1] *Mue., for* dissimilitudines.   [2] *Aldus, for* XXIII.

---

§ 26. [a] Spoken in sarcasm.   [b] Slightly longer than
solar hours.   [c] In relation to the month ; non-existent, but
assumed for purpose of argument.

Equator to the Tropic of Cancer, and from there to the Arctic Circle, is not also its counterpart, extending from the Tropic of Capricorn in the other direction, likewise divided into equal sections ? Is it not a fact that as far as the North Pole is removed from the Arctic Circle and this from the Tropic of Cancer, around which the sun travels when it comes to the summer solstice, so far the South Pole is from that Circle which the astronomers call the Antarctic, and this from the Tropic of Capricorn ? Is it not true that in the fashion in which each constellation has risen in the sky this year, in just the same fashion it rises each and every year ?

25. The sun does not come in one way from the Tropic of Capricorn to the Equator, does it, and on the other hand, when it comes to the Tropic of Cancer, return in a different way to the Equator and thence to Capricorn ? The moon, when it goes away from the sun to the north and returns from there into the same path which the sun pursues, goes on from there to the south and comes back again in just the same way, does it not ? But why should I speak further of the stars, in the case of which there is unusual difficulty in finding any irregularity which exists or takes place in their motions ?

XIX. 26. But in the sea, I suppose, the motions do not have the twofold likenesses [a]—the motions which in twenty-four lunar [b] hours change themselves four times, and when the tides have risen for six hours, and have ebbed for just as many, they likewise rise again, and in the same fashion ebb after this time. Or do they keep this Regularity for a day's space, and not likewise for a month, since similarly they have another set of motions [c] which

457

habeant aliis[3] inter se convenientes ? De quibus in libro quem de *A*estuariis feci scripsi.

XX. 27. Non in terra in sationibus servata analogia ? Nec cuius modi in praeterito tempore fructuum genera reddidit, similia in praesenti reddit, et cuius modi tritico iacto reddidit segetes, sic *h*ordeo sato proportione reddidit parilis ? Non, ut Europa habet flumina lacus, montis campos, sic habet Asia ?

XXI. 28. Non in volucribus generatim servatur analogia ? Non ex aquilis aquilae atque ut ex turdis qui procreantur turdi, sic ex reliquis sui[1] cuiusque generis ? XXII. An aliter hoc fit quam in aere in aqua ? Non hic conchae inter se generatim innumerabili numero similes ? Non pisces ? An e[2] mura*e*na fit lupus aut merula? Non bos ad bovem collatus similis, et qui ex his progenerantur inter se vituli ? Etiam ubi dissimilis fetus,[3] ut ex ⟨asino et⟩[4] equa mulus, tamen ibi analogia : quod ex quocumque asino et equa nascitur id est mulus aut mula, ut ex equo et asina hinnulei.

XXIII. 29. Non sic ex viro et muliere omnis similis partus, quod pueri et puellae ? Non horum ita inter se[1] omnia similia membra, ut separatim in suo utroque genere similitudine sint[2] paria ? Non, omnes cum sint ex anima et corpore, partes quo*q*ue[3] horum proportione similes ?

---

[3] *Reiter, for* alios.

§ 28. [1] *Aug., with* B, *for* suis.   [2] an e *Aug., for* sane.
[3] *Aug., for* faetus.   [4] *Added by L. Sp. ; Aug., with* B, *added* et asino *after* equa.

§ 29. [1] *Sciop. deleted* non *after* se.   [2] *Aug., for* similitudines intra.   [3] *M, p, Laetus, for* quaque.

agree with one another ? Of these I have written in
the book which I composed *On Tidal Inlets.*

XX. 27. On the earth, is not Regularity preserved in the case of plantings ? Does it not give us
to-day fruits of precisely the same kind as it has
given us in the past ? Does it not regularly return to
us a crop of barley when barley has been sown, even
as it returns a crop of wheat when wheat has been
sown ? Does not Asia have rivers and lakes, mountains and plains, even as Europe has ?

XXI. 28. Is not Regularity preserved among the
birds, according to their kind ? As the progeny of
eagles are eagles and the progeny of thrushes are
thrushes, are not the progeny of the other birds all of
their own proper and special kind ? XXII. Does
the process go on in another way in the water, than
in the air ? Are not the shell-fish here all like their
own kind, despite their countless number ? Are not
the fishes ? Is a sea-bass or a sea-carp produced of
a moray ? Is not one head of cattle like another,
when compared, and so also the calves which are
procreated by them ? Even where the offspring is
unlike the parents, as the mule born of a he-ass and
a mare, even there there is Regularity none the less :
the offspring of any ass and mare whatsoever is a
mule, male or female, as the offspring of a stallion
and a she-ass is a hinny.

XXIII. 29. Are not in this way all the offspring
of man and woman alike, in that they are boys and
girls ? Do these not have all their limbs mutually
alike, in such a way that item by item they are pairs
in likeness, in their own special kinds ? As all are
made up of soul and body, are not also the parts of
soul and body alike with the same regularity ?

30. Quid ergo cum omnes animae hominum sint[1] divisae in octonas partes, hae[2] inter se non proportione similes ? Quinque quibus sentimus, sexta qua cogitamus, septuma qua progeneramus, octava qua voces mittimus ? Igitur quoniam qua loquimur voce oratio est,[3] hanc quoque necesse est natura habere analogias: itaque habet.

XXIV. 31. An non vides, ut Graeci habeant eam quadripertitam, unam in qua si⟨n⟩t[1] casus, alteram in qua tempora, tertiam in qua neutrum, quartum in qua utrumque, sic nos habere ? Ecquid[2] verba nescis ut apud illos sint alia finita, alia non,[3] sic utra⟨que⟩[4] esse apud nos ?

32. Equidem non dubito, qui⟨n⟩ animadverteris[1] item in ea[2] innumerabilem similitudin*um*[3] numerum, ut trium temporum verb⟨i⟩ aut[4] trium personarum. XXV. Quis enim potest non una animadvertisse in omni oratione esse ut legebam lego[5] legam si⟨c⟩[6] lego legis legit, cum haec eadem dicantur alias ut singula, alias ut plura significentur ? Quis est tam tardus qui illas quoque non animadvert⟨er⟩it[7] similitudines, quibus utimur ⟨in⟩[8] imperando, quibus in optando, quibus

§ 30.   [1] *H*, *Laetus*, *for* sunt.   [2] *G, Rhol.*, *for* heae. [3] *L. Sp.*, *for* orationem.
§ 31.   [1] *Mue., for* sit.   [2] *Sciop., for* et quid.   [3] *Aug., with B, for* ne.   [4] *Aug., for* utra.
§ 32.   [1] *Sciop., for* qui animaduertunt.   [2] *L. Sp., for* eam.   [3] *Sciop., for* similitudinem.   [4] *L. Sp., for* uerba ut.   [5] lego *is repeated in F.*   [6] *Bentinus, for* si.   [7] *L. Sp., for* animaduertit.   [8] *Added by Sciop.*

§ 30.   [a] Sight, hearing, taste, smell, touch.
§ 31.   [a] *Cf.* viii. 44.   [b] *Cf.* viii. 45.
§ 32.   [a] That is, the verb-forms used in commands (im-

30. What then of the fact that the souls of men are divided into eight parts—are these parts not mutually alike with regularity ? Five with which we perceive,[a] the sixth with which we think, the seventh with which we procreate, the eighth with which we utter articulate words ? Therefore since the word with which we talk is speech, speech also must by nature have its Regularities ; and it does.

XXIV. 31. Do you not see that the Greeks have divided speech into four parts, one in which the words have cases, a second in which they have indications of time, a third in which they have neither, a fourth in which they have both [a]—and that in the same way we have all these divisions ? Do you not know that among them some words are definite, others not [b]—and that both kinds are present in our language also ?

32. For my part I have no doubt that you have observed the countless number of likenesses in speech, such as those of the three tenses of the verb, or its three persons. XXV. Who indeed can have failed to join you in observing that in all speech there are the three tenses *lego* ' I read,' *legebam* ' I was reading,' *legam* ' I shall read,' and similarly the three persons *lego* ' I read,' *legis* ' thou readest,' *legit* ' he reads,' though these same forms may be spoken in such a way that sometimes one only is meant, at other times more ? Who is so slow-witted that he has not observed also those likenesses which we use in commands,[a] those which we use in wishes, those in questions, those in the case of matters not

peratives and subjunctives) exhibit certain regular resemblances ; and so do those used in wishes, etc.

in interrogando, quibus in infectis rebus, quibus in perfectis, sic in aliis discriminibus ?

XXVI. 33. Quare qui negant esse rationem[1] analogiae, non vide⟨n⟩t[2] naturam non solum orationis, sed etiam mundi ; qui autem vident et sequi negant oportere, pugnant contra naturam, non contra analogian, et pugnant volsillis, non gladio, cum pauca excepta verba ex pelago sermonis ⟨po⟩puli[3] minus ⟨usu⟩[4] trita afferant, cum dicant propterea analogias non esse, similiter ut, si quis viderit mutilum bovem aut luscum hominem claudicantemque equum, neget in[5] bovum hominum et equorum natura similitudines proportione constare.

XXVII. 34. Qui autem duo genera esse dicunt analogiae, unum naturale, quod ut ex satis[1] nascuntur ⟨lentibus⟩[2] lentes[3] sic ex ⟨lupino⟩[4] lupinum, alterum voluntarium, ut in fabrica, cum vident scaenam ut in dexteriore parte sint ostia, sic esse in sinisteriore simili ratione factam, de his duobus generibus naturalem esse analogian, ut sit in motibus caeli, voluntariam non esse, quod ut quo⟨i⟩que[5] fabro lubitum sit possit facere partis scaenae : sic in hominum partibus esse analogias, quod ea⟨s⟩[6] natura faciat, in verbis non esse, quod ea homines ad suam quisque voluntatem fingat, itaque de eisdem rebus alia verba habere Graecos, alia Syros, alia Latinos : ego declinatus verborum et voluntarios et naturalis

§ 33.   [1] *For* orationem.   [2] *For* uidet.   [3] *Canal, for* puli.   [4] *Transferred to this place by Fay ; added by GS. before* populi.   [5] *Sciop. deleted* cornibus *after* in.

§ 34.   [1] *Vertranius, after Aug., for* natis.   [2] *Added by L. Sp.*   [3] *For* lentis.   [4] *L. Sp. ;* ex lupinis *Aug., with* B ; *for* et.   [5] *B, for* quoque.   [6] *Laetus, for* ea.

§ 34.   a The expected continuation is, " They are in error."

completed and those for matters completed, and
similarly in other differentiations ?

XXVI. 33. Therefore those who say that there is
no logical system of Regularity, fail to see the nature
not only of speech, but also of the world. Those
who see it and say that it ought not to be followed,
are fighting against nature, not against the principle
of Regularity, and they are fighting with pincers,
not with a sword, since out of the great sea of speech
they select and offer in evidence a few words not
very familiar in popular use, saying that for this
reason the Regularities do not exist : just as if one
should have seen a dehorned ox or a one-eyed man
and a lame horse, and should say that the likenesses
do not exist with regularity in the nature of cattle,
men, and horses.

XXVII. 34. Those moreover who say that there
are two kinds of Regularity, one natural, namely
that lentils grow from planted lentils, and so does
lupine from lupine, and the other voluntary, as in the
workshop, when they see the stage as having an
entrance on the right and think that it has for a like
reason been made with an entrance on the left ; and
say further, that of these two kinds the natural
Regularity really exists, as in the motions of the
heavenly bodies, but the voluntary Regularity is not
real, because each craftsman can make the parts of
the stage as he pleases : that thus in the parts of
men there are Regularities, because nature makes
them, but there is none in words, because men shape
them each as he wills, and therefore as names for the
same things the Greeks have one set of words, the
Syrians another, the Latins still another [a]—I firmly
think that there are both voluntary and natural

esse puto, voluntarios quibus homines vocabula
imposuerint[7] rebus quaedam, ut ab Romulo Roma,
ab Tibure[8] Tiburtes, naturales ut ab impositis vocabulis quae inclinantur in tempora[9] aut in casus,
ut ab Romulo Romuli Romulum et ab dico dicebam
dixeram.

35. Itaque in voluntariis declinationibus incon-
stantia est, in naturalibus constantia ; quae utrasque
quoniam iei non debeant negare esse in oratione,
quom[1] in mundi partibus omnibus sint, et declinationes verborum innumerabiles, dicendum est esse
in his analogias. Neque ideo statim ea in omnibus
verbis est sequenda : nam si qua perperam declinavit
verba consuetudo, ut ea aliter ⟨non possint efferri⟩[2]
sine offensione multorum, hinc rationem[3] verborum
praetermittendam ostendit loquendi ratio.

XXVIII. 36. Quod ad universam pertinet cau-
sam, cur similitudo et sit in oratione et debeat
observari et quam ad finem quoque, satis dictum.
Quare quod sequitur de partibus singulis deinceps
expediemus ac singula crimina quae dicunt ⟨contra⟩[1]
analogias solvemus.

37. In quo animadvertito natura quadruplicem
esse formam, ad quam in declinando accommodari
debeant verba : quod debeat subesse res quae[1]

---

[7] *For* imposierint.   [8] *For* tybere.   [9] *For* tempore.

§ 35. [1] *Mue., with a, for* quam.   [2] *Added by GS., after
Aldus* efferri non possit (*Aug.,* possint).   [3] *Sciop., a, for*
orationem.

§ 36. [1] *Added by L. Sp. ; cf.* ix. 7.

§ 37. [1] *Rhol., for* resque.

---

§ 35. [a] That is, a regular form must be discarded in

derivations of words, voluntary for the things on which men have imposed certain names, as Rome from Romulus and the *Tiburtes* ' men of Tibur ' from Tibur, and natural as those which are inflected for tenses or for cases from the imposed names, as genitive *Romuli* and accusative *Romulum* from *Romulus*, and from *dico* ' I say ' the imperfect *dicebam* and the pluperfect *dixeram*.

35. Therefore in the voluntary derivations there is inconsistency, and in the natural derivations there is consistency. Inasmuch as they ought not to deny the presence of both of these in speech, since they are in all parts of the world, and the derivative forms of words are countless, we must say that in words also the Regularities are present. And yet Regularity does not for this reason have to be followed in all words ; for if usage has inflected or derived any words wrongly, so that they cannot be uttered in any other way without giving offence to many persons, the logic of speaking shows us that because of this offence the logic of the words must be set aside.[a]

XXVIII. 36. As far as concerns the general cause why likeness is present in speech and ought to be observed, and also to what extent this should be done, enough has now been said. Therefore in the following we shall set forth its several parts item by item, and refute the individual charges which they bring against the Regularities.

37. In this matter, you should take notice that by nature there are four elements in the basic situation to which words must be adjusted in inflection : there must be an underlying object or idea to be de-

favour of an irregular form if the feeling (*Sprachgefühl*) of the speakers rebels against it.

designetur,[2] et ut sit *ea* res[3] in usu, et ut vocis natura
ea sit quae significavit, ut declinari possit, et similitudo figura⟨e⟩[4] verbi ut sit ea quae ex se declinat*u*[5]
genus prodere certum poss*i*t.[6]

38. Quo neque a terra terrus ut dicatur postulandum est, quod natura non subest, ut in hoc alterum
maris, alterum feminae debeat esse; sic neque
propter usum, ut Terentius significat unum, plures
Terentii, postulandum est, ut sic dicamus faba *et*
fabae : non enim in simili us⟨u⟩[1] utrumque ; neque
ut dicimus ab Terentius Terentium, sic postulandum
ut inclinemus ab A et B, quod non omnis vox natura
habet declinatus.

39. Neque in forma collata qu*a*erendum solum,
quid habeat in figura simile, sed etiam nonnunquam
in eo quem habeat effectum. Sic enim lana Gallicana
et Apula videtur imperito similis propter speciem,
cum peritus Apulam emat pluris, quod in usu firmior
sit. Haec nunc strictim dicta apertiora fient infra.
Incipiam hinc.

XXIX. 40. Quod rogant ex qua parte oporteat
simile esse verbum, a *v*oce an a[1] significatione, re-
spondemus a voce ; sed tamen nonnunquam qu*a*erimus
genere similiane sint quae significantur ac nomen

---

[2] *Laetus, for* designentur.   [3] *G, H, a, Laetus, for* cares.
[4] *Mue., for* figura.   [5] *L. Sp., for* declinata.   [6] *Aug., for*
possunt.
   § 38.   [1] *L. Sp., for* similius.
   § 40.   [1] *After Laetus*, ab voce an, *for* aboceana.

---

   § 38.   [a] The singular *faba* was used also collectively for the
plural or mass idea ; *cf.* Priscian, ii. 176 Keil.   [b] Names of
letters.
   § 39.   [a] *Cf.* § 92.
   40.   [a] *Cf.* viii. 40.

signated ; this object or idea must be in use ; the nature of the utterance which has designated it, must be such that it can be inflected ; and the resemblance of the word's form to other words must be such that of itself it can reveal a definite class in respect to inflection.

38. Therefore it is not to be demanded that from *terra* ' earth ' there should be also a *terrus*, because there is no natural basis that in this object there ought to be one word for the male and another for the female. Similarly, with respect to usage, while *Terentius* designates one person of the name and *Terentii* designates several, it is not to be demanded that in this way we should say *faba* ' bean ' and *fabae* ' beans,' for the two are not subject to the same use.[a] Nor is it to be demanded that as we say acc. *Terentium* from nom. *Terentius*, we should make case-forms from *A* and *B*,[b] because not every utterance is naturally fitted for declensional forms.

39. The likeness which the word has in its shape must be investigated not in the comparison of the basis merely, but also sometimes in the effect which it has. For thus the Gallic wool and the Apulian wool seem alike to the inexperienced on account of their appearance, though the expert buys the Apulian at a higher price because in use it lasts better. These matters, which have been touched upon hastily here, will become clearer in a later discussion.[a] Now I shall start.

XXIX. 40. To their question in what respect a word ought to be similar, sound or meaning,[a] we answer that it should be so in sound. But yet sometimes we ask whether the objects designated are like in kind, and compare a man's name with a man's,

467

virile cum virili conferimus, feminae cum muliebri :
non quod id quod significant vocem commoveat, sed
quod nonnunquam in re dissim⟨ili par⟩ilis[2] figurae
formas in simil*i*[3] imponunt disp*a*riles,[4] ut calcei muliebres sint an viriles dicimus ad similitudinem figurae,
cum tamen sciamus nonnunquam et mulierem habere
calceos viriles et virum muliebris.

41. Sic dici virum Perpennam ut A*l*fenam[1]
muliebri forma[2] et contra parietem ut abietem esse
forma[3] similem, quo⟨m⟩[4] alterum vocabulum dicatur
virile, alterum muliebre et utrumque natura neutrum
si*t*.[5] Itaque ea virilia dicimus non quae virum[6]
significant, sed quibus proponimus hic et hi, et sic
muliebria in quibus dicere poss*u*mus[7] haec aut hae.

XXX. 42. Quare nihil[1] est, quod dicunt Theona
et Diona non esse similis, si alter est A*e*thiops, alter
al*b*us,[2] si analogia rerum dissimilitudines adsumat ad
discernendum vocis verbi figuras.

XXXI. 43. Quod dicunt simile sit necne nomen
nomini impudenter Aristar*c*hum praecipere oportere spectare non solum ex recto, sed etiam ex
eorum vocandi casu, esse[1] enim derid*i*culum, si similes

[2] *GS. ;* dissim⟨ili sim⟩ilis *Mue. ; for* dissimilis.   [3] *GS. ;*
in ⟨re⟩ simili *Mue. ; for* indissimiles.   [4] *For* disperiles.
§ 41. [1] ut Alfenam *Mue., for* aut plenam ; *cf.* viii. 41.
[2] *Laetus, for* formam.   [3] *Aldus, for* formam.   [4] *Mue. ;*
cum *Aug. ; for* quo.   [5] *Ant. Miller and Reiter, for* sic.
[6] *Aldus, for* utrum.   [7] *M, Laetus, for* possimus.
§ 42.   [1] *For* nichil.   [2] *Mue., for* gallus ; *cf.* viii. 41.
§ 43.   [1] *L. Sp., C. F. W. Mueller, Madvig, for* esset.

§ 41.   *a Cf.* viii. 41.   *b* The forms of *hic haec hoc* are
regularly used by the grammarians to indicate the case,
number, and gender of a word.

a woman's name with a woman's : not because that which they designate affects the word, but because sometimes in case of an unlike thing they set upon it forms of an equivalent appearance, and on a like thing they set unequal forms, as we call shoes women's shoes or men's shoes by the likeness of the shape, although we know that sometimes a woman wears men's shoes and a man wears women's shoes.

41. In like fashion, we say, a man is called *Perpenna*, like *Alfena*, with a feminine form[a] ; and on the other hand *paries* ' house-wall ' is like *abies* ' fir-tree ' in form, although the former word is used as a masculine, the latter as a feminine, and both are naturally neuter. Therefore those which we use as masculines are not those which denote a male being, but those before which we employ *hic* and *hi*, and those are feminines with reference to which we can say *haec* or *hae*.[b]

XXX. 42. For this reason it amounts to nothing, that on the premise that Regularity adopts the unlikenesses of the objects as a criterion for difference in the forms[a] of the spoken word,[b] they say that *Theon* and *Dion* are not alike if the one is an Ethiopian and the other is a white man.[c]

XXXI. 43. As to what they say,[a] that Aristarchus was shameless in his instructions that to see whether one name was like another you should view it not only from the nominative, but also from the vocative —for the same persons say that it is absurd to judge

§ 42.   [a] One of the rare examples of the accusative of the *gerund* with an object.   [b] The word as sound is *vox*, while the word as symbol of meaning is *verbum* ; the *vox verbi* is therefore the sound, or series of sounds, which represent the symbol of meaning. *Cf.* viii. 40.   [c] *Cf.* viii. 41.

§ 43.   [a] *Cf.* viii. 42.

inter se parentes sint, de filiisi udicare[2] : errant, quod non ab eo⟨rum⟩[3] obliquis casibus fit, ut recti simil*i*[4] facie ostendantur, sed propter eos facilius perspici similitudo potest eorum quam vim habeat,[5] ut lucerna in tenebris allata non facit ⟨ut⟩[6] quae ibi sunt posita similia sint, sed ut videantur, quae sunt quoius ⟨mo⟩di sint.[7]

44. Quid similius videtur quam in his est extrema littera crux *Phry*x[1] ? Quas, qui audit voces, auribus discernere potest nemo, cum easdem non esse similes ex ⟨declin⟩a*t*is[2] verbis intellegamus, quod cum sit cruces et *Phryges*[3] et de his extremis syllabis exemp-*t*um[4] sit E, ex altero fit ut ex C et S crux, ex altero G et S *Phry*x.[1] Quod item apparet, cum est dempt-tum S : nam fit unum cruce,[5] alterum *Phryge*.[6]

XXXII. 45. Quod aiunt, cum in maiore parte orationis non sit similitudo, non esse analogian, dupliciter stulte dicunt, quod et in maiore parte est et si in minore parte[1] sit, tamen sit,[2] nisi etiam nos calceos negabunt habere, quod in maiore parte corporis calceos non habeamus.

---

[2] *L. Sp. deleted* qui *after* iudicare.   [3] *L. Sp., for* eo.
[4] *Laetus, for* simile.   [5] *Laetus, for* habeant.   [6] *Added by L. Sp.*   [7] *L. Sp., for* dissint.
§ 44. [1] *Aldus, for* frix.   [2] *GS., for* aliis.   [3] *Aldus, for* friges.   [4] *Aldus, for* exemplum.   [5] *L. Sp., for* cruci.
[6] Phruge *L. Sp.,* Phrygi *Aldus ; for* frigi.
§ 45. [1] *Here L. Sp., following other slightly different deletions, deleted a repeated* est et si in minore.   [2] *After* sit, *L. Sp. deleted* in maiore.

---

§ 44.   [a] For *Phryx* and its forms, Augustinus (with B) read *frux*, etc. ; but nom. *frux* was no longer used in Varro's

from the children whether the parents are alike : those who say this are mistaken, for it does not come about from their oblique cases that the nominatives are shown to be of like appearance, but through the oblique cases can be more easily seen what evidential force lies in the likeness of the nominatives—even as a lamp in the dark, when brought, does not cause that the things which are there should be alike, but that they should be seen in their real character.

44. What seems more closely alike than the last letter in the words *crux* ' cross ' and *Phryx* ' Phrygian ' ? [a] No one who hears the spoken words can by his ears distinguish the letters,[b] although we know from the declined forms of the words that though alike they are not identical ; because when the plurals *cruces* and *Phryges* are taken and E is removed from the last syllables, from the one there results *crux*, with X from C and S, and from the other comes *Phryx*, from G and S. And the difference is likewise clear, when S is removed ; for the one becomes *cruce*, the other *Phryge*.[c]

XXXII. 45. As to what they say,[a] that since likeness does not exist in the greater part of speech, Regularity does not exist, they speak foolishly in two ways, because Regularity is present in the greater part of speech, and even if it should exist only in the smaller part, still it is there : unless they will say that we do not wear any shoes, because on the greater part of our body we do not wear any.

---

time, *cf.* ix. 75-76.   [b] The usual confusion of letters and sounds.   [c] Abl. sing. : the manuscript has forms ending in *-i*, which are datives, but the removal of *s* from *cruces* and *Phryges* leaves forms ending in *e*, not in *i*.

§ 45.   [a] *Cf* viii. 37.

XXXIII. 46. Quod dicunt nos dissimilitudinem
⟨potius gratam acceptamque habere quam simili-
tudinem⟩[1] : itaque in vestitu in supellectile delectari
varietate, non paribus subuculis uxoris, respondeo, si
varietas iucunditas, magis varium esse in quo alia
sunt similia, alia non sunt : itaque sicut abacum
argento ornari, ut alia ⟨paria sint, alia⟩[2] disparia, sic
orationem.

47. Rogant, si similitudo sit sequenda, cur malimus
habere lectos alios ex ebore, alios ex testudine, sic
item genere aliquo alio. Ad quae dico non dis⟨simili-
tudines solum nos, sed⟩[1] similitudines quoque sequi
saepe. Itaque ex eadem supellectili licet videre :
nam nemo facit triclinii lectos nisi paris et materia et
altitudine et figura. Qui⟨s⟩[2] facit mappas triclinaris
non similis inter se ? Quis pulvinos ? Quis denique
cetera, quae unius generis sint plura ?

48. Cum, inqui⟨un⟩t,[1] utilitatis causa introducta
sit oratio, sequendum non quae habebit similitudinem,
sed quae utilitatem. Ego utilitatis causa orationem
factam concedo, sed ut vestimenta : quare ut hic
similitudines sequimur,[2] ut virilis tunica sit virili
similis, item toga togae, sic mulierum stola ut sit
stola⟨e⟩[3] proportione et pallium pallio simile, sic

§ 46. [1] *Added by GS., following other attempts (Aug.,
with B, inserted* sequi *after* nos ; *but cf.* § 47, *where* sequi *is
actually found*). [2] *Added by Aug., with B.*
§ 47. [1] *Added by Mue.* [2] *Aldus, for* qui.
§ 48. [1] *Vertranius, for* inquit. [2] *Sciop., for* sequere-
mur. [3] *Aug., for* stola.

XXXIII. 46. As to what they say,[a] that we find unlikeness pleasing and acceptable rather than likeness, and therefore in clothing and in furniture we take pleasure in variety, and not in having our wives' undertunics all identical: I answer, that if variety is pleasure, then there is greater variety in that in which some things are alike and others are not ; and just as a side-table is adorned with silver in such a way that some ornaments are alike and others are unlike, so also is speech adorned.

47. They ask why, if likeness is to be followed, we prefer to have some couches inlaid with ivory, others with tortoise-shell, and so on with some other kind of material. To which I say that unlikenesses are not the only thing which we follow, but often we follow likenesses. And this may be seen from the same piece of furniture ; for no one makes the three couches of the dining-room other than alike in material and in height and in shape. Who makes the table-napkins not like each other ? Or the cushions ? And finally the other things which are several in number but of one sort ?

48. Since speech, they say,[a] was introduced for the sake of utility, we should follow not that kind of speech which has likeness, but that which has utility. I grant that speech has been produced for utility's sake, but in the same way as garments have : therefore as in the latter we follow the likenesses, so that a man's tunic is like a man's, and a toga like a toga, and a woman's dress is like a dress regularly and a cloak like a cloak, so also, as words that are names

§ 46. [a] *Cf.* viii. 31 32.
§ 48. [a] *Cf.* viii. 28-29.

cum sint nomina utilitatis causa, tamen virilia inter
se similia, item muliebria inter se sequi debemus.

XXXIV. 49.   Quod aiunt ut persedit et perstitit
sic ⟨periacuit et⟩[1] percubuit quoniam non si⟨n⟩t,[2]
non esse analogian, et[3] in hoc e⟨r⟩rant[4] : quod duo
posteriora ex prioribus declinata non sunt, cum
analogia polliceatur ex duobus similibus similiter
declinatis similia fore.

XXXV. 50.   Qui dicunt quod sit ab Romulo Roma
et non Romula neque ut ab ove ovilia[1] sic a bove
bovilia,[2] ⟨non⟩[3] esse analogias, errant, quod nemo
pollicetur e vocabulo vocabulum declinari recto casu
singulari in rectum singularem, sed ex duobus
vocabulis similibus casus similiter declinatos similes
fieri.

XXXVI. 51.   Dicunt, quod vocabula litterarum
Latinarum non declinentur in casus, non esse analogias.   Hi ea quae natura declinari non possunt,
eorum declinatus requirunt,[1] proinde et non eo⟨rum⟩[2]
dicatur esse analogia quae ab similibus verbis similiter esse⟨nt⟩[3] declinata.   Quare non solum in vocabulis litterarum haec non requirenda analogia, sed ⟨ne⟩[4]
in syllaba quidem ulla, quod dicimus hoc BA, huius
BA, sic alia.

§ 49.   [1] *Added by Canal.*   [2] *Kent, for* sit.   [3] *Aug.,*
for ut.   [4] *B, Rhol., for* erant.

§ 50.   [1] *Aug., for* ovilla.   [2] *Aug., for* bovilla.   [3] *Added*
by Stephanus.

§ 51.   [1] *B, G, H, a, Aug., for* sequirunt.   [2] *L. Sp., for*
eo *F*[1], ca *F*[2].   [3] *L. Sp. ;* esset *M, a, Aug. ; for* esse.
[4] *Added by Aldus.*

§ 49.   [a] Referring to a passage now lost.   [b] The two
verbs are not attested in any form.

§ 50.   [a] *Cf.* viii. 54 and 80.

of persons exist for the purpose of utility, we ought still to employ men's names that are like one another, and women's names that also have mutual resemblances.

XXXIV. 49. As to the fact that they say [a] that Regularity does not exist because there are no perfects *periacuit* 'remained lying' and *percubuit* 'remained lying,' like *persedit* 'remained sitting' and *perstitit* 'remained standing,' in this also they are mistaken : for the two perfects have no presents [b] from which to be inflected, whereas Regularity promises only that from two like words inflected in like manner there will be like forms.

XXXV. 50. Those who say [a] that there are no Regularities because from *Romulus* there is *Roma* and not *Romula* and there is no *bovilia* 'cow-stables' from *bos* 'cow' as there is *ovilia* 'sheepfolds' from *ovis* 'sheep,' are in error ; because nobody professes that one word is derived from another word, from nominative singular to nominative singular, but only that from two like words like case-forms develop when they are inflected in like manner.

XXXVI. 51. They say [a] that because the words denoting the Latin letters are not inflected into case-forms the Regularities do not exist. Such persons are demanding the declension of those words which by nature cannot be inflected ; just as if Regularity were not said [b] to belong merely to those forms which had already been inflected in like fashion from like words. Therefore not only in the names of the letters must this kind of Regularity not be sought, but not even in any syllable, because we say nominative *ba*, genitive *ba*, and so on.

§ 51. [a] *Cf*. viii. 64. [b] *Cf*. viii. 23.

52. Quod si quis in hoc quoque velit dicere esse analogias rerum, tenere potest : ut eni⟨m⟩[1] dicunt ipsi alia nomina, quod quinque habeant figuras, habere quinque casus, alia quattuor, sic minus alia, dicere poterunt esse litteras ac syllabas in voce quae singulos habeant casus, in rebus pluris[2] ; quemadmodum inter se conferent ea quae quaternos habebunt vocabulis casus, item ea inter se qua⟨e⟩ ternos,[3] sic qua*e*[4] singulos habebunt, ut conferant inter se dicentes, ut sit hoc A, huic A, esse hoc E,[5] huic E.

XXXVII. 53. Quod dicunt esse quaedam verba quae habeant declinatus, ut caput ⟨capitis, nihil nihili⟩,[1] quorum par reperiri quod non possit, non esse analogias, respondendum sine dubio, si quod est singulare verbum, id non habere analogias : minimum duo esse debent verba, in quibus sit similitudo. Quare in hoc tollunt esse analogias.

54. Sed ni*hil*um[1] vocabulum recto casu apparet in hoc :

Quae dedit i*ps*a[2] cap*it*[3] neque dispendi facit hilum,

§ 52. [1] *For* eni. [2] *GS. ;* plureis *Canal ; for* plurimis. [3] *Koeler, for* quaternos. [4] *For* sicque. [5] *After* hoc E, L. Sp. *deleted* huiusce E.
§ 53. [1] *Added by Reitzenstein.*
§ 54. [1] *Lachmann ;* in nihil *Sciop. ; for* initium. [2] *Sciop., for* ira. [3] *Scaliger, for* caput.

§ 52. [a] *Cf.* viii. 63. [b] That is, words indeclinable in form have only one case-form, but still have all the case-uses.
§ 53. [a] There is no corresponding passage in Book VIII. [b] That is, when they select a unique word as basis for argument.

52. But if any one should wish to say that in this also there are Regularities in the things, he can maintain it. For as they themselves say [a] that some nouns, because they have five forms, have five cases, and others have four, and others fewer in like manner, they will be able to say that the letters and syllables which have one case-form apiece in sound, have several in connexion with the things [b] ; as they will compare only with each other those which have four case-forms for the words, and likewise those which have three apiece, so let them compare with each other those which have only one form each, saying that nominative E, dative E is like nominative A, dative A.

XXXVII. 53. As to the fact that they say [a] that there are certain words which have declensional forms, like *caput* ' head,' genitive *capitis*, and *nihil* ' nothing,' genitive *nihili*, a match for which cannot be found, and therefore the Regularities do not exist, answer must be made that unquestionably any word which is the only one of its kind is outside the systems of Regularity ; there must be at least two words for a likeness to be existent therein. Therefore, in this case,[b] they eliminate the possible existence of the Regularities.

54. But the word *nihilum* ' nothing ' is found in the nominative in the following [a] :

> The body she's given
> Earth doth herself take back, and of loss not a whit
> does she suffer,

§ 54. [a] Ennius, *Ann.* 14 Vahlen² ; *R.O.L.* i. 6-7 Warmington ; *cf.* v. 60 and 111. The neuter accusative, having the same form as the nominative, is used as a proof of the nominative form.

quod valet nec dispendii facit quicquam. Idem hoc
obliquo apud Plautum :

> Video enim[4] te nihili[5] pendere prae Philolacho[6] omnis
> homines,

quod est ex ne et hili : quare dictus est nihili[5] qui non
hili erat. Casus tantum[7] commutantur de quo dicitur, ⟨ut⟩[8] de homine : dicimus enim hic homo
nihili[9] et huius hominis nihili et hunc hominem
nihili. Si in illo commutaremus, diceremus ut hoc
linum et libum,[10] sic nihilum, non hic nihili, et ⟨ut⟩[11]
huic lino et libo[12], sic nihilo, non huic nihili. Potest
dici patricus casus, ut ei praeponantur[13] nomina[14]
plura, ut hic casus Terentii, hunc casum Terentii,
hic miles legionis, huius militis legionis, hunc militem
legionis.

XXXVIII. 55. Negant, cum omnis natura sit aut
mas aut femina aut neutrum, ⟨non⟩[1] debuisse ex
singulis vocibus ternas figuras vocabulorum fieri,
ut albus alba album ; nunc fieri in multis rebus
binas, ut Metellus Metella,[2] Aemi⟨li⟩us Aemi⟨li⟩a,[3]
nonnulla singula, ut tragoedus, com⟨o⟩edus[4] ; sic
esse Marcum, Numerium, at Marcam, at Numeriam

---

[4] *Enim is Varro's addition ; it is not found in the manuscripts of Plautus.*   [5] *For* nichili.   [6] *The manuscripts
of Plautus have* Philolache.   [7] *Fay, for* tum cum.
[8] *Added by GS.*   [9] *After* nihili, *L. Sp. deleted* est.
[10] *Mue., for* limum.   [11] et ut *Mue. ;* ut *L. Sp. ; for* et.
[12] *Mue., for* limo.   [13] *Mue., for* praeponuntur.   [14] *Kent,
for* praenomina.
   § 55.   [1] *Added by Mue.*   [2] *Laetus, for* metelle.
[3] *Wackernagel ;* Ennius Ennia *Laetus ; for* enuus enua.
[4] *Christ, for* tragoedia comedia.
478

which is the same as ' nor of loss does she suffer anything.' This same word is found in an oblique case in Plautus [b] :

I see, beside Philolaches you count all men as nothing.

The word is from *ne* ' not ' and genitive *hili* ' whit ' ; therefore he has been called *nihili* ' of naught ' who was not *hili* ' of a whit ' in value. Change is made only in the case-forms of that about which the speaking is done, as about a man ; for we say a man *nihili* ' of no account ' in nominative, in genitive, in accusative, changing the forms of *homo* but not changing the form *nihili*. If we were to make changes in it, then we should say not *hic nihili* [c] but *nihilum* as the nominative, like *linum* ' flax ' and *libum* ' cake,' and dative not *huic nihili* [d] but *nihilo* like *lino* and *libo*. The genitive case [e] can however be said with various nouns set before it, like nominative *casus* ' mishap ' *Terentii* ' of Terence,' accusative *casum Terentii*, and nominative *miles* ' soldier ' *legionis* ' of the legion,' genitive *militis legionis*, accusative *militem legionis*.

XXXVIII. 55. They say [a] that since every nature is either male or female or neuter, from the individual spoken words there should not fail to be forms of the words in sets of three, like *albus, alba, album* ' white ' ; that now in many things there are only two, like *Metellus* and *Metella*, *Aemilius* and *Aemilia*, and some with only one, like *tragoedus* ' tragic actor ' and *comoedus* ' comic actor ' ; that there are the names *Marcus* and *Numerius*, but no

[b] Plautus, *Most.* 245.   [c] The genitive *nihili* depending on a nominative.   [d] The genitive *nihili* depending on a dative.   [e] Such as the form *nihili*.
§ 55.   [a] *Cf.* viii. 47.

479

VARRO

non esse ; dici corvum,[5] turdum, non[6] dici corvam,[5] turdam ; contra dici pantheram, merulam, non dici pantherum, merulum ; nullius nostrum[7] filium et filiam non apte[8] discerni marem ac feminam, ut Terentium[9] et Terentiam, contra deorum liberos et servorum non itidem,[10] ut Iovis filium et filiam, Iovem[11] et Iovam ; item magnum numerum vocabulorum in hoc genere non servare analogias.

56.   Ad haec dicimus, omnis orationis quamvis res naturae subsit, tamen si ea in usu⟨m⟩[1] non pervenerit, eo non pervenire verba : ideo equus dicitur et equa : in usu enim horum discrimina[2] ; corvus et corva non, quod sine usu id, quod dissimilis natura⟨e⟩.[3] Itaque quaedam al⟨i⟩ter olim ac nunc : nam et tum omnes mares et feminae dicebantur columbae, quod non erant in eo usu domestico quo nunc, ⟨et nunc⟩[4] contra, propter domesticos usus quod internovimus, appellatur mas columbus, femina columba.

57.   Natura cum tria genera transit et id est in usu discriminatu⟨m⟩, tum[1] denique apparet, ut est in doctus[2] et docta et doctum : doctrina enim per tria haec transire potest et usus docuit discriminare doctam rem ab hominibus et in his marem ac feminam. In mare et femina et neutro neque natura maris[3]

---

[5] *Aldus, for* corbum *and* corbam.   [6] *Aldus, for* non non.
[7] *Aug., for* neutros.   [8] *Aug., with B, for* apta.   [9] *For* terentium et terentium.   [10] *Ed. Veneta, for* ididem.
[11] *For* iouem iouem.

§ 56.   [1] *Aug., with B, for* usu.   [2] *Aug., for* discrimine.
[3] *Vertranius, for* natura.   [4] *Added by L. Sp.*
§ 57.   [1] *Reiter, for* discrimina totum.   [2] *Aug., with B, for* docto.   [3] *L. Sp., for* mares.

---

[b] *Numeria* is in fact found, but as a divine name.   [c] *Cf.* § 59.

§ 56.   [a] For the expression, *cf.* ix. 37.

Marca and *Numeria* [b]; that *corvus* ' raven ' and *turdus* ' thrush ' are said, but the feminines *corva* and *turda* are not said; that on the other hand *panthera* ' panther ' and *merula* ' blackbird ' are used, but the masculines *pantherus* and *merulus* are not; that there is no one of us whose son and daughter are not suitably distinguished as male and female, as *Terentius* and *Terentia*; that on the other hand the children of gods and slaves are not distinguished in the same way,[c] as by *Iovis* and *Iova* for the son and the daughter of Jupiter; that likewise a great number of common nouns do not in this respect preserve the Regularities.

56. To this we say that although the object is basic [a] for the character of all speech, the words do not succeed in reaching the object if it has not come into our use; therefore *equus* ' stallion ' and *equa* ' mare ' are said, but not *corva* beside *corvus*, because in that case the factor of unlike nature is without use to us. But for this reason some things were formerly named otherwise than they are now: for then all doves, male and female, were called *columbae*, because they were not in that domestic use in which they are now, and now, on the other hand, because we have come to make a distinction on account of their uses as domestic fowl, the male is called *columbus* and the female *columba*.

57. When the nature goes through the three genders and this distinction is made in use, then finally it is seen, as it is in *doctus* ' learned man ' and *docta* ' learned woman ' and *doctum* ' learned thing '; for learning can go across through these three, and use has taught us to differentiate a learned thing from human beings, and among the latter to distinguish the male and the female. But in a male or a female

VARRO

transit neque feminae neque neutra, et ideo non
dicitur feminus femina feminum, sic reliqua : itaque
singularibus ac secretis vocabulis appellati sunt.

58. Quare in quibus rebus non subest similis
natura aut usus, in his vocabulis huiusce modi ratio
quaeri non debet : ergo dicitur ut surdus vir, surda
mulier, sic surdum theatrum, quod omnes tres ⟨res⟩[1]
ad auditum sunt comparatae ; contra nemo dicit
cubiculum surdum, ⟨quod⟩[2] ad silentium, non ad
auditum ; at si fenestram non habet, dicitur caecum,
ut caecus et caeca, quod omnia ⟨non⟩[3] habent ⟨quod⟩[3]
lumen habere debent.

59. Mas et femina habent inter se natura quandam
societatem, ⟨nullam societatem⟩[1] neutra cum his,
quod sunt diversa ; inter se[2] quoque de his perpauca
sunt quae habeant quandam co⟨m⟩munitatem. Dei
et servi nomina quod non item ut libera nostra transeunt, eadem e⟨s⟩t[3] causa, quod ad usum attinet ⟨et⟩[4]
institui opus fuit de liberis, de reliquis nihil attinuit,
quod in servis gentilicia natura non subest in usu, in
nostri⟨s⟩ nominibus qui sumus in Latio et liberi,
necessaria. Itaque ibi apparet analogia ac dicitur
Terentius vir, Terentia femina, Terentium genus.

§ 58. [1] tres res *Mue.*; res *Bentinus* ; *for* tres. [2] *Added
by Canal* ; quod id *Mue.* ; quod sit *Sciop.* [3] *Added by
Fay.*

§ 59. [1] *Added by A. Sp., after L. Sp. and Mue.* [2] *B,
G, H, Aug., for* interest. [3] *L. Sp., for* et. [4] *Added by
L. Sp.*

§ 58. [a] Varro means a theatre in which it is difficult to
hear ; but the term is applicable also to an audience which
is inattentive. [b] Rather, things are called ' blind ' because
they hinder vision by darkness or by walls without openings,
such as windows and doors.

or what is neither, the nature of the male does not shift, nor that of the female, nor the neuter nature, and for this reason there is no saying of *feminus*, *femina*, *feminum*, and so with the rest. Therefore they are called by special and separate words.

58. Wherefore in the names of those things in which there is no likeness of nature or of use as the basis, a relation of this sort ought not to be sought. Accordingly, as a *surdus* 'deaf' man is a current term, and a *surda* woman, so also is a *surdum* theatre,[a] because all three things are equally intended for the act of hearing. On the other hand, nobody says a *surdum* sleeping-room, because it is intended for silence and not for hearing ; but if it has no window, it is called *caecum* 'blind,' as a man is called *caecus* and a woman *caeca*, because not all sleeping-rooms have the light which they ought to have.[b]

59. The male and the female have by nature a certain association with each other ; but the neuters have no association with them, because they are different from them in kind, and even of these neuters there are very few which have any elements in common with other neuters. As for the fact that the names of a god and of a slave do not vary like our free names, there is the same reason, namely that the variation is connected with use, and had to be established with reference to free persons, but as to the rest had no consequence, because among slaves the clan quality has no foundation in practice, but it is necessary in the names of us who are in Latium and are free. Therefore in that class Regularity makes its appearance, and we say *Terentius* for a man, *Terentia* for a woman, and *Terentium* for the *genus* 'stock.'

60. In praenominibus ideo non fit item, quod haec instituta ad usum singularia, quibus discernerentur nomina gentilicia, ut ab numero Secunda, Tertia, Quarta ⟨in mulieribus⟩,[1] in viris ut Quintus, Sextus, Decimus, sic ab aliis rebus. Cum essent duo Terentii aut plures, discernendi causa, ut aliquid singulare haberent, notabant, forsitan ab eo, qui mane natus diceretur, ut is Manius esset, qui luci, Lucius,[2] qui post patris mortem, Postumus.

61. E quibus ⟨ae⟩que[1] cum item accidisset feminis, proportione ita appellata declinarant praenomina mulierum antiqua, Mania, Lucia, Postuma : videmus enim Maniam matrem Larum dici, Luciam Volumniam[2] Saliorum Carminibus appellari, Postumam a multis post patris mortem etiam nunc appellari.

62. Quare quocumque progressa est natura cum usu vocabuli,[1] similiter proportione propagata est analogia, cum in quibus declinatus voluntarii[2] maris et feminae et neutri, quae voluntaria, non debeant similiter declinari, sed in quibus naturales, sint de-

§ 60. [1] *Placed here by GS. ; added before* Secunda *by L. Sp.* [2] *p, Aldus, for* lucilius.
§ 61. [1] *A. Sp., for* que. [2] *Aug., for* Volaminiam.
§ 62. [1] *Aug., with B, for* vocabula. [2] *L. Sp., for* declinationibus voluntariis.

§ 60. [a] Seemingly a contamination of *ab eo quod* with *sic . . . ut.* [b] Properly, as the ' last ' child ; but not to be associated with *post humum* ' after (burial in the) earth,' though this popular etymology gave a later spelling *posthumus* and the English *posthumous.*
§ 61. [a] *Mania* is perhaps not related etymologically to *Manius* ; see Marbach in Pauly-Wissowa's *Encyc. d. cl. Alt.-wiss.* xiv. 1110. [b] More probable than the *Volaminia* of *F*,

60. In first names the situation is not the same, because these were in practice established as individual names, by which the clan names might be differentiated; from the numerals came Secunda, Tertia, Quarta for women, Quintus, Sextus, Decimus for men, and similarly other names from other things. When there were two or more persons of the name Terentius, then that they might have something individual to distinguish them they marked them perhaps in this way,[a] that he should be Manius who was said to have been born *mane* ' in the morning,' and he who has been born *luci* ' at dawn ' should be Lucius, and he who was born *post* ' after ' his father's death should be Postumus.[b]

61. When any of these things happened to females as well, they derived the first names of women regularly in this manner—that is, in former times—and called them by them, for example, *Mania, Lucia, Postuma* : for we see that the mother of the Lares is called *Mania*,[a] that *Lucia Volumnia* [b] is addressed in the *Hymns of the Salians*,[c] and that even now many give the name *Postuma* to a daughter born after the death of her father.

62. Therefore as far as the nature and the use of a word have jointly advanced, so far has Regularity been extended in like manner by a corresponding relationship, since of the words in which there are voluntary inflections of male and female and neuter, those which are voluntary in inflection ought not to be inflected in similar manner, but in those in which there are natural inflections there are those regular

not found elsewhere; several members of the *gens Volumnia* are mentioned at Rome during Varro's time.   [c] Frag. 5, page 336 Maurenbrecher; page 4 Morel.

clinatus hi qui esse reperiuntur. Quocirca in tribus
generibus nominum in⟨i⟩que[3] tollunt analogias.

XXXIX. 63. Qui autem eas reprehendunt, quod
alia vocabula singularia sint solum, ut cicer, alia multitudinis solum, ut scalae, cum debuerint omnia esse
duplicia, ut equus equi, analogiae fundamentum esse
obliviscuntur naturam et usu⟨m⟩.[1] Singulare est
quod natura unum significat, ut equus, aut quod
coniuncta quodammodo ad unum usu,[2] ut bigae :
itaque ⟨ut⟩[3] dicimus una Musa, sic dicimus unae
bigae.

64. Multitudinis vocabula sunt unum infinitum,
ut Musae, alterum finitum, ut duae, tres, quattuor :
dicimus enim ut hae Musae sic unae bigae et binae
et trinae bigae, sic deinceps. Quare tam unae et uni
et una quodammodo singularia sunt quam unus et una
et unum ; hoc modo mutat, quod altera in singularibus, altera in coniunctis rebus ; et ut duo tria sunt
multitudinis, sic bina trina.

65. Est tertium quoque genus singulare ut in
multitudine, uter, in quo multitudinis ut utrei[1] ; uter

---

[3] *Aldus, for* inquae.
  § 63. [1] *p, Mue., for* usu.   [2] *A. Sp., for* usum.
[3] *Added by L. Sp.*
  § 65. [1] *A. Sp., for* utre ·I·.

---

§ 62.   [a] Crates and his followers, who uphold Anomaly.
§ 63.   [a] *Cf.* viii. 48.   [b] *Cf.* x. 54.
§ 64.   [a] The first is the generic or collective, without speci-
fication of the number or of the individuals ; the second is
numerical, in which the number of the individuals is given or
their identity is clearly implied.   [b] A word like *bigae*,

inflections which are actually found to exist. Therefore in the matter of the three genders they [a] are
unfair in setting aside the Regularities.

XXXIX. 63. Moreover those who find fault [a]
with the Regularities, because some words are
singulars only, like *cicer* ' chickpea,' and others are
plural only, like *scalae* ' stairs,' [b] although all ought
to have the two forms, like *equus* ' horse ' and *equi*
' horses,' forget that the foundation of Regularity
is nature and use taken in combination. That is
singular which by nature denotes one thing, like
equus ' horse,' or which denotes things that by use
are joined together in some way, like *bigae* ' two-horse
team.' Therefore just as we say *una Musa* ' one
Muse,' we say *unae bigae* ' one two-horse team.'

64. Plural words are of two sorts,[a] the one indefinite, like *Musae* ' Muses,' the other definite, like
duae ' two,' *tres* ' three,' *quattuor* ' four ' ; for as we
say *Musae* in the plural, so also we say *unae bigae* ' one
two-horse team,' and *binae* ' two ' and *trinae* [b] *bigae*
' three two-horse teams,' and so on. Wherefore
unae and the masc. *uni* and the neut. *una* are in
a certain manner as much singulars as *unus* and *una*
and *unum* : the word changes in this way because
the one set of forms is said of individual things, the
other of things joined together in sets ; and just as
duo and *tria* are plurals, so also are *bina* and *trina*.

65. There is also a third class which is singular
though expressed by a plural form, namely *uter*
' which of two,' in which the plural form is for ex-

already plural in form, can be pluralized in meaning only by
the use of a numerical modifier ; for this purpose, distributive numerals such as *bini* are used. For the singular idea,
the plural form of *unus* is used.

poeta singulari, utri poetae multitudinis est. Qua
explicata natura apparet non debere omnia vocabula
multitudinis habere par singulare : omnes enim
numeri ab duobus susum versus multitudinis sunt
neque eorum quisquam habere potest singulare
compar. Iniuria igitur postulant, si qua sint singularia, oportere habere multitudinis.

XL. 66.   Item qui reprehendunt, quod non dicatur
ut unguentum unguenta vinum vina sic acetum aceta
garum gara, faciunt imperite : qui ibi desiderant
multitudinis vocabulum, quae sub mensuram ac pon-
dera potius quam sub numerum succedunt : nam in
plumbo,[1] a⟨r⟩ge⟨n⟩to,[2] cum incrementum accessit,
dicimus[3] multum,[4] sic multum plumbum, argentum ;
non[5] plumba, argenta, cum quae ex hisce fiant, dicamus plumbea et argentea (aliud enim cum argenteum :
nam id tum cum iam vas : argent⟨e⟩um[6] enim, si
pocillum aut quid item) : quod pocilla argentea
multa, non quod argentum multum.

67.   Ea, natura in quibus est mensura, non
numerus, si genera in se habe⟨n⟩t[1] plura et ea in
usum venerunt, a genere multo, sic vina et unguenta,
dicta : alii generis enim vinum quod Chio, aliud[2]

§ 66.   [1] *After* plumbo, *L. Sp. deleted* oleo.   [2] *Aug., for*
aceto.   [3] *After* dicimus, *Aldus deleted* enim.   [4] *After*
multum, *L. Sp. deleted* oleum.   [5] *After* non, *L. Sp. deleted*
multa olea.   [6] *Aug., with* B, *for* argentum.
    § 67.   [1] *Laetus, for* habet.   [2] *For* aliut.

§ 65.   [a] The old spelling of the nominative plural, still
more or less in use in Varro's time, though rarely attested in
the manuscripts.
    § 66.   [a] *Cf.* § 67.   [b] Derivative adjectives, 'made of
lead ' and ' made of silver '; supply *vasa* ' utensils.'

ample *utrei* [a] : *uter poeta* ' which of two poets ' in the
singular, *utri poetae* ' which of two sets of poets ' in
the plural. Now that the nature of this has been
explained it is clear that plural nouns are not all
under obligations to have a like singular form ; for
all the numerals from two upwards are plural, and
no one of them can have a singular to match it.
Therefore it is quite wrongly that they demand that
all singulars that there are, must have a corresponding plural form.

XL. 66. Likewise those who find fault because
there are no plurals *aceta* and *gara* to *acetum* ' vinegar '
and *garum* ' fish-sauce ' like *unguenta* to *unguentum*
' perfume ' and *vina* to *vinum* ' wine,' [a] act ignorantly ;
they are looking for a plural name in connexion
with things which come under the categories of
quantity and weight rather than under that of
number. For in *plumbum* ' lead ' and *argentum* ' silver,' when there has been added an increase, we say
multum ' much ': thus *multum plumbum* or *argentum*,
not *plumba* ' leads ' and *argenta* ' silvers,' since articles
made of these we call *plumbea* and *argentea* [b] (silver
is something else when it is *argenteum*, for that is
what it is when it has now become a utensil ; thus
argenteum if it is a small cup or the like), because in
this case we speak of many *argentea* ' silver ' cups,
and not of much *argentum* ' silver.'

67. But if those things which have by nature the
idea of quantity rather than that of number, exist in
several kinds and these kinds have come into use,
then from the plurality of kinds they are spoken of
in the plural, as for example *vina* ' wines ' and *unguenta* ' perfumes.' For there is wine of one kind,
which comes from Chios, another wine which is from

quod Lesbo,[3] sic ex regionibus aliis. ⟨Ae⟩que[4] ipsa
dicuntur nunc melius unguenta,[5] cui nunc genera
aliquot. Si item discrimina magna essent olei et
aceti et sic ceterarum rerum eiusmodi in usu co⟨m⟩-
muni, dicerentur sic olea et ⟨aceta ut⟩[6] vina. Quare
in utraque re ⟨i⟩nique[7] rescindere conantur analogias,
et[8] cum in dissimili usu similia vocabula qu*aerant*[9] et
cum item ea quae metimur atque ea quae numeramus
dici putent oportere.

XLI. 68. Item reprehendunt analogias, quod
dicantur multitudinis nomine publicae balneae, non
balnea, contra quod privati dicant unum balneum,
quo*m*[1] plura balnea ⟨non⟩[2] dicant. Quibus respon-
der*i*[3] potest non esse reprehendendum, quod scalae
et aquae caldae, pleraque[4] cum causa, multitudinis
vocabulis sint appellata neque eorum singularia in
usum venerint ; idemque item contra. Primum
balneum (nomen e⟨s⟩t[5] Graecum), ⟨cum⟩[6] introiit in
urbem, publice ibi consedit, ubi bina essent coniuncta aedificia lavandi causa, unum ubi viri, alterum
ubi mulieres lavarentur ; ab eadem ratione domi
suae quisque ubi lavatur balneum dixerunt et, quod
non erant duo, balnea dicere non consuerunt, cum

---

[3] *V, p, Aldus, for* Lesbio.   [4] *A. Sp., for* quae.   [5] *For*
unguentia.   [6] *Added by L. Sp.*   [7] *Canal, for* denique.
[8] *Aug., for* analogiam set.   [9] *L. Sp., for* querunt.
  § 68.   [1] *Canal, for* quod.   [2] *Added by Popma.*   [3] *Aldus, for* respondere.   [4] *After* pleraque, *L. Sp. deleted* quae.
[5] *GS., for* et.   [6] *Added by GS.*

---

§ 68.   *a* The word is a heteroclite in form, with a different

Lesbos, and so on from other localities. Likewise *unguenta* 'perfumes' themselves are now properly spoken of in the plural, for of perfume there are now a number of kinds. If in like fashion there were great differences in olive-oil and vinegar and the other articles of this sort, in common use, then we should employ the plurals *olea* and *aceta*, like *vina*. Therefore in both these matters their attempt to destroy the Regularities is unfair, since they expect that the words will be alike though their uses are different, and since they think that articles which we measure and objects which we count should be spoken of in the same way.

XLI. 68. Likewise they find fault with the Regularities, because public baths are spoken of as *balneae*, with the form in the plural, and not as *balnea*, in the singular; and on the other hand they speak of one *balneum* of a private individual, though they do not use the plural *balnea*.[a] To them answer can be made, that fault ought not to be found because *scalae* 'stairs' and *aquae caldae* 'hot springs,' mostly with good reason, have been called by plural names and the corresponding singulars have not come into use : and *vice versa*.[b] The first *balneum* 'bath-room' (the name is Greek), when it was brought into the city of Rome, was as a public establishment set in a place where two connected buildings might be used for the bathing, in one of which the men should bathe and in the other the women. From the same logical reasoning each person called the place in his own house where baths were taken, a *balneum* ; and they were not accustomed to speak of *balnea* in the plural,

meaning in the two numbers. But the plural *balnea* began to be used in the time of Augustus.   [b] *Cf.* § 69.

hoc antiqui non balneum, sed lavatrinam[7] appellare
consuessent.[8]

69. Sic aquae caldae ab loco et aqua, quae ibi
scateret, cum ut colerentur venissent in usum nostris,
cum aliae ad alium morbum idoneae essent, eae cum
plures essent, ut Puteolis et in Tuscis, quibus uteban-
tur, multitudinis potius quam singulari vocabulo
appellarunt. Sic scalas, quod ab scandendo dicuntur
et singulos gradus scanderent, magis erat quaeren-
dum, si appellassent singulari vocabulo scalam, cum
origo nominatus ostenderet contra.

XLII. 70. Item reprehendunt de casibus, quod
quidam nominatus habent rectos, quidam obliquos,
quod dicunt utrosque in vocibus oportere. Quibus
idem responderi potest, in quibus usus aut natura
non subsit, ibi non esse analogiam. . . .

71. Sed ne in his ⟨quidem⟩[1] vocabulis quae
declinantur, si transeunt e recto casu in rectum
casum : quae tamen fere non discedunt ab ratione
sine iusta[2] causa, ut hi qui gladiatores Faustini[2] :
nam quod plerique dicuntur, ut tris extremas syllabas

[7] *Aug., with B, for* lauiatrinam.   [8] *B, Ed. Veneta, for*
consuescent.

§ 71.   [1] *Added here by L. Sp. ; added after* vocabulis *by*
Madvig.   [2] *Mue., for* faustinos.

---

[c] More commonly in the contracted form *latrina*, and in
Varro's time meaning ' water-closet, privy.'

§ 69.   [a] At least nine places in Etruria bore the name
Aquae.

§ 70.   [a] *Cf.* viii. 49.   [b] There seems to be a lacuna here,
as examples illustrating this point of the refutation are lacking.

§ 71.   [a] That is, by derivation with suffixes, not merely by

because they did not have two in one house—though our forbears were accustomed to call this not a *balneum*, but a *lavatrina* [c] ' wash-room.'

69. So also, the hot springs, on account of the locality and the water which gushed out there, came to be frequented for our use, since some of the springs were beneficial to one disease and others to another ; and because those which they used were several in number, as at Puteoli and in Etruria,[a] they called them by a plural word rather than by a singular. So also with the *scalae* ' stairs ' ; because they are named from *scandere* ' to mount ' and there were separate steps to be mounted, it would be a more difficult problem to answer if they had called them *scala*, in the singular, inasmuch as the origin of the name shows their plural nature.

XLII. 70. Likewise they find fault [a] about the cases, because some nouns have nominative forms only, and others have only oblique forms : whereupon they say that all words ought to have both the nominative and the oblique forms. To them the same answer can be given, that there is no Regularity in those instances which lack a relationship in use or in nature. . . .[b]

71. But they should not look for complete Regularity even in these names which are derived by passage from one nominative form to another.[a] Still, such words do not in general depart from the path of logic without valid reason, such as there is for those gladiators who are called *Faustini* [b] ; for though most gladiators are spoken of in such a way that they

case-inflection.   [b] The troops of gladiators were designated by adjectives of this sort which were derived from the names of the owners.

habeant easdem, Cascelliani, ⟨Caeciliani⟩,[3] Aquiliani,
animadvert*a*nt,[4] unde oriuntur, nomina dissimilia
Cascellius,[5] C*a*ecilius, Aquilius, ⟨Faustus : quod si
esset⟩[6] Faustius, recte dicerent Faustianos ; si⟨c⟩[7]
a Scipione quidam male dicunt Scipioninos : nam est
Scipionarios. Sed, ut dixi, quod ab huiuscemodi
cognominibus raro declinantur cognomina neque in
usum etiam perducta, natant quaedam.

XLIII. 72. Item dicunt, cum sit simile stultus
luscus et dicatur stultus stultior stultissimus, non
dici luscus luscior luscissimus, sic in hoc genere
multa. Ad quae dico ideo fieri, quod natura nemo
lusco magis sit luscus, cum stultior fieri videatur.

XLIV. 73. Quod rogant, cur ⟨non⟩[1] dicamus mane
man*i*us manissime, item de vesper*i* : in[2] tempore vere
magis et minus esse non potest, ante et post potest.
Itaque prius est hora prima quam secunda, non
magis hora. Sed magis mane surgere tamen dicitur :
qui primo mane surgit, ⟨magis mane surgit⟩[3] quam
qui non pri⟨m⟩o[4] : ut enim dies non potest esse
magis quam ⟨dies, sic mane non magis quam⟩[5] mane ;

---

[3] *Placed here by L. Sp. ; added after* Aquiliani *by Aug.*
[4] *Aug., for* animaduertunt. [5] Cascelius *Aug., for* Cas-
sellius F. [6] *Added by Mue.* [7] *M,* Laetus, *for* si.
§ 73. [1] *Added by Aug.* [2] Popma, *for* uespertino.
[3] *Added by GS.* [4] Stephanus, *for* prior. [5] *Added by
L. Sp.*

---

§ 72. [a] *Cf.* viii. 75.
§ 73. [a] *Cf.* viii. 76. [b] The usual phrase is *multo mane* ;
evidently, to the Romans, *mane* was not completely an adverb
like English *early*. [c] The Latin corresponding to this
(English) sentence should perhaps, as GS. suggest, be placed
before the sentence beginning *Itaque prius* ; the argument
then develops more logically.

494

have the last three syllables alike, *Cascelliani, Caeciliani, Aquiliani,*[b] let them take note that the names from which these come, *Cascellius, Caecilius, Aquilius* on the one hand, and *Faustus* on the other, are unlike : if the name were *Faustius,* they would be right in saying *Faustiani.* In the same way, from *Scipio* some make the bad formation *Scipionini* ; it is properly *Scipionarii.* But, as I have said, since appellations are rarely derived from surnames of this kind and they are not fully at home in use, some such formations fluctuate in form.

XLIII. 72. Likewise they say,[a] that although *stultus* ' stupid ' and *luscus* ' one-eyed ' are like words, and *stultus* is compared with *stultior* and *stultissimus,* the forms *luscior* and *luscissimus* are not used with *luscus,* and similarly with many words of this class. To which I say that this happens for the reason that by nature no one is more one-eyed than a one-eyed man, whereas he may seem to become more stupid.

XLIV. 73. To their question [a] why we do not say *mane* ' in the morning,' comparative *manius,* superlative *manissime,* with a similar question about *vesperi* ' in the evening,' I reply that in matters of time there is properly no ' more ' and ' less,' but there can be before and after. Therefore the first hour is earlier than the second, but not ' more hour.' But nevertheless to rise *magis mane* ' more in the morning ' is an expression in use ; he who rises in the first part of the morning rises *magis mane* [b] ' more in the morning ' than he who does not rise in that first part. For as the day cannot be said to be more than day, so *mane* cannot be said to be more than *mane.*[c] Therefore that very *magis* ' more '

VARRO

itaque ipsum hoc quod dicitur magis sibi non constat,
quod magis mane significat primum mane, magis
vespere novissimum vesper.

XLV. 74. Item ab huiuscemodi ⟨dis⟩similitu-
dinibus[1] reprehenditur analogia, quod cum sit anus
cadus simile et sit ab anu anicula anicilla, a cado duo
reliqua quod non sint propagata, sic non dicatur a
piscina piscinula piscinilla. Ad ⟨haec respondeo⟩[2]
huiuscemodi vocabul*is*[3] analogias esse, ut dixi, ubi
magnitudo animadvertenda sit in unoquoque gradu
eaque[4] sit in usu co⟨m⟩muni, ut est cista cistula
cistella et canis catulus catellus, quod in pecoris usu
non est. Itaque consuetudo frequentius res in binas
dividi partis ut maius et minus, ut lectus et lectulus,
arca et arcula, sic alia.

XLVI. 75. Quod dicunt casus alia non habere
rectos, alia obliquos et ideo non esse analogias, falsum
est. Negant habere rectos ut in hoc frugis frugi
frugem, item cole⟨m⟩ colis cole,[1] obliquos non habere
ut in hoc Diespiter Diespitri Diespitrem, Maspiter
Maspitri Maspitrem.

§ 74. [1] L. Sp., for similitudinibus.   [2] Added by L. Sp.
[3] L. Sp., for vocabula.   [4] Mue., for ea quae.
§ 75. [1] A. Sp.; colis coli colem Mue.; for role rolis role.

§ 74. [a] Cf. viii. 79.   [b] The diminutives are not ety-
mological derivatives of canis, but are of quite distinct origin.
[c] Curiously, none of the Latin words denoting sheep and
goats, cattle and horses, had a diminutive in regular use in
Varro's time or earlier, except that Varro himself used equulus
and equula. Plautus, Asin. 667, coined the words agnellus
'little lamb,' haedillus 'little kid,' vitellus 'little calf,' as
terms of endearment, but they do not appear again.   [d] The
normal, undiminished object.
§ 75. [a] Cf. viii. 49 ; the subject-matter of § 75 seems to
come closely after that of § 70, but there seems to be no sure

which is commonly said is not consistent with itself, because *magis mane* means the first part of the *mane*, and *magis vespere* the last part of the evening.

XLV. 74. Similarly, Regularity is found fault with on account of unlikenesses of this sort,[a] that although *anus* ' old woman ' and *cadus* ' cask ' are like words, and from *anus* there are the diminutives *anicula* and *anicilla*, the other two are not formed from *cadus*, nor from *piscina* ' fish-pond ' are *piscinula* and *piscinilla* made. To this I answer that words of this kind have the Regularities, as I have said, only when the size must be noted in each separate stage, and this is in common use, as is *cista* ' box,' *cistula*, *cistella*, and *canis*[b] ' dog,' *catulus* ' puppy,' *catellus* ' little puppy '; this is not indicated in the usage connected with flocks.[c] Therefore the usage is more often that things be divided into two sets, as larger [d] and smaller, like *lectus* ' couch ' and *lectulus*, *arca* ' strong-box ' and *arcula*, and other such words.

XLVI. 75. As to their saying [a] that some words lack the nominative and others lack the oblique cases, and that therefore the Regularities do not exist, this is an error. For they say that the nominative is lacking in such words as *frugis frugi frugem* [b] ' fruit of the earth ' and *colem colis cole* [c] ' plant-stalk,' and the oblique cases are lacking in such as *Diespiter* ' Jupiter,' dat. *Diespitri*, acc. *Diespitrem*, and *Maspiter* ' Mars,' *Maspitri*, *Maspitrem*.[d]

way of rearranging the order of the text.   [b] Gen., dat., acc.
[c] Acc., gen., abl., unless the manuscript readings are to be more seriously altered ; the word is more properly *caul-*, but Cato and Varro prefer the country forms, with *o* from *au*.
[d] For *Dies pater* and *Mars pater* ; the addition of *pater* is found only in nom. and voc. (*Iuppiter*, older *Iupiter*, is a voc. form).

76. Ad haec respondeo et priora habere nominandi et posteriora obliquos. Nam et frugi rectus est natura frux, at secundum consuetudinem dicimus ut haec avis, haec ovis, sic haec frugis ; sic secundum naturam nominandi est casus *cols*,[1] secundum consuetudinem colis,[2] cum utrumque conveniat ad analogian, quod et id quod in consuetudine non est cuius modi debeat esse apparet, et quod est in consuetudine nunc in recto casu, eadem est analogia ac pleraque, quae ex multitudine cum transeunt in singulare, difficulter efferuntur ore. Sic cum transiretur ex eo quod dicebatur haec oves, una non est dicta ovs sine *I*,[3] sed additum I ac factum ambiguum verbum nominandi an patrici esse⟨t⟩[4] casus. Ut ovis, et avis.

77. Sic in obliquis casibus cur negent esse Diespitri Diespitrem non video, nisi quod minus est tritum in consuetudine quam Diespiter ; quod in nihil argumentum est : nam tam casus qui non tritus est quam qui est. Sed est⟨o⟩[1] in casuum serie alia vocabula non habere nominandi, alia de obliquis aliquem: nihil enim ideo quo minus siet[2] ratio percellere poterit hoc crimen.

§ 76. [1] *Mue., for* rois.   [2] *Mue., for* rolis.   [3] *L. Sp., for* una.   [4] *L. Sp., for* esse.

§ 77. [1] *L. Sp., for* est.   [2] *Mue., for* si et ; *on the possibility of the use of* siet *in Varro's time, cf. Cicero,* Orator 47. 157.

---

§ 76. [a] *Frux* is found in Ennius, *Ann.* 314 (' honest man ') and 431 Vahlen[2] = *R.O.L.* i. 116-117 and 150-151 Warmington ; but nom. *frugis* is not quotable from a text.   [b] *Colis* may be cited from Lucilius, 135 Marx, and Varro, *R. R.* i. 41. 6.   [c] Varro is speaking on the basis that the relation is nom. sing. ending in -*s*, nom. pl. in -*es*, as in *dux*, pl. *duces*.   [d] *Haec* before *oves* is the sign of the nom. pl. fem. ; Varro appears to use *hae* before consonants, *haec*

76. To this I answer that the former have nominatives and the latter have oblique case-forms. For the nominative of *frugi* is by nature *frux*, but by usage we say *frugis*,[a] like *avis* ' bird ' and *ovis* ' sheep ' ; so also, the nominative of the other word is by nature *cols* and by usage *colis*.[b] Both of these agree with the principle of Regularity, because it is perfectly clear of what sort that form ought to be which is not in use, and in that which is now in use in the nominative there is the same kind of Regularity as most words have that are hard to pronounce when they pass from the plural to the singular.[c] So when the passage was made from the spoken plural *oves*,[d] the form which was pronounced was not *ovs* without I, but an I was added and the word became ambiguous as to whether the case was nominative or genitive.[e] Like the nominative *ovis* is also the nominative *avis*.

77. Thus I do not see why they say that in the oblique cases *Diespitri* and *Diespitrem* are lacking, except because they are less common in use than *Diespiter*. But the argument amounts to nothing ; for the case-form which is uncommon is just as much a case-form as that which is common. But let us grant that in the list of case-forms some words lack the nominative and others lack some one of the oblique cases ; for this charge will not for that reason be able in any way to destroy the existence of a logical relationship[a] among the forms.

before vowels as here (and at the sentence-end, as at v. 75).
[e] Varro is of course unaware of the fact that some nouns of the third declension had stems ending in *i* and therefore had a right to nominatives in *is*, while others had stems ending in consonants and could have the ending *is* only by analogy with the *i*-stems.

§ 77.   [a] That is, Regularity.

78. Nam ut signa quae non habent caput[1] aut aliquam aliam partem, nihilo minus[2] in reliquis membris eorum esse possunt analogiae, sic in vocabulis casuum possunt item fieri ⟨iacturae. Potest etiam refingi⟩[3] ac reponi quod aberit, ubi patietur natura et consuetudo : quod nonnunquam apud poetas invenimus factum, ut in hoc apud Naevium in Clastidio :

Vita insepulta laetus in patriam redux.

XLVII. 79. Item reprehendunt, quod dicatur haec strues, hic Hercules,[1] hic homo : debuisset enim dici, si esset analogia, hic Hercul, haec strus, hic hom⟨en. N⟩on[2] haec ostendunt no⟨mi⟩na[3] non analogian esse, sed obliquos casus non habere caput ex sua analogia. Non, ut si in Alexandri statua imposueris caput Philippi, membra conveniant ad rationem, sic[4] et Alexandri membrorum simulacro[5] caput quod respondeat item sit ? Non, si quis tunicam in usu ita consuit, ut altera plagula[6] sit angustis clavis, altera latis, utraque pars in suo genere caret analogia.

XLVIII. 80. Item negant esse analogias, quod

---

§ 78. [1] *After* caput, *M and Laetus deleted* et.   [2] *For* nihil hominus.   [3] *Added by GS.; but the lost part may be somewhat longer.*
§ 79. [1] *p, Laetus, for* Herculis.   [2] *GS.;* homen Canal*;* *for* homon.   [3] *Kent, for* noua.   [4] *G, H, Aug., for* sit.   [5] *A. Sp., for* simulacrum.   [6] *Aldus, for* placula.

---

§ 78. [a] *By regular formation.*   [b] *Trag. Rom. Frag., Praet.* II Ribbeck[3].   [c] *Redux,* not elsewhere found in the nom. sing.
§ 79. [a] If the nominatives were of the usual types, which replace the genitive ending -IS by -S or by nothing at all, like *sus, animal, nomen,* genitives *suis, animalis, nominis.*   [b] That is, the nominatives are not formed ' regularly ' from the oblique cases, but from these nominatives of variant types

78. For as some statues lack the head or some other part without destroying the Regularities in their other limbs, so in words certain losses of cases can take place, with as little result. Besides, what is lacking can be remade [a] and put back into its place, where nature and usage permit ; which we sometimes find done by the poets, as in this verse of Naevius, in the *Clastidium* [b] :

> With life unburied, glad, to fatherland restored. [c]

XLVII. 79. Likewise they find fault with the nominatives *strues* ' heap,' *Hercules*, *homo* ' man ' ; for if Regularity actually existed, they say, these forms should have been *strus, Hercul, homen*. [a] These nouns do not show that Regularity is non-existent, but that the oblique cases do not have a head or starting-point according to their type of Regularity. [b] Is it not a fact that, if you should put a head of Philip on a statue of Alexander and the limbs should be proportionately symmetrical, then the head which does correspond to the statue of Alexander's limbs [c] would likewise be symmetrical ? And it is not a fact that if one should in practice sew together a tunic in such a way that one breadth of the cloth has narrow border-stripes and the other has broad stripes, each part lacks regular conformity within its own class. [d]

XLVIII. 80. Likewise they say that the Regu-

the oblique cases are formed regularly.   [c] That is, the heads or nominatives may be varied, but the limbs or oblique cases are of uniform type.   [d] For there are tunics with the broad stripe, worn by senators, and tunics with the narrow stripe, worn by knights ; therefore, though the two halves in the example do not belong together, each has its regular precedent.

alii dicunt cupressus, alii cupressi, item de ficis
platanis et plerisque arboribus, de quibus alii extremum US, alii EI faciunt. Id est falsum : nam
debent dici E et I, fici ut nummi, quod est ut num-
mi⟨s⟩ fici⟨s⟩,[1] ut nummorum ficorum. Si essent
plures ficus, essent ut manus ; diceremus ut manibus,
sic ficibus, et ut manuum, sic ficuum, neque has ficos
diceremus, sed ficus, ut non manos appellamus, sed
⟨manus, nec⟩[2] consuetudo diceret singularis obliquos
casus huius fici neque hac fico, ut non dici⟨t⟩[3] huius
mani,[4] sed huius manus, ⟨n⟩ec[5] hac mano, sed hac
manu.

XLIX. 81. Etiam illud putant esse causae, cur
non sit[1] analogia, quod Lucilius scribit :

> Decu⟨s⟩is,[2]
> Sive decusibus est.

Qui errant, quod Lucilius non debuit dubitare, quod
utrumque : nam in aere usque ab asse ad centussis
numerus aes adsignificat, et eius numero finiti casus
omne*s*[3] ab dupondio sunt, quod dicitur a multis
duobus modis hic dupondius et hoc dupondium, ut

---

§ 80. [1] *L. Sp., for* nummi fici.   [2] *Added by Mue. ;*
manus neque *L. Sp.*   [3] *Aug., for* dici.   [4] *M, Laetus, for*
manui.   [5] *L. Sp., for* et.
§ 81. [1] *After* sit, *Aldus deleted* in.   [2] *Lachmann ;*
decussi *Mue. ; for* decuis.   [3] *For* omnis.

---

§ 80. [a] As belonging to the fourth and the second declensions respectively.   [b] This shows that Varro wrote the
nominative plural of the second declension with EI, and not
with I ; but it would be pedantic to substitute such spellings
throughout his works, or even merely in this section.
[c] As type of the second declension.   [d] As type of the
fourth declension.

larities do not exist, because some say *cupressus*
' cypress-trees ' in the plural and others say *cupressi*,[a]
and similarly with fig-trees, plane-trees, and most
other trees, to which some give the ending US and
others give EI. This is wrong ; for the tree-names
ought to be spoken with E and I,[b] *fici* like *nummi* [c]
' sesterces,' because the ablative is *ficis* like *nummis*,
and the genitive is *ficorum* like *nummorum*. If the
plural were *ficus*, then it would be like *manus* [d]
' hand ' ; we should say ablative *ficibus* like *manibus*,
and genitive *ficuum* like *manuum*, and we should not
say accusative *ficos*, but *ficus*, just as we do not say
accusative *manos* but *manus* ; nor would usage speak
the oblique cases of the singular genitive *fici* and
ablative *fico*, just as it does not say genitive *mani* but
manus, nor ablative *mano* but *manu*.

XLIX. 81. Moreover, they think that there is
proof of the non-existence of Regularity, in the fact
that Lucilius writes [a] :

Priced a ten-*as*, or else we may say at ten-*asses.*[b]

They are in error, because Lucilius should not have
been uncertain as to the form, since both are right.
For in copper money, from the *as* to the hundred-*as*,
the number adds to itself the meaning of the copper
coin, and all its case-forms are limited by its numerical
value,[c] starting from the *dupondius* ' two-*as* piece,'
which is used by many in two ways, masculine
dupondius and neuter *dupondium*, like *gladius* and

§ 81.   [a] Lucilius, 1153-4 Marx.   [b] Or *decussis, decus-sibus* ; but the single S is elsewhere attested in these words,
and Lucilius may well have followed the older orthography,
which doubled no consonants. On the *as, cf.* v. 169.   [c] As
first element in the compound.

hoc gladium et hic gladius ; ab tressibus virilia multitudinis hi tresses et " his tressibus confido," singulare
" hoc tressis habeo " et " hoc tres⟨s⟩is[4] confido," sic
deinceps a⟨d⟩[5] centussis. Deinde numerus aes non
significa*t*.[6]

82. Numeri qui *a*es non significant, usque a quattuor ad centum, triplicis habent formas, quod dicuntur hi quattuor, hae quattuor, haec quattuor ; cum
perventum est ad mille, quartum assumit singulare
neutrum, quod dicitur hoc mille denarium, a quo
multitudinis fit milia denari*um*.[1]

83. Quare *quo*⟨nia⟩m[1] ad analogias quod pertineat
non ⟨opus⟩[2] est ut omnia similia dicantur, sed ut
in suo quaeque genere similiter declinentur, stulte
qu*a*erunt, cur as et dupondius et tressis non dicantur
proportione, cum a*s*[3] sit simple*x*,[4] d*u*pondius[5] fictus,
quod duo asses pendebat,[6] tressis ex tribus aeris quod
sit. Pro assibus nonnunquam aes dicebant antiqui, a

[4] *For* tresis.   [5] *Aug.*, *for* a.   [6] *Aug.*, *for* significans.
   § 82.   [1] *Aug.*, *for* denaria.
   § 83.   [1] *Mue.*, *for* cum.   [2] *Added by GS.*   [3] as sit
Aldus, *for* adsit.   [4] *For* simples.   [5] *For* dipondius.
[6] *Aug.*, *for* pendebant.

[d] *Cf.* v. 116 and viii. 45.   [e] The value-names *tressis* to
centussis were invariable in the singular, but had a full set
of cases in the plural, without multiplying the value of the
term ; thus *tresses* in the plural still means 'three *asses*'
precisely like the singular.
   § 82.   [a] One invariable form serves for three genders.
[b] *Mille* is not only an indeclinable plural adjective, of three
genders, but also a neuter noun in the singular, upon which
a genitive depends ; and in this last capacity it has a plural,
which is declinable.   [c] The *denarius* was a Roman silver
coin, equivalent to the Greek drachma, and in modern times

gladium.ᵈ From *tressis* ' three-*as* ' there is a masculine plural, *tresses* in the nominative and *tressibus* in
the ablative, as in " I trust in these three *asses*,"
singular *tressis* as in " I have this three-*as* " and " I
trust in this three-*as*." The same usage is followed
all the way to *centussis* ' hundred-*as*.' ᵉ From here on,
the numeral does not denote money any more than
other things.

82. The numerals which do not signify money,
from *quattuor* ' four ' to *centum* ' hundred,' have forms
of triple function,ᵃ because *quattuor* is masculine,
feminine, and neuter. When *mille* ' thousand ' is
reached, it takes on a fourth function,ᵇ that of a
singular neuter, because the expression in use is
mille ' thousand ' of *denarii*,ᶜ from which is made a
plural, *milia* ' thousands ' of *denarii*.

83. Since therefore so far as concerns the Regularities it is not essential that all words that are
spoken should be alike in their systems, but only that
they should be inflected alike each in its own class,
those persons are stupid who ask why *as* and *dupondius*
and *tressis* are not spoken according to a regular
scheme ; for the *as* is a single unit, the *dupondius* is a
compound term indicating that it *pendebat* ' weighed '
duo ' two ' *asses*, and the *tressis* is so called ᵃ because
it is composed of *tres* ' three ' units of *aes* ' copper.'
Instead of *asses*, the ancients used sometimes to say
aes ᵇ ; a usage which survives when we hold an *as* in

to the Swiss franc (about 1s. 4d. English, or 32 cents U.S.A.,
in 1936).
    § 83. ᵃ From *tres* and *as*, not from *tres* and *aes*.   ᵇ But
in the genitive, if with a numeral ; just as we say " four
o'clock," = " four (hours) of the clock " ; in the singular,
aes might mean ' money ' collectively, like the French *argent*,
and sometimes even a ' copper piece.'

quo dicimus assem tenentes " hoc[7] aere aeneaque
libra " et " mille *a*eris legasse."

84. Quare quod ab tressis usque ad centussis[1]
numeri ex ⟨partibus⟩[2] eiusdem modi sunt compositi,
eiusdem modi habent similitudinem : dupondius,
quod dissimilis est, ut debuit, dissimilem habet
rationem. Sic as, quoniam simplex est ac principium,
et unum significat et multitudinis habet suum infinitum : dicimus enim asses, quos cum finimus,
dicimus dupondius et tressis et sic porro.

85. Sic videtur mihi, quoniam finitum et infinitum
habeat dissimilitudinem, non debere utrumque item
dici, eo magis quod in ipsis vocabulis[1] ubi additur
certus numerus miliar⟨i⟩is[2] aliter atque in reliquis
dicitur : nam sic loquontur, hoc mille denarium, non
hoc mille denari⟨orum⟩,[3] et haec duo milia denari*um*,[4]
non duo milia denari⟨orum⟩.[5] Si esset denarii in
recto casu atque infinitam multitudinem significaret,
tunc in patrico denariorum dici oportebat ; et non
solum in denariis, victoriatis, *d*rachmis,[6] nummis, sed
etiam in viris idem servari oportere, cum dicimus

<hr/>

[7] *After* hoc, *Brissonius deleted* ab.
§ 84. [1] *Aug., for* ducentussis. [2] *Added by GS.*
§ 85. [1] *M, Laetus, for* vocalibus. [2] *Mue. ;* milliariis
L. Sp. ; for militaris. [3] *L. Sp., for* denarii. [4] *Aug., for*
denaria. [5] *Christ, for* denarii. [6] *Rhol., for* et rachmis.

<hr/>

[c] A legal survival used in symbolic sales, *cf.* v. 163; for the
ancient *as libralis* (*cf.* v. 169) had long since been decreased
in weight and was not coined after 74 B.C.
§ 84. [a] Even as *dies* and *annus* were not modified by the
lower numerals ; for such phrases the Romans substituted
biduum, triduum, biennium, triennium, etc. So for sums

the hand and say " with this *aes* ' copper piece ' and *aenea libra* ' pound of copper,' " [c] and also in the legal formula " to have bequeathed a thousand (*asses*) of *aes* ' copper.' "

84. Therefore, because the numerals from *tressis* to *centussis* are compounded of parts of the same kind, they have a likeness of the same kind ; but the word *dupondius*, because it is different in formation, has a different system of declension, as it should have. So also the *as*, because it is a single unit and is the beginning, means one and has its own indefinite plural, for we say *asses* ; but when we limit them numerically, we say *dupondius* and *tressis* and so on.[a]

85. Thus it seems to me that since the definite and the indefinite have an inherent difference, the two ought not to be spoken in the same fashion, the more so because in the words themselves, when they are attached to a definite number in the thousands, a form is used which is not the same as that used in other expressions. For they speak thus : *mille denarium* [a] ' thousand of *denarii*,' not *denariorum*, and two *milia denarium* ' thousands of *denarii*,' not *denariorum*. If it were *denarii* in the nominative and it denoted an indefinite quantity, then it ought to be *denariorum* in the genitive ; and the same distinction must be preserved, it seems to me, not only in *denarii*, *victoriati*,[b] *drachmae*, and *nummi*, but also in *viri*, when we say

from 2 to 100 *asses*, the compound words were used, and not *asses* with the numeral.

§ 85. [a] For names of weights and measures, and for some other words, the old genitive in *-um* continued in use long after the new form in *-orum* had been generalized. [b] The *victoriatus* was a silver coin stamped with a figure of Victory, and worth half a *denarius*.

iudicium fuisse triumvirum, decem⟨virum, centum⟩-
virum,[7] non ⟨triumvirorum, decemvirorum⟩,[8] centum-
virorum.

86. Numeri antiqui habent analogias, quod omnibus est una[1] regula, duo actus, tres gradus, sex decuriae, qua⟨e⟩[2] omnia similiter inter se respondent.
Regula[3] est numerus novenarius, quod, ab uno ad
novem cum pervenimus, rursus redimus ad unum et
V⟨IIII⟩[4]; hinc et LX⟨XXX⟩[5] et nongenta[6] ab una
sunt natura novenaria; sic ab octonaria, et deo⟨r⟩sum
versus ad singularia perveniunt.

87. Actus primus est ab uno ⟨ad⟩[1] DCCCC, secundus a mille ad nongenta[2] milia; quod idem valebat
unum et mille, utrumque singulari nomine appellatur:
nam ut dicitur hoc unum, haec duo, ⟨sic hoc mille,
haec duo⟩[3] milia et sic deinceps multitudinis in duobus
actibus reliqui omnes item numeri. Gradus singularis est in utroque actu ab uno ad novem, denari*us*[4]
gradus ⟨a⟩[5] decem ad LX⟨XXX⟩,[6] centenarius a centum ⟨ad⟩[7] DCCCC. Ita tribus gradibus sex decuriae
fiunt, tres miliariae, tres[8] minores. Antiqui his
numeris fuerunt contenti.

---

[7] *Added by L. Sp.*   [8] *Added by A. Sp., after* Aldus.
§ 86. [1] *After* una, *L. Sp. deleted* non novenaria (*Aug.
deleted* non).   [2] *Rhol., for* qua.   [3] *Sciop., for* regulae.
[4] novem *L. Sp., for* V.   [5] nonaginta *Aldus, for* LX.
[6] *L. Sp.;* nongenti *G, H; for* nungenti.
§ 87. [1] *Added by Aug.*   [2] *For* nungenta.   [3] *Added
by Gronov.*   [4] *Aug., for* denarios.   [5] *Added by Aug.*
[6] nonaginta *Aug., for* LX.   [7] *Added by Aug.*   [8] *L. Sp.,
for* miliaria etres.

---

[e] The *tresviri* or *triumviri capitales*, in charge of prisons and

that there has been a decision of the triumvirs,[c] the decemvirs,[d] the centumvirs,[e] all of which have the genitive *virum* and not *virorum*.

86. The old numbers have their Regularities, because they all have one rule, two acts, three grades, and six decades, all of which show regular internal correspondences. The rule is the number nine, because, when we have gone from one to nine, we return again to one and nine [a]; hence both ninety and nine hundred are of that one and the same nine-containing nature. So there are numbers of eight-containing nature,[b] and going downwards they arrive at those which are merely ones.

87. The first act [a] is from one to nine hundred. the second from one thousand to nine hundred thousand. Because one and thousand are alike unities, both are called by a name in the singular ; for as we say ' this one ' and ' these two,' so we say ' this thousand ' and ' these two thousands,' and after that all the other numbers in the two acts are likewise plural. The unitary grade is found in both acts, from one to nine ; the denary grade extends from ten to ninety ; the centenary grade from hundred to nine hundred. Thus from the three grades, six decades are made, three in the thousands, and three in the smaller numbers. The ancients were satisfied with these numerals.

executions. [d] The *decemviri stlitibus iudicandis*, a permanent board with jurisdiction over cases involving liberty or citizenship. [e] The *centumviri* or board of judges with jurisdiction over civil suits, especially those involving inheritances.

§ 86. [a] As multiples of ten ; and then as multiples of one hundred. [b] But these do not constitute the ' rule.'

§ 87. [a] Technical term, taken from the drama.

88. Ad[1] hos tertium et quartum actum ⟨addentes⟩[2] ab decie⟨n⟩s ⟨et ab deciens miliens⟩[2] minores imposuerunt vocabula, neque ratione, sed tamen non contra est eam de qua scribimus analogiam. Nam[3] deciens[4] cum dicatur hoc deciens ut mille hoc mille, ut sit utrumque sine casibus vocis, dicemus ut hoc mille, huius mille, sic hoc deciens, huius deciens, neque eo minus in altero, quod est mille, praeponemus hi mille, horum mille, ⟨sic hi deciens, horum deciens⟩.[5]

L. 89. Quoniam in eo est nomen co⟨m⟩mune, quam vocant ὁμωνυμίαν,[1] obliqui casus ab eodem capite, ubi erit ὁμωνυμία,[2] quo minus dissimiles fiant, analogia non prohibet. Itaque dicimus hic Argus, cum hominem dicimus, cum oppidum, Graec⟨e Graec⟩an⟨i⟩ceve[3] hoc Argos, cum Latine ⟨hi⟩[4] Argi. Item faciemus, si eadem vox nomen et[5] verbum significabit,[6] ut et in casus et in tempora dispariliter declinetur, ut faciemus a Meto quod nomen est Metonis Metonem, quod verbum est metam metebam.

§ 88. [1] *For* ab. [2] *Added by Kent, after Mue.* (actum ab deciens minorem, ⟨a deciens miliens maiorem addentes⟩, imposuerunt). [3] *After* nam, *L. Sp. deleted* ut. [4] *Aug., for* decienis. [5] *Added by L. Sp.; there may have been other text also in the lacuna.*

§ 89. [1] *For* omonimyan. [2] *For* omonimya; *after which Aug. deleted* obliqui casus. [3] *Fay, cf.* x. 71; graecanice *Pius; for* graecancaene. [4] *Added by Vertranius;* ⟨hei⟩ *Aug.* [5] *Pius, for* nominet. [6] *Pius, for* significavit.

---

§ 88. [a] Elliptic for *decies centena milia* 'ten times a hundred thousands.' [b] Similarly elliptic for *decies milies centena milia.* [c] Varro seems not to know the abl. sing. *milli,* found in Plautus, *Bac.* 928 (assured by the metre), and in Lucilius, 327 and 506 Marx (assured by Gellius, i. 16. 10-13).

88. To these, their descendants added a third and a fourth act, imposing names which started from *deciens* [a] ' million ' and *deciens miliens* [b] ' thousand million ' ; and though the names were not formed by logical relation with the lower numerals, still their formation is not in conflict with the Regularity about which we are writing. For inasmuch as *deciens* is used as a neuter singular like *mille*, so that both words are without change of form for the various cases,[c] we shall use *deciens* unchanged as nominative and as genitive, even as we do *mille* ; and none the less shall we set before *mille* the signs of nominative and of genitive plural, because *mille* is also in the other number—and so also shall we speak of ' these *deciens* ' in the same cases.

L. 89. When a noun is the same in the nominative though it has more than one meaning, in which instance they call it a homonymy, Regularity does not prevent the oblique cases from the same starting form in which the homonymy is, from being dissimilar. Therefore we say *Argus* in the masculine, when we mean the man, but when we mean the town we say, in Greek or in the Greek fashion, *Argos* [a] in the neuter, though in Latin it is *Argi*, masculine plural. Likewise, if the same word denotes both a noun and a verb, we shall cause it to be inflected both for cases and for tenses, with different inflection for noun and verb, so that from *Meto* as a noun, a man's name, we form gen. *Metonis*, acc. *Metonem*, but from *meto* as a verb, ' I reap,' we form the future *metam* and the imperfect *metebam*.

§ 89. [a] The homonymy is not perfect, since the forms are *Argus* and *Argos* ; the neuter *Argos* is found in Latin only in nom. and acc.

LI. 90.   Reprehendunt, cum ab eadem voce plura
sunt vocabula declinata, quas συνωνυμίας[1] appellant,
ut[2] Alc⟨m⟩aeus[3] et Alc⟨m⟩aeo,[3] sic Geryon, Geryo-
n⟨e⟩us,[4] Geryones.   In hoc genere quod casus perperam permutant quidam, non reprehendunt analogiam, sed qui eis utuntur imperite ; quod quisque
caput prenderit, sequi debet eius consequenti⟨s⟩[5]
casus in declinando ac non facere, cum dixerit recto
casu Alc⟨m⟩aeus,[6] in obliquis[7] Alc⟨m⟩aeoni[6] et
Alc⟨m⟩aeonem[6] ; quod si miscuerit et non secutus
erit analogias, reprehendendum.

LII. 91.   ⟨Reprehendunt⟩[1] Aristarchum, quod
haec nomina Melicertes et Philomedes similia neget
esse, quod vocandi casus habet alter Melicerta, alter
Philomede⟨s⟩,[2] sic qui dicat lepus et lupus non esse
simile, quod alterius vocandi casus sit lupe, alterius
lepus, sic socer, macer, quod in transitu fiat ab
altero trisyllabum soceri, ab altero bisyllabum macri.

92.   De hoc etsi supra responsum est, cum dixi
de lana, hic quoque[1] amplius adiciam similia non solum

§ 90.   [1] *For* synonimyas.   [2] *After* ut, *Aug. deleted*
sapho et.   [3] *Kent, for* alceus *and* alceo, *usually corrected
to* Alcaeus, Alcaeo, *though a variant nominative* Alcaeo *is
unknown ; whereas* Alcumēus *occurs in* Plautus, Capt. 562,
and Alcmaeo *in* Cicero, Acad. Priora ii. 28. 89, *and elsewhere.*   [4] *Mue., for* gerionus.   [5] *L. Sp., for* consequenti.
[6] *Kent, for* alceus, alceoni, alceonem ; *cf. crit. note* 3.
[7] *After* obliquis, *Mue. deleted* dicere.
§ 91.   [1] *Added by* L. Sp., *after* Aug.   [2] *Mue., for*
philomede.
§ 92.   [1] *For* hic hic quoque.

§ 90.   [a] Son of Amphiaraus and Eriphyle, who killed his
mother at the command of his father, because she tricked him
into going to a war in which he was destined to die ; *cf.* also
the critical note.   [b] The three-bodied giant whom Hercules

LI. 90. They find fault when from the same utterance two or more word-forms are derived, which they call synonymns, such as *Alcmaeus* and *Alcmaeo,*[a] and also *Geryon, Geryoneus, Geryones.*[b] As to the fact that in this class certain speakers interchange the case-forms wrongly—they are not finding fault with Regularity, but with the speakers who use those case-forms unskillfully : each speaker ought to follow, in his inflection, the case-forms which attend upon the nominative which he has taken as his start, and he ought not to make a dative *Alcmaeoni* and an accusative *Alcmaeonem* when he has said *Alcmaeus* in the nominative ; if he has mixed his declensions and has not followed the Regularities, blame must be laid upon him.

LII. 91. They find fault[a] with Aristarchus for saying that the names *Melicertes* and *Philomedes* are not alike, because one has as its vocative *Melicerta,* and the other has *Philomedes*[b] ; and likewise with those who say that *lepus* 'hare' and *lupus* 'wolf' are not alike, because the vocative case of one is *lupe* and of the other is *lepus,* and with those who say the same of *socer* 'father-in-law' and *macer* 'lean,' because in the declensional change there comes from the one the three-syllabled genitive *soceri* and from the other the two-syllabled genitive *macri.*

92. Although the answer to this was given above[a] when I spoke about the kinds of wool, I shall make here some further statements : the likenesses of

overpowered and robbed of his cattle ; all three forms are known in Greek, but only *Geryon* and *Geryones* in Latin.

§ 91. [a] *Cf.* viii. 68. [b] The Greek nominatives end in -ης, but the vocatives end in -α and -ες respectively.

§ 92. [a] *Cf.* ix. 39.

a facie dici, sed etiam ab aliqua coniuncta vi et
potestate, quae et oculis et auribus latere soleant :
itaque saepe gemina facie mala negamus esse
similia, si sapore sunt alio ; sic equos eadem facie
nonnullos negamus esse similis, ⟨s⟩i[2] natione s⟨unt⟩[3]
ex procreante dissimiles.[4]

93. Itaque in hominibus emendis, si natione alter
est melior, emimus pluris. Atque in hisce omnibus
similitudines non sumimus tantum a figura, sed
etiam aliu⟨n⟩de, ut in equis aetas, ut in ⟨asin⟩is[1]
cuius modi faciant pullos, ut in pomis quo sint suco.
Si igitur idem sequitur in similitudine verborum quis,
reprehendundus non est.

94. Quare similitudin*u*m[1] discernendarum causa
nonnunquam ut pronomen assumitur, sic casum
aliquem assumi⟨mus⟩,[2] ut in his nemus, lepus, hic
lepus, hoc nemus : itaque discedunt ac dicuntur hi
lepores, haec nemora. Sic aliud si quid assumptum
erit extrinsecus, quo similitudo penitus perspici
possit, non nim⟨is⟩[3] erit remotum ab natura : neque
enim magnetas lapides duo inter se similes sint
necne, perspicere possis, nisi minutum extrinsecus
prope apposueris ferrum, quod similes lapides
similiter ducunt, dissimiliter dissimiles.

[2] *Sciop., for* in.   [3] *L. Sp. ;* natione *Vertranius ; for*
nationes.   [4] *For* dissimilis.
  § 93.   [1] *Lachmann, for* ut inis.
  § 94.   [1] *L. Sp., for* similitudinem.   [2] *L. Sp., for* assumi.
[3] *A. Sp., for* enim.

  § 93.   [a] For example, Cappadocians were notoriously
worthless as slaves.

spoken words rest not only upon their form, but also upon some attached strength and power which is usually hidden from our eyes and ears. Therefore we often say that two apples that are identical in appearance are not alike, if they are of different flavour ; and we say that some horses of the same appearance are not alike, if by breed they are different on the sire's side.

93. Therefore in buying human beings as slaves, we pay a higher price for one that is better by nationality.[a] And in all these matters we take the points of likeness not merely from the appearance, but also from other factors, as in horses their age, in asses the kind of colts that they beget, in fruits the flavour of their juice. If therefore one proceeds in the same way in deciding whether words are alike, he is not to be found fault with.

94. Wherefore as the pronoun [a] is sometimes taken as an aid to distinguish the resemblances, so we take some case-form, as in *nemus* ' grove ' and *lepus* ' hare,' *lepus* being shown by it to be masculine and *nemus* neuter : therefore they go in different directions and the plurals are *lepores* and *nemora*. So also, if anything else whatsoever is taken from outside to enable a thorough examination of the problem of likeness to be made, it will not be too far from the natural qualities : for you cannot even see whether two magnetic stones are alike or not, unless you have brought close to them from outside a particle of steel, which like magnets attract to a like degree, and magnets different in strength attract with different powers.

§ 94. [a] Specifically, the demonstrative *hic* and its forms, used as indicative of gender and of case.

VARRO

95. Quod ad nominatuom[1] analogia⟨m⟩[2] pertinet,
ita deli⟨q⟩uatum[3] arbitror, ut omnia quae dicuntur
contra ad respondendum ab his fontibus sumi possit.
LIII. Quod ad verborum temporalium rationem
attinet, cum partes sint quattuor, tempora, personae,
genera, divisiones,[4] ex omni parte quoniam reprehendunt, ad singula respondebo.

LIV. 96. Primum quod aiunt analogias non servari
in temporibus, cum dicant legi lego legam et sic
simili⟨ter⟩[1] alia : nam quae sint ut legi rem[2] perfectam significare, duo reliqua lego et legam[3] in-
choatam, iniuria reprehendunt : nam ex eodem
genere et ex divisione idem verbum, quod sumptum
est, per tempora traduci ⟨infecti⟩[4] potest, ut discebam
disco discam, et eadem perfecti, ut didiceram didici
didicero. LV. Ex quo licet scire verborum
ratione⟨m⟩[5] constare, sed eos, qui trium temporum
verba pronuntiare velint, ⟨in⟩scienter[6] id facere ;

97. item[1] illos qui reprehendunt, quod dicamus
amor amabor amatus sum : non enim debuisse in una
serie unum verbum esse duplex, cum duo simplicia
essent. Neque ex divisione si unius modi ponas

§ 95. [1] *L. Sp., for* nominatiuom. [2] *Aug., for* analogia.
[3] *GS., for* declinatum. [4] *L. Sp., for* personarum generum
diuisionum.
§ 96. [1] *L. Sp., with H, for* simile. [2] *C. F. W. Mueller*
(legi *Aug.*), *for* legerem. [3] *After* legam, *L. Sp. deleted* et
lego (*Aug. deleted* lego et *before* legam). [4] *Added here by*
GS. ; *after* ut, *by L. Sp. ; after* tempora, *by Christ.* [5] *Aug.,*
for ratione. [6] *L. Sp., for* scienter.
§ 97. [1] *Aug., for* idem.

§ 95. [a] Apparently a *genus* of verbs is a group of verbs
which make their forms similarly ; but it may also be a set
of forms having one function, and hence equal to ' mood,'
cf. § 102 ; it is not clear whether Varro includes ' voice '
516

95. That which concerns the Regularity of nouns has, I think been so cleared up that material for answering all objections can be drawn from these sources. LIII. We now come to the logical system of verbs ; this has four parts : tenses, persons, kinds,*a* and divisions.*b* As they find fault with respect to each and every part, I shall make answer to the objections one by one.

LIV. 96. First as to their saying that the Regularities are not preserved in the tenses, when they give perfect *legi* ' I have read,' present *lego* ' I read,' future *legam* ' I shall read,' and others in just the same way : they are wrong in finding fault with those forms like *legi* as denoting completed actions and the other two, *lego* and *legam*, as denoting action only begun ; for the same verb which has been taken from the same kind and the same division, can be paraded through the tenses of non-completion, like *discebam* ' I was learning,' *disco* ' I learn,' *discam* ' I shall learn,' and the same of completion, thus *didiceram* ' I had learned,' *didici* ' I have learned,' *didicero* ' I shall have learned.' LV. From this one may know that the logical system of verbs is consistent with itself, but that those who try to speak the verbs in their three tenses, do this in an ignorant way ;

97. that likewise those do so ignorantly who find fault because we say *amor* ' I am loved,' *amabor* ' I shall be loved,' *amatus sum* ' I have been loved '; for, they say, in one and the same series there ought not to be one verb made up of two words while the other two verbs are each of one word. Yet if you would

under *genus*.   *b* There were two divisions, one comprising the tenses of incomplete action, and the other the tenses of completed action.

verba, discrepant inter se : nam infecta omnia simplicia similia sunt, et perfecta duplicia inter se paria
in omnibus verbis, ut haec amabar amor amabor,
amatus ⟨eram amatus sum amatus⟩[2] ero.

98. Quare item male dicunt ferio feriam percussi,
quod est ordo ⟨ferio⟩[1] feriam feriebam, percussi
percussero percusseram.[2] Sic deinceps in reliquis
temporibus reprehendenti responderi potest.

LVI. 99. Similiter errant qui dicunt ex utraque
parte verba omnia commutare syllabas oportere aut
nullum, in his pungo pungam pupugi, tundo tundam
tutudi : dissimilia enim conferunt, verba infecti cum
perfectis. Quod si infecta modo conferrent, omnia
verbi principia incommutabilia viderentur, ut in his
pungebam pungo pungam et contra ex utraque parte
commutabilia, si perfecta ponerent, ut pupugeram
pupugi pupugero.

LVII. 100. Item male conferunt fui sum ero, quod
fui est perfectum, cuius series sibi, ut debet, in omnibus partibus[1] constat, quod est fueram fui fuero ; de
infectis sum quod nunc dicitur olim dicebatur esum
et in omnibus personis constabat, quod dicebatur

---

[2] *Added by L. Sp.*
  § 98.   [1] *Added here by Mue. ; added after* feriam *by G, H,
Aldus.*   [2] *Mue., for* percutio percutiam *; see note b.*
  § 100.   [1] *A. Sp., for* personis.

---

§ 98.   [a] In this section Varro changes the order in which
he cites the tenses.   [b] *Ferio* is found only in the present
tense-system ; in the perfect tense-system it is replaced by
percussi, the present tense-system of which is relatively little
used. This justifies the emendation of the text.

put down verb-forms from a division of one kind,
they would not differ from one another; for all the
forms denoting incomplete action are alike single,
and the forms of completed action are in all verbs
double, quite like one another: such as *amabar, amor,
amabor,* and *amatus eram, amatus sum, amatus ero.*

98. Wherefore likewise they do ill to cite *ferio*
' I strike,' future *feriam,* perfect *percussi*; because
the proper order is *ferio, feriam, feriebam,*[a] and *percussi,
percussero, percusseram.*[b] And in this fashion answer
can be made to the one who finds fault in the matter
of the other tenses.

LVI. 99. They make a similar mistake who say
that all verbs ought to change the radical syllables
in both divisions, or no verb should—as in *pungo*
' I prick,' future *pungam,* perfect *pupugi,* and *tundo*
' I pound,' *tundam, tutudi*; for they are comparing
unlikes, namely verbs of the incomplete phase with
the completed. But if they were comparing only
the incomplete, then all the stems of the verb would
be seen to be unchangeable, as in *pungebam, pungo,
pungam,* and on the other hand changeable, if they
instanced the completed, as in *pupugeram, pupugi,
pupugero.*

LVII. 100. Likewise they do ill to compare *fui*
' I was,' *sum* ' I am,' *ero* ' I shall be '; for *fui* is a form
of completed time, whose series is consistent with
itself in all its parts, as it should be, namely *fueram,
fui, fuero.* Of the incomplete, that which is now
pronounced *sum* used to be spoken *esum,*[a] and the
series is consistent in all its persons, because they

§ 100. [a] This form seems to have been invented by Varro
to suit his argument; all the evidence is against its ever
having existed.

esum es est, eram eras erat, ero eris erit ; sic huiusce
modi cetera servare analogiam videbis.

LVIII. 101. Etiam in hoc reprehendunt, quod
quaedam verba neque personas habent ternas neque
tempora terna : id imperite reprehendunt, ut si quis
reprehendat naturam, quod non unius modi finxerit
animalis omnis. Si[1] enim natura non omnes formae
verborum terna habent[2] tempora, ternas personas,
non habent totidem verborum divisiones. Quare
cum imperamus, natura quod infecta ⟨ver⟩ba[3] solum
habe⟨n⟩t,[4] cum aut[5] praesenti aut absenti imperamus,
fiunt terna, ut lege legito legat : perfectum enim
imperat nemo. Contra quae sunt indicandi,[6] ut lego
legis legit, novena fiunt verba infecti, novena perfecti.

LIX. 102. Quocirca non si genus cum genere
discrepat,[1] sed in suo quique[2] genere si quid deest,
requirendum. Ad haec addita si erunt ea quae de
nominatibus[3] supra sunt dicta, facilius omnia sol-
ventur. Nam ut illic externi⟨s⟩[4] caput rectus casus,
sic hic in forma est persona eius qui loquitur et tempus
praesens, ut scribo lego.

§ 101.   [1] *Aug.*, *for* sic.   [2] *G*, *H*, *a*, *for* habeant.
[3] *Mue.*, *with G*, *for* infectaba.   [4] *Christ.*, *with G*, *for* habet.
[5] *L. Sp.*, *for* et.   [6] *L. Sp.*, *for* imperandi.
§ 102.   [1] *Laetus*, *for* discrepant.   [2] *Abl.* quique *Lachmann*, *for* quisque.   [3] *L. Sp.*, *for* nominatiuis.   [4] *Fay*,
for externi.

§ 101.   [a] Present imperative, future imperative, present
subjunctive.   [b] The indicative mood.   [c] Varro disregards the plural forms in this calculation.
§ 102.   [a] Meaning ' mood '; *cf.* § 95, note *a*.   [b] *Cf.*
ix. 75-79.

used to say present *esum es est*, imperfect *eram eras erat*, future *ero eris erit*. In this same fashion you will see that the other verbs of this kind preserve the principle of Regularity.

LVIII. 101. Besides, they find fault with Regularity in this matter, that certain verbs have not the three persons, nor the three tenses ; but it is with lack of insight that they find this fault, as if one should blame Nature because she has not shaped all living creatures after the same mould. For if by nature not all forms of the verbs have three tenses and three persons, then the divisions of the verbs do not all have this same number. Therefore when we give a command, a form which only the verbs of uncompleted time have—when we give a command to a person present or not actually present, three verb-forms [a] are made, like *lege* ' read (thou),' *legito* ' read (thou) ' or ' let him read,' *legat* ' let him read ' : for nobody gives a command with a form denoting action already completed. On the other hand, in the forms which denote declaration,[b] like *lego* ' I read,' *legis* ' thou readest,' *legit* ' he reads,' there are nine verb-forms of uncompleted action and nine of completed action.[c]

LIX. 102. For this and similar reasons the question that should be asked is not whether one kind [a] disagrees with another kind, but whether there is anything lacking in each kind. If to these there is added what I said above [b] about nouns, all difficulties will be easily resolved. For as the nominative case-form is in them the source for the derivative cases, so in verbs the source for other forms is in the form which expresses the person of the speaker and the present tense : like *scribo* ' I write,' *lego* ' I read.'

103. Quare ut illic fit, si[1] hic item acciderit, in
formula ut aut caput non sit aut ex alieno genere sit,
proportione eadem quae illic dicimus, cur nihilominus[2]
servetur analogia. Item, sicut illic caput suum
habebit et in obliquis casibus transitio erit in ali⟨am⟩
quam[3] formulam, qua assumpta reliqua facilius
possint videri verba, unde sint declinata (fit enim, ut
rectus casus nonnunquam sit ambiguus), ut in hoc
verbo volo, quod id duo significat, unum a voluntate,
alterum a volando ; itaque a volo intellegimus et
volare et velle.

LX. 104. Quidam reprehendunt, quod pluit et
luit dicamus in praeterito et praesenti tempore, cum
analogiae sui cuiusque temporis verba debeant discriminare. Falluntur : nam est ac putant aliter,
quod in praeteritis U dicimus longum pluit ⟨luit⟩,[1]
in praesenti breve pluit luit : ideoque in lege vendi-
tionis fundi " ruta caesa " ita dicimus, ut U produ-
camus.

LXI. 105. Item reprehendunt quidam, quod
putant idem esse sacrifico[1] et sacrificor, lavat[2] et
lavatur ; quod sit an non, nihil commovet analogian,
dum sacrifico[3] qui dicat servet sacrificabo et sic per

§ 103. [1] *Mue., for* sic.   [2] *For* nichilominus.   [3] *Mue.,*
for aliquam.
§ 104. [1] *Added by Aug.*
§ 105. [1] *Aug., for* sacrificio.   [2] *L. Sp. ;* sacrificor et
lavat *Aug. ; for* sacrifico relauat.   [3] *Aug., for* sacrifici.

§ 103. [a] *Cf.* ix. 76.
§ 104. [a] Found in older Latin, but seemingly shortened
by about Varro's time.   [b] One might exempt from inclu-
sion in the sale of a property all things dug up (sand, chalk,
etc.) and all things cut down (timber, etc.), even though they
were still unwrought materials.   [c] The *u* is short in the
compounds *erutus, obrutus,* etc.

103. Wherefore, if it has happened in verbs as it does happen in nouns, that in the pattern the starting-point is lacking or belongs to a different kind, we give the same arguments here which we gave there,[a] with suitable changes in application, as to why and how Regularity is none the less preserved. And as in nouns the word will have its own peculiar starting-point and in the oblique cases there will be a change to some other pattern, on the assumption of which it can be more easily seen from what the word-forms are derived (for it happens that the nominative case-form is sometimes ambiguous), so it is in verbs, as in this verb *volo*, because it has two meanings, one from wishing and the other from flying ; therefore from *volo* we appreciate that there are both *volare* ' to fly ' and *velle* ' to wish.'

LX. 104. Certain critics find fault, because we say *pluit* ' rains ' and *luit* ' looses ' both in the past tense and in the present, although the Regularities ought to make a distinction between the verb-forms of the two tenses. But they are mistaken ; for it is otherwise than they think, because in the past tense we say *pluit* and *luit* with a long U,[a] and in the present with a short U ; and therefore in the law about the sale of farms we say *ruta caesa* ' things dug up and things cut,'[b] with a lengthened *u*.[c]

LXI. 105. Likewise certain persons find fault, because they think that active *sacrifico* ' I sacrifice ' and passive *sacrificor*, active *lavat* ' he bathes ' and passive *lavatur*, are the same[a] : but whether this is so or not, has no effect on the principle of Regularity, provided that he who says *sacrifico* sticks to the future

§ 105. [a] With the same meaning ; but the passive of these verbs sometimes has true passive meaning.

totam formam, ne dicat sacrificatur[4] aut sacrificatus
sum : haec enim inter se non conveniunt.

106. Apud Plautum, cum dicit :

> Piscis ego credo qui usque dum vivunt lavant
> Diu minus lavari[1] quam haec lavat Phronesium,

ad lavant lavari non convenit, ut I^2 sit postremum,
sed E ; ad lavantur analogia lavari reddit : quod
Plauti aut librarii mendum si est, non ideo analogia,
sed qui scripsit est reprehendendus. Omnino et
lavat[3] et lavatur dicitur separatim recte in rebus certis,
quod puerum nutrix lava⟨t⟩,[4] puer a nutrice lavatur,
nos in *b*alneis et lavamus et lavamur.

107. Sed consuetudo alterum utrum cum satis
haberet, in toto corpore potius utitur lavamur, in
partibus lavamus, quod dicimus lavo manus, sic pedes
et cetera. Quare e balneis non recte dicunt lavi, lavi
manus recte. Sed quoniam in balneis lavor lautus
sum, sequitur, ut contra, quoniam est soleo, oporte⟨a⟩t[1]
dici solui, ut Cato et Ennius scribit, non ut dicit
volgus, solitus sum, debere dici ; neque propter haec,
quod discrepant in sermone pauca, minus est analogia,
ut supra dictum est.

---

[4] *L. Sp., for* sacrificaturus.
 § 106. [1] *Plautus has* minus diu lavare. [2] *H, for* T.
[3] *H, for* lauant. [4] *For* laua.
 § 107. [1] *Mue., for* oportet.

---

 § 106. [a] *Truc.* 322-323.
 § 107. [a] The passive form as a middle or reflexive, but the
active form as a transitive requiring an object. [b] *Frag.
inc.* 54 Jordan. [c] *Frag. inc.* 26 Vahlen[2]. [d] *Cf.* ix. 33.

sacrificabo and so on in the active, through the whole paradigm, avoiding the passive *sacrificatur* and *sacrificatus sum* : for these two sets do not harmonize with each other.

106. In Plautus, when he says [a] :

> The fish, I really think, that bathe through all their life,
> Are in the bath less time than this Phronesium,

lavari ' are in the bath,' with final I instead of E, does not attach to *lavant* ' bathe ' : Regularity refers *lavari* to *lavantur*, and whether the error belongs to Plautus or to the copyist, it is not Regularity, but the writer that is to be blamed. At any rate, *lavat* and *lavatur* are used with a difference of meaning in certain matters, because a nurse *lavat* ' bathes ' a child, the child *lavatur* ' is bathed ' by the nurse, and in the bathing establishments we both *lavamus* ' bathe ' and *lavamur* ' are bathed.'

107. But since usage approves both, in the case of the whole body one uses rather *lavamur* ' we bathe ourselves,' and in the case of portions of the body *lavamus* ' we wash,' in that we say *lavo* ' I wash ' my hands, my feet, and so on.[a] Therefore with reference to the bathing establishments they are wrong in saying *lavi* ' I have bathed,' but right in saying *lavi* ' I have washed ' my hands. But since in the bathing establishments *lavor* ' I bathe ' and *lautus sum* ' I have bathed,' it follows that on the other hand from *soleo* ' I am wont,' which is in the active, one ought to say *solui* ' I have been wont,' as Cato [b] and Ennius [c] write, and that *solitus sum*, as the people in general say, ought not to be used. But as I have said above,[d] Regularity exists none the less for these few inconsistencies which occur in speech.

LXII. 108. Item cur non sit analogia, afferunt,[1]
quod ab similibus similia non declinentur, ut ab dolo
et colo : ab altero enim dicitur dolavi, ab altero colui ;
in quibus assumi solet aliquid, quo facilius reliqua
dicantur, ut i⟨n⟩[2] M*y*rmecidis[3] operibus minutis solet
fieri : igitur in verbis temporalibus, quo⟨m⟩[4] similitudo s*a*epe sit confusa, ut discerni nequeat, nisi trans-
ieris in aliam personam aut in tempus, quae pro-
posita sunt no⟨n e⟩sse[5] similia intellegitur, cum transitum est in secundam personam, quod alterum est
dolas, alterum colis.

109. Itaque in reliqua forma verborum suam
utr⟨um⟩que[1] sequitur formam. Utrum in secunda
⟨persona⟩[2] forma verborum temporal*i*⟨um⟩[3] habeat
in extrema syllaba AS ⟨an ES⟩ an ĪS a⟨u⟩t ĪS,[4] ad
discernendas similitudines interest : quocirca ibi
potius index analogiae quam in prima, quod ibi
abstrusa est dissimilitudo, ut apparet in his meo, neo,
ruo : ab his enim dissimilia fiunt transitu, quod sic
dicuntur meo meas, neo nes, ruo ruis, quorum
unumquodque suam conservat similitudinis formam.

LXIII. 110. Analogiam item de his quae appellantur participia reprehendunt mult*i*[1] ; iniuria : nam
non debent dici terna ab singulis verbis amaturus
amans amatus, quod est ab amo amans et amaturus,

§ 108. [1] adferunt *Aug.*, *for* asserunt.   [2] *Aug.*, *for* uti.
[3] *Pius*, *for* murmecidis.   [4] *Aug.*, *for* quo.   [5] *Vertranius*,
for nosse.
    § 109. [1] *Sciop.*, *for* uterque.   [2] *Added by L. Sp.*   [3] *L.
Sp.*, *for* temporale.   [4] *L. Sp.* (aut ES *Canal*), *for* as anis
at si.
    § 110. [1] *GS.*, *for* multa.

§ 108.   [a] Just as we nowadays take the infinitive to show
the conjugation, adding the perfect active and the passive

LXII. 108. Likewise, they present as an argument against the existence of Regularity the fact that like forms are not derived from likes, as from *dolo* ' I chop ' and *colo* ' I till ' ; for one forms the perfect *dolavi* and the other forms *colui*. In such instances something additional is wont to be taken to aid in the making of the other forms,[a] just as we do in the tiny art-works of Myrmecides [b] : therefore in verbs, since the likeness is often so confusing that the distinction cannot be made unless you pass to another person or tense, you become aware that the words before you are not alike when passage is made to the second person, which is *dolas* in the one verb and *colis* in the other.

109. Thus in the rest of the paradigm of the verbs each follows its own special type. Whether in the second person the paradigm of verbs has in the final syllable AS or ES or IS or ĪS, is of importance for distinguishing the likenesses. Wherefore the mark of Regularity is in the second person rather than in the first, because in the first the unlikeness is concealed, as appears in *meo* ' I go,' *neo* ' I sew,' *ruo* ' I fall ' ; for from these there develop unlike forms by the change from first to second person, because they are spoken thus : *meo meas, neo nes, ruo ruis*, each one of which preserves its own type of likeness.

LXIII. 110. Likewise, many find fault with Regularity in connexion with the so-called participles ; wrongly : for it should not be said that the set of three participles comes from each individual verb, like *amaturus* ' about to love,' *amans* ' loving,' *amatus* ' loved,' because *amans* and *amaturus* are from

participle to make up the " principal parts " which are our guide.   [b] *Cf.* vii. 1.

ab amor[2] amatus. Illud analogia quod praestare
debet, in suo quicque genere habet, casus, ut amatus
amato et amati amatis ; et sic in muliebribus amata
et amatae ; item amaturus eiusdem modi habet
declinationes, amans paulo aliter ; quod hoc genus
omnia sunt in suo genere similia proportione, sic
virilia et muliebria sunt eadem.

LXIV. 111. De eo quod in priore libro extremum
est, ideo non es⟨se⟩ analogia⟨m⟩,[1] quod qui de ea
scripserint aut inter se non conveniant aut in quibus
conveniant ea cum consuetudinis discrepent[2] verbis,
utrumque ⟨est leve⟩[3] : sic enim omnis repudiandum
erit artis, quod et in medicina et in musica et in
aliis multis discrepant scriptores ; item in quibus
conveniunt in[4] scriptis, si e⟨a⟩ tam⟨en⟩[5] repudiat[6]
natura : quod ita ut dicitur non sit ars, sed artifex
reprehendendus, qui ⟨dici⟩[7] debet in scribendo non
vidisse verum, non ideo non posse scribi verum.

112. Qui dicit hoc monti et hoc fonti, cum alii
dicant hoc monte et hoc fonte, sic alia quae duobus
modis dicuntur, cum alterum sit verum, alterum
falsum, non uter peccat tollit analogias, sed uter
recte dicit confirmat ; et quemadmodum is qui[1]
peccat in his verbis, ubi duobus modis dicuntur, non

---

[2] *Aug. ;* amaturus ab amabar *Rhol. ; for* ab amaturus
amabar.
    § 111. [1] *Mue., for* est analogia. [2] *Mue., for* dis-
crepant. [3] *Added by GS. ;* falsum *A. Sp. ;* falsum est
Popma. [4] *A. Sp., for* ut. [5] *GS., for* etiam. [6] *For*
repudiant. [7] *Added by GS.*
    § 112. [1] *L. Sp., for* quicum.

---

    § 112. [a] *Cf.* viii. 66.

the active *amo*, and *amatus* is from the passive *amor*. But that which Regularity can offer, which the participles have, each in its own class, is case-forms, as *amatus*, dative *amato*, and plural *amati*, dative *amatis* ; and so in the feminine, *amata* and plural *amatae*. Likewise *amaturus* has a declension of the same kind. *Amans* has a somewhat different declension ; because all words of this kind have a regular likeness in their own class, *amans*, like others of its class, uses the same forms for masculine and for feminine.

LXIV. 111. About the last argument in the preceding book, that Regularity does not exist for the reason that those who have written about it do not agree with one another, or else the points on which they agree are at variance with the words of actual usage, both reasons are of little weight. For in this fashion you will have to reject all the arts, because in medicine and in music and in many other arts the writers do not agree ; you must take the same attitude in the matters in which they agree in their writings, if none the less nature rejects their conclusions. For in this way, as is often said, it is not the art but the artist that is to be found fault with, who, it must be said, has in his writing failed to see the correct view ; we should not for this reason say that the correct view cannot be formulated in writing.

112. As to the man who uses as ablatives *monti* ' hill ' and *fonti* ' spring ' while others say *monte* and *fonte*,[a] along with other words which are used in two forms, one form is correct and the other is wrong, yet the person who errs is not destroying the Regularities, but the one who speaks correctly is strengthening it ; and as he who errs in these words where they are used in two forms is not destroying logical

tollit rationem cum sequitur falsum, sic etiam in his
⟨quae⟩[2] non[3] duobus dicuntur, si quis aliter putat
dici oportere atque oportet, non scientiam tollit
orationis, sed suam inscientiam denudat.

LXV. 113.   Quibus rebus solvi arbitraremur posse
quae dicta sunt priori libro contra analogian, ut potui
brevi percucurri.   Ex quibus si id confecissent[1] quod
volunt, ut in lingua Latina esset anomalia, tamen
nihil egissent[2] ideo, quod in omnibus partibus mundi
utraque natura inest, quod alia inter se ⟨similia⟩,[3]
alia ⟨dissimilia⟩[3] sunt, sicut in animalibus dissimilia
sunt, ut equus bos ovis homo, item alia, et in uno
quoque horum genere inter se similia innumerabilia.
Item in piscibus dissimilis muraena lupo, is[4] soleae,
haec muraenae[5] et mustelae, sic aliis, ut maior ille
numerus sit similitudinum earum quae sunt separatim
in muraenis, separatim in asellis, sic in generibus
aliis.

114.   Quare cum in inclinationibus verborum
numerus sit magnus a dissimilibus verbis ortus, quod
etiam vel maior est in quibus similitudines reperiuntur, confitendum[1] est esse analogias.   Itemque[2] cum
ea non multo minus quam in omnibus verbis patiatur
uti consuetudo co⟨m⟩munis, fatendum illud quoquo

---

[2] *Added by* Aug.   [3] *After* non, *Aug. deleted* in.
§ 113.   [1] *For* conficissent.   [2] *Aug., for* legissent.
[3] *Added by* Mue.   [4] *L. Sp., for* his.   [5] *G, H, Aldus, for*
nerene.
§ 114.   [1] *Aug., for* conferendum.   [2] *Aug., for* item
quae.

---

[b] That is, wrong forms not recognized as having a limited
currency, but practically individual with the speaker.
§ 113.   [a] The identification of the various kinds of fish is

system when he follows the wrong form, so even in those words which are not spoken in two ways, a person who thinks they ought to be spoken otherwise than they ought,[b] is not destroying the science of speech, but exposing his own lack of knowledge.

LXV. 113. The considerations by which we might think that the arguments could be refuted which were presented against Regularity in the preceding book, I have touched upon briefly, as best I could. Even if by their arguments they had achieved what they wish, namely that in the Latin language there should be Anomaly, still they would have accomplished nothing, for the reason that in all parts of the world both natures are present : because some things are like, and others are unlike, just as in animals there are unlikes such as horse, ox, sheep, man, and others, and yet in each kind there are countless individuals that are like one another. In the same way, among fishes, the moray is unlike the sea-bass, the sea-bass is unlike the sole, and this is unlike the moray and the codfish, and others also ; though the number of those resemblances is still greater, which exist separately among morays, among hakes, and in other kinds of fish, class by class.[a]

114. Now although in the derivations of words a great number develop from unlike words, still the number of those in which likenesses are found is even greater, and therefore it must be admitted that the Regularities do exist. And likewise, since general usage permits us to follow the principle of Regularity in almost all words, it must be admitted that we ought

in some instances uncertain, but is not important for Varro's argument.

$m\langle o\rangle do^3$ analogian sequi nos debere universos, singulos autem praeterquam in quibus verbis offensura sit consuetudo co⟨m⟩munis, quod ut dixi aliud debet praestare populus, aliud e populo singuli homines.

115. Neque id mirum est, cum singuli quoque non sint eodem iure : nam liberius potest poeta quam orator sequi analogias. Quare cum hic liber id quod pollicitus est demonstraturum absolveri*t*,[1] faciam finem ; proxumo deinceps de declinatorum verborum forma[2] scribam.

---

[3] *Canal ;* quoque modo *Mue. ;* quodammodo *Aug. ; for* quo quando.

§ 115. [1] *Aldus, for* absoluerim. [2] *Pius, for* firma.

as a body to follow Regularity in every way, and individually also except in words the general use of which will give offence [a] ; because, as I have said,[b] the people ought to follow one standard, the individual persons ought to follow another.

115. And this is not astonishing, since not all individuals have the same privileges and rights ; for the poet can follow the Regularities more freely than can the orator. Therefore, since this book has completed the exposition of what it promised to set forth, I shall bring it to a close ; and then in the next book I shall write about the form of inflected words.

§ 114. [a] That is, will offend the feeling for idiom.   [b] Cf. ix. 5.

M. TERENTI VARRONIS
DE LINGUA LATINA

AD CICERONEM LIBER VIIII EXPLICIT ; INCIPIT

X

I. 1. In verborum declinationibus disciplina loquendi
dissimilitudinem an similitudinem sequi deberet,
multi quaesierunt. Cum ab his ratio quae ab similitudine oriretur vocaretur analogia, reliqua pars
appellaretur anomalia : de qua re primo libro quae
dicerentur cur dissimilitudinem ducem haberi oporteret, dixi, secundo contra quae dic⟨er⟩entur,[1] cur
potius similitudinem[2] conveniret praeponi : quarum
rerum quod nec fundamenta, ut deb⟨u⟩it,[3] posita ab
ullo neque ordo ac natura, ut res postulat, explicita,
ipse eius rei formam exponam.

2. Dicam de quattuor rebus, quae continent
declinationes[1] verborum : quid sit simile ac dissimile,
quid ratio quam appellant λόγον, quid pro portione[2]

---

§ 1. [1] *Aldus, for* dicentur.   [2] *Aldus, for* dissimilitudinem.   [3] *Aug., for* debita.
§ 2.   [1] *L. Sp., for* declinationibus.   [2] *Plasberg, for* proportione.

---

§ 1.   [a] Book VIII., which begins a fresh section of the
entire work.   [b] Book IX.

MARCUS TERENTIUS VARRO'S
ON THE LATIN LANGUAGE

ADDRESSED TO CICERO

BOOK IX ENDS, AND HERE BEGINS

BOOK X

I. 1. Many have raised the question whether in the inflections of words the art of speaking ought to follow the principle of unlikeness or that of likeness. This is important, since from these develop the two systems of relationship : that which develops from likeness is called Regularity, and its counterpart is called Anomaly. Of this, in the first book,[a] I gave the arguments which are advanced in favour of considering unlikeness as the proper guide ; in the second,[b] those advanced to show that it is proper rather to prefer likeness. Therefore, as their foundations have not been laid by anyone, as should have been done, nor have their order and nature been set forth as the matter demands, I shall myself sketch an outline of the subject.

2. I shall speak of four factors which limit the inflections of words : what likeness and unlikeness are ; what the relationship is which they call *logos* ; what " by comparative likeness " is, which they call

535

quo*d*[3] dicunt ἀνὰ λόγον,[4] quid consuetudo ; quae
explicat*ae* declarabunt analogiam et anomalia⟨m⟩,[5]
unde sit, quid sit, cuius modi sit.

II. 3.   De similitudine et dissimilitudine ideo
primum dicendum, quod ea res est fundamentum
omnium declinationum ac continet rationem verborum.   Simile est quod res plerasque habere videtur
easdem quas illud cuiusque simile : dissimile est
quod videtur esse contrarium huius.   Minimum ex
duobus constat omne simile, item dissimile, quod
nihil potest esse simile, quin alicuius sit simile, item
nihil dicitur dissimile, quin addatur quoius sit dissimile.

4.   Sic dicitur similis homo homini, equus equo,
et dissimilis homo equo : nam similis est homo homini
ideo, quod easdem figuras membrorum habent, quae
eos dividunt ab reliquorum animalium specie.   In
ipsis hominibus simili de causa vir viro similior quam
vir mulieri, quod plures habent easdem partis ; et
sic senior seni similior quam puero.   Eo porro
similiores sunt qui facie quoque p*ae*ne eadem, habitu
corporis, filo : itaque qui plura habent eadem,
dicuntur similiores ; qui proxume accedunt ad id,
ut omnia habeant eadem, vocantur gemini, simillimi.

5.   Sunt qui tris naturas rerum putent esse, simile,
dissimile, neutrum, quod alias vocant non simile, alias

[3] *Aug.*, *for* quid.   [4] *Plasberg*, *for* analogon.   [5] *Pius*,
for anomalia.

§2.   [a] *Cf*. x. 37.

" according to *logos* " [a] ; what usage is. The explanation of these matters will make clear the problems connected with Regularity and Anomaly : whence they come, what they are, of what sort they are.

II. 3. The first topic to be discussed must be likeness and unlikeness, because this matter is the foundation of all inflections and set limits to the relationship of words. That is like which is seen to have several features identical with those of that which is like it, in each case : that is unlike, which is seen to be the opposite of what has just been said. Every like or unlike consists of two units at least, because nothing can be like without being like something else, and nothing can be unlike without association with something to which it is unlike.

4. Thus a human being is said to be like a human being, and a horse to be like a horse, and a human being to be unlike a horse ; for a human being is like a human being because they have limbs of the same shape, which separate human beings from the category of the other animals. Among human beings themselves, for a like reason a man is more like a man than a man is like a woman, because men have more physical parts the same ; and so an elderly man is more like an old man than he is like a boy. Further, they are more like who are of almost the same features, the same bearing of person, the same shape of body ; therefore those who have more points of identity, are said to be more like ; and those who come nearest to having them all alike, are called most like, as it were, twins.

5. There are those who think that things have three natures, like, unlike, and neutral, which last they sometimes call the not like, and sometimes the

537

non dissimile (sed quamvis tria sint simile dissimile neutrum, tamen potest dividi etiam in duas partes sic, quodcumque conferas aut simile esse aut non esse); simile esse et dissimile, si videatur esse ut dixi, neutrum, si in neutram partem praeponderet, ut si duae res quae conferuntur vicenas habent partes et in his denas habeant easdem, denas alias ad similitudinem et dissimilitudinem aeque animadvertendas : hanc naturam plerique subiciunt sub dissimilitudinis nomen.

6.   Quare quoniam fit[1] ut potius de vocabulo quam de re controversia esse videatur, illud est potius advertendum, quom simile quid esse dicitur, cui[2] parti simile dicatur esse (in hoc enim solet esse error), quod potest fieri ut homo homini similis[3] non sit,[4] ut multas partis habeat similis et ideo dici possit similis habere oculos, manus, pedes, sic alias res separatim et una plures.

7.   Itaque quod diligenter videndum est in verbis, quas partis et quot modis oporteat similis habere ⟨quae similitudinem habere⟩[1] dicuntur, ut infra apparebit, is locus maxime lubricus est.   Quid enim similius potest videri indiligenti quam duo verba haec suis et suis ?   Quae non sunt, quod alterum[2] significat suere, alterum suem.   Itaque similia vocibus

---

§ 6.   [1] *Aug., for* fuit.   [2] quoi *L. Sp., for* quin cui.
[3] *V, p, C. F. W. Mueller, for* simile.   [4] non sit *Rhol., for* sit non sit.

§ 7.   [1] *Added by GS., cf.* § 12 *end ;* quae similia esse, *added by L. Sp. ;* ut similia, *by Canal.*   [2] *After* alterum, *p and Aug. deleted* non.

not unlike ; but although there are the three, like, unlike, neutral, there can also be a division into two parts only, in such a way that whatever you compare with something else either is like or is not. They think that a thing is like and is unlike if it is seen to be of such a kind as I have described, and neutral, if it does not have greater weight on one side than on the other ; as if the two things which are being compared have twenty parts each, and among these should have ten to be noted as identical and ten likewise to be noted as different, in respect to likeness and unlikeness. This nature most scholars include under the name of unlikeness.

6. Therefore since it happens that the question in dispute seems rather to be about the name than about the thing, attention must rather be directed, when something is said to be like, to the problem to what part it is said to be like ; for it is in this that any mistake ordinarily rests. This must be noted, I say, because it can happen that a man may not be like another man even though he has many parts like the other's, and can be said therefore to have like eyes, hands, feet, and other physical features in considerable number, separately and taken together, like the other man's.

7. Therefore because careful watch must be kept in words to see what parts those words which are said to show likeness ought to have alike, and in what ways, the inquirer is on this topic especially likely to slip into error, as will appear below. For to the careless person what can seem more alike than the two words *suis* and *suis* ? But they are not alike, because one is from *suere* ' to sew ' and means ' thou sewest,' and the other is from *sus* and means ' of a swine.' There-

esse ac syllabis confitemur, dissimilia esse partibus orationis videmus, quod alterum habet tempora, alterum casus, quae duae res vel maxime discernunt analogias.

8. Item propinquiora genere inter se verba similem saepe pariunt errorem, ut in hoc, quod nemus[1] et lepus videtur esse simile, quom[2] utrumque habeat eundem casum rectum ; sed non est simile, quod eis[3] certae similitudines opus sunt, in quo est ut in genere nominum sint eodem, quod in his non est : nam in virili genere[4] est lepus, ex neutro nemus ; dicitur enim hic lepus et hoc nemus. Si eiusdem generis esse⟨n⟩t,[5] utrique praeponeretur idem ac diceretur aut hic lepus et hic nemus aut hoc nemus, hoc lepus.

9. Quare quae et cuius modi sunt genera similitudinum ad hanc rem, perspiciendum ei qui declinationes verborum proportione sintne quaeret. Quem[1] locum, quod est difficilis, qui de his rebus scripserunt aut vitaverunt aut inceperunt neque adsequi potuerunt.

10. Itaque in eo dissensio neque ea unius modi apparet : nam alii de omnibus universis discriminibus posuerunt numerum, ut Dionysius Sidonius, qui scripsit ea[1] esse septuaginta unum,[2] alii partis[3] eius quae habet[4] casus, cuius eidem hic cum dicat esse

§ 8. [1] H, Rhol., for numerus. [2] Mue., for quod cum. [3] Aug., for eas. [4] After genere, Aug. deleted nominum sint eodem, repeated from the previous line. [5] Aug., for esset.

§ 9. [1] Mue., for quod.
§ 10. [1] L. Sp., for eas. [2] L. Sp., for unam. [3] Mue., for partes. [4] Mue., for habent.

§ 8. [a] That is, so far as the termination is concerned.
§ 10. [a] That is, schemes of inflection. [b] A pupil of Aristarchus.

fore we admit that they are alike as spoken words
and in their separate syllables, but we see that
they are unlike in their parts of speech, because
one has tenses and the other has cases ; and tenses
and cases are the two features which in the highest
degree serve to distinguish the different systems of
Regularity.

8. Likewise, words that are even nearer alike in
kind often cause a similar mistake, as in the fact that
nemus ' grove ' and *lepus* ' hare ' seem to be alike since
both have the same nominative [a] ; but it is not an
instance of likeness, because they stand in need of
certain factors of likeness, among which is that they
should be in the same noun-gender. But these two
words are not, for *lepus* is masculine and *nemus* is
neuter ; for we say *hic* ' this ' with *lepus* and *hoc* with
nemus. If they were of the same gender, the same
form would be set before both, and we should say
either *hic lepus* and *hic nemus,* or *hoc nemus* and *hoc
lepus.*

9. Therefore he who asks whether the inflections
of words stand in a regular relation, must examine
to see what kinds of likenesses there are and of what
sort they are, which pertain to this matter. And just
because this topic is difficult, those who have written
of these subjects either have avoided it or have begun
it without being able to complete their treatment of it.

10. Therefore in this there is seen a lack of agreement, and not merely of one kind. For some have
fixed the number of all the distinctions [a] as a whole,
as did Dionysius of Sidon,[b] who wrote that there were
seventy-one of them ; and others set the number of
those distinctions which apply to the words which have
cases : the same writer says that of these there are

discrimina quadr*a*gint*a*[5] septem, Aristocles re*t*tulit[6] in litteras XIIII, Parmeniscus VIII, sic alii pauciora aut plura.

11. Quarum similitudinum si esset origo recte capta et inde orsa ratio, minus erraret⟨ur⟩[1] in declinationibus v⟨er⟩borum.[2] Quarum *e*go principia prima duum generum sola arbitror esse, a*d* qu*ae*[3] similitudines ex*i*gi[4] oporteat : e quis unum positum in verborum materia, alterum ut in materiae figura, quae ex declinatione fit.

12. Nam debet esse unum, ut verbum verbo, unde declinetur, sit simile ; alterum, ut e verbo in verbum declinatio, ad quam conferetur, eiusdem modi sit : alias enim ab similibus verbis similiter declinantur, ut ab erus[1] ferus, ero[2] fero, alias dissimiliter erus[1] ferus, eri[3] ferum. Cum utrumque et verbum verbo erit simile et declinatio declinationi, tum denique dicam esse simile[4] ac duplicem et perfectam similitudinem habere, id quod postulat analogia.[5]

13. Sed ne astutius videar posuisse duo genera esse similitudinum sola, cum utriusque inferiores species sint plures, si de his reticuero, ut mihi relin-

---

[5] *M, Laetus, for* quadringenta.   [6] *Mue. ;* retulit *Laetus ; for* rutulit.

§ 11. [1] *Vertranius, for* erraret.   [2] *For* uborum.   [3] *Aldus, for* atque.   [4] *For* exegi.

§ 12. [1] *For* herus.   [2] *For* hero.   [3] *For* heri.   [4] *L. Sp., for* similem.   [5] *For* analogiam.

---

[c] Probably Aristocles of Rhodes, a contemporary of Varro.
[d] A pupil of Aristarchus.

forty-seven, Aristocles *c* reduced them to fourteen headings, Parmeniscus *d* to eight, and others made the number smaller or larger.

11. If the origin of these likenesses had been correctly grasped and their logical explanation had proceeded from that as a beginning, there would be less error in regard to the inflections of words. Of these likenesses there are, I think, first principles of two kinds only, by which the likenesses ought to be tested ; of which one lies in the substance of the words,*a* the other lies, so to speak, in the form *b* of that substance, which comes from inflection.

12. For there must be one, that the word be like the word from which it is inflected, and two, that in comparison from word to word the inflectional form with which the comparison is made should be of the same kind. For sometimes there are like forms reached by inflection from like words, such as datives *ero* and *fero* from *erus* ' master ' and *ferus* ' wild,' and sometimes unlike forms, such as genitive *eri* and accusative *ferum*, from *erus* and *ferus*. When both principles are fulfilled and word is like word and inflectional form like inflectional form, then and not before will I pronounce that the word is like, and has a twofold and perfect likeness to the other—which is what Regularity demands.

13. But I wish to avoid the appearance of trickiness in having declared that there are only two kinds of likenesses when both have a number of sub-forms —if I say nothing about these, you may think that I am intentionally leaving myself a place of refuge ; I

§ 11. *a* That is, its form and ending, in the form which is the starting point for inflection. *b* The inflectional form ; *cf.* § 12.

quam latebras, repetam ab origine similitudinum quae
in conferendis verbis et inclinandis sequendae aut
vitandae sint.

14. Prima divisio in oratione, quod alia verba
nusquam declinantur,[1] ut haec vix mox, alia declinantur, ut ab lima limae,[2] a fero ferebam, et cum nisi
in his verbis quae declinantur non possit esse analogia,
qui dicit simile esse mox et nox errat, quod non est
eiusdem generis utrumque verbum, cum nox succedere debeat sub casuum ratione⟨m⟩,[3] mox neque
debeat neque possit.

15. Secunda divisio est de his verbis quae declinari possunt, quod alia sunt a voluntate, alia a
natura. Voluntatem appello, cum unus quivis a
nomine aliae ⟨rei⟩[1] imponit nomen, ut Romulus
Romae ; naturam dico, cum universi acceptum nomen
ab eo qui imposuit non requirimus quemadmodum
is velit declinari, sed ipsi declinamus, ut huius Romae,
hanc Romam, hac Roma. De his duabus partibus
voluntaria declinatio refertur ad consuetudinem,
naturalis ad rationem.[2]

16. Quare proinde ac simile conferre[1] non oportet
ac dicere, ut sit ab Roma Romanus, sic ex Capua dici
oportere Capuanus, quod in consuetudine vehementer
natat, quod declinantes imperite rebus nomina imponunt, a quibus cum accepit consuetudo, turbulenta

§ 14. [1] *For* declimantur.   [2] *GS., for* limabo.   [3] *Lachmann, for* ratione.
§ 15. [1] *Added by GS.*   [2] *Aug., for* orationem.
§ 16. [1] *Stephanus, for* conferri.

shall therefore go back and start from the origin of the likenesses which must be followed or avoided in the comparison of words and in their inflections.

14. The first division in speech is that some words are not changed into any other form whatsoever, like *vix* ' hardly ' and *mox* ' soon,' and others are inflected, like genitive *limae* from *lima* ' file,' imperfect *ferebam* from *fero* ' I bear ' ; and since Regularity cannot be present except in words which are inflected, he who says that *mox* and *nox* ' night ' are alike, is mistaken, because the two words are not of the same kind, since *nox* must come under the system of caseforms, but *mox* must not and cannot.

15. The second division is that, of the words which can be changed by derivation and inflection, some are changed in accordance with will, and others in accordance with nature. I call it will, when from a name a person sets a name on something else, as *Romulus* gave a name to *Roma* ; I call it nature, when we all accept a name but do not ask of the one who set it how he wishes it to be inflected, but ourselves inflect it, as genitive *Romae*, accusative *Romam*, ablative *Roma*. Of these two parts, voluntary derivation goes back to usage, and natural goes back to logical system.

16. For this reason we ought not to compare *Romanus* ' Roman ' and *Capuanus* ' Capuan ' as alike, and to say that *Capuanus* ought to be said from *Capua* just as *Romanus* is from *Roma* ; for in such there is in actual usage an extreme fluctuation, since those who derive the words set the names on the things with utter lack of skill, and when usage has accepted the words from them, it must of necessity speak confused names variously derived. Therefore

545

necesse est dicere. Itaque neque Aristarchei[2] neque
alii in analogiis defendendam eius susceperunt cau-
sam, sed, ut dixi, hoc genere declinatio in co⟨m⟩-
muni consuetudine verborum *a*egrotat, quod oritur
e populo multiplici ⟨et⟩[3] imperito : itaque in hoc
genere in loquendo[4] magis anomalia quam analogia.

17. Tertia divisio est : quae verba declinata
natura ; ea divid*u*ntur[1] in partis quattuor : in unam
quae habet casus neque tempora, ut docilis et facilis ;
in alteram quae tempora neque casus, ut docet facit ;
in tertiam quae utraque, ut docens faciens ; in
quartam quae neutra, ut docte et facete. Ex hac
divisione singulis partibus tres reliqu*ae*[2] dissimiles.
Quare nisi in sua parte inter se collata erunt verba,
si[3] conveniunt, non erit ita simile, ut debeat facere
idem.

18. Unius cuiusque part*is*[1] quoniam species plures,
de singulis dicam. Prima pars casualis dividitur in
partis duas, in nominatus *scilicet*[2] ⟨et articulos⟩,[3]
quod *a*eque[4] finitum ⟨et infinitum⟩[5] est ut hic et quis ;
de his generibus duobus utrum sumpseris, cum

---

[2] *Kent, for* Aristarchii *; cf.* viii. 63.　　[3] *Added by Groth.*
[4] *For* loquenda.
§ 17.　[1] *L. Sp., for* dividitur.　　[2] *Mue., for* reliquere.
[3] *After* si, *Canal deleted* non.
§ 18.　*The text of this § stands in the manuscripts between*
§ 20 *and* § 21 ; *the shift of position was made by Mueller, who
left* unius cuiusque partis *at the end of* § 20 ; *A. Spengel
transferred these words also.*　　[1] *Sciop., for* partes.
[2] *Laetus, for* § (=sunt).　　[3] *Added by Mue.*　　[4] *L. Sp., for*
neque.　　[5] *Added by L. Sp. ; cf.* viii. 45.

---

§ 16.　[a] This is shown even to-day in the new technical
terminology of some near-sciences.　　[b] Varro is somewhat

neither the followers of Aristarchus nor any others have undertaken to defend the cause of voluntary derivation as among the Regularities ; but, as I have said, this kind of derivation of words in common usage is an ill thing, because it springs from the people, which is without uniformity and without skill.[a] Therefore, in speaking, there is in this kind of derivation rather Anomaly than Regularity.[b]

17. There is a third division, the words which are by their nature inflected. These are divided into four subdivisions : one which has cases but not tenses,[a] like *docilis* ' docile ' and *facilis* ' easy ' ; a second, which has tenses but not cases,[b] like *docet* ' teaches,' *facit* ' makes ' ; a third which has both,[c] like *docens* ' teaching,' *faciens* ' making ' ; a fourth which has neither,[d] like *docte* ' learnedly ' and *facete* ' wittily.' The individual parts of this division are each unlike the three remaining parts. Therefore, unless the words are compared with one another in their own subdivision, even if they do agree the one word will not be so like the other that it ought to make the same inflectional scheme.

18. Since there are several species in each part, I shall speak of them one by one. The first subdivision, characterized by the possession of cases, is divided into two parts, namely into nouns and articles, which latter class is both definite and indefinite, as for example *hic* ' this ' and *quis* ' who.' Whichever of these two kinds you have taken, it must not be compared with the other, because they belong

unfair here, since derivation by suffixes, though varied, is not without its regular principles.
§ 17. [a] Nouns, pronouns, adjectives (except participles).
[b] Finite verbs.   [c] Participles.   [d] Adverbs.

reliquo non conferendum, quod inter se dissimiles habent analogias.

19. In articulis vix adumbrata est analogia et magis rerum quam vocum ; in nomin⟨at⟩ibus[1] magis expressa ac plus etiaɱ in vocibus ac ⟨syllabarum⟩[2] similitudinibus quam in rebus suam optinet rationem. Etiam illud accedit ut in articulis habere analogias ostendere sit difficile, quod singula sint verba, hic contra facile, quod magna sit copia similium nominatuum. Quare non tam hanc partem ab illa[3] dividendum quam illud videndum, ut satis sit verecundi⟨ae⟩[4] etiam illam in eandem arenam vocare pugnatum.

20. Ut in articulis duae partes, finitae et infinitae, sic in nominatibus[1] duae, vocabulum et nomen : non enim idem oppidum et Roma, cum oppidum sit vocabulum, Roma nomen, quorum discrimen in his reddendis rationibus alii discernunt, alii non ; nos sicubi opus fuerit, quid sit et cur, ascribemus.[2]

21. Nominatui[1] ut similis sit nominatus, habere debet ut sit eodem genere, specie eadem, sic casu, exitu eodem[2] : specie,[3] ut si nomen est quod conferas, cum quo conferas sit nomen ; genere,[4] ut non solum ⟨unum sed⟩[5] utrumque sit virile ; casu,[6] ut si alterum sit dandi, item alterum sit dandi ; exitu, ut quas

§ 19. [1] L. Sp., for nominibus. [2] Added by GS.
[3] After illa, Aug. deleted ab. [4] Kent, for uerecundi.
§ 20. [1] L. Sp., for uocabulis. [2] Sciop., for ascribimus.
§ 21. [1] Mue., for nominatus (Sciop. changed the second nominatus to -tui). [2] Mue., for eius. [3] Lübbert, for genere, transposing with specie (note 4). [4] Lübbert, for specie (cf. preceding note) ; after this, L. Sp. deleted simile. [5] Added by Mue. ; sed added by Aug. [6] After casu, L. Sp. deleted simile.

§ 21. [a] Here, as often in Varro, including adjective as well as substantive.

to schemes of Regularity which are different from each other.

19. In the articles, Regularity is hardly even a shadow, and more a Regularity of things than of spoken words ; in nouns, it comes out better, and consummates itself rather in the spoken words and the likeness of the syllables than in the things named. There is also the additional fact that it is difficult to show that Regularities reside in the articles, because they are single words ; but in nouns it is easy, because there is a great abundance of like name-words. Therefore it is not so much a matter of dividing this part from that other part, as of see-ing to it that the investigator should be too much ashamed even to call that other part into the same arena to do battle.

20. As there are two groups in the articles, the definite and the indefinite, so there are in the nouns, the common nouns and the proper names ; for *oppidum* ' town ' and *Roma* ' Rome ' are not the same, since *oppidum* is a common noun, and *Roma* is a proper name. In their account of the systems, some make this distinction, and others do not ; but we shall enter in our account, at the proper place, what this difference is and why it has come to be.

21. That noun [a] may be like noun, it ought to have the qualities of being of the same gender, of the same kind, also in the same case and with the same ending : kind, that if it is a proper name which you are com-paring, it be a proper name with which you compare it ; gender, that not merely one, but both words be masculine ; case, that if one is in the dative, the other likewise be in the dative ; ending, that what-

549

unum haḃeat extremas litteras, easdem alterum
habeat.

22. Ad hunc quadruplicem fontem ordines derigun-
tur bini, uni transversi, alteri derecti, ut in tabula
solet in qua latrunculis[1] ludunt. Transversi sunt
qui ab recto casu obliqui declinantur, ut albus albi
albo ; derecti sunt qui ab recto casu in rectos
declinantur, ut albus alba album ; utrique sunt partibus senis. Transversorum ordinum partes *appellantur*[2] casus, derectorum gen*era*,[3] utrisque inter se
implicatis forma.[4]

23. Dicam prius de transversis. Casuum vocabula alius alio modo appellavit ; nos dicemus, qui
nominandi causa dicitur, nominandi vel nomina-
tivum. . . .[1]

HIC DESUNT TRIA FOLIA IN EXEMPLARI[2]

24. . . . ⟨dicuntur una⟩e[1] scopae, non dicitur una
scopa : alia enim natura, quod priora simplicibus,

§ 22. [1] *Bentinus, for* latrunculus.   [2] *Aldus, for* expel-
lantur.   [3] *Aug., for* genere.   [4] *Aug., for* formam.
§ 23.   [1] *There is blank space here in F, for the rest of the
page (18 lines), all the next page (39 lines), and the first part
of the following (8 lines).*   [2] *F², in margin.*
§ 24.   [1] *Added and altered by Kent, for* et ; *cf.* viii. 7.

§ 22. [a] The ' men ' in a game like draughts or checkers
were called *latrunculi* ' mercenary soldiers ' by the Romans.
[b] Varro did not arrange his paradigm of adjectives as we do,
but set the cases of the same number and gender in one line
across the page, while the other genders followed in the next
two lines, and then the three genders of the plural in the
succeeding lines.   [c] Varro counts his six genders by considering the genders of the plural as additional genders.
§ 23. [a] The cases.   [b] Varro's names for the remaining

ever last letters the one has, the other also have the same.

22. To this fourfold spring two sets of lines are drawn up, the ones crosswise and the others vertical, as is the regular arrangement on a board on which they play with movable pieces.[a] Those are crosswise which are the oblique cases formed from a nominative,[b] like *albus* ' white,' genitive *albi*, dative *albo* ; those are vertical which are inflected from one nominative to other nominatives, as masculine *albus*, feminine *alba*, neuter *album*. Both sets of lines are of six members.[c] Each member of the crosswise lines is called a case ; each member of the vertical lines is a gender ; that which belongs to both in their crossed arrangement, is a form.

23. I shall speak first of the crosswise lines.[a] Scholars have given various sets of names to the cases ; we shall call that case which is spoken for the purpose of naming, the case of naming or nominative . . .[b]

HERE THREE LEAVES ARE LACKING IN THE MODEL
COPY[c]

24. . . . To indicate one ' broom ' the plural *scopae* is used, not the singular *scopa*.[a] For they[b] are different by nature, because the names first men-

cases, which were listed in the lost text, are : *casus patricus* or *patrius*, *casus dandi*, *casus accusandi* or *accusativus*, *casus vocandi*, *casus sextus*. The names *genetivus*, *dativus*, *vocativus*, *ablativus* appear in Quintilian and Gellius.   [c] In the lost text stood the remainder of the discussion of cases, all the discussion of gender, and almost all concerning number, which is concluded in § 30.

§ 24.   [a] *Cf.* viii. 7.   [b] The nouns in the preceding discussion, of which *scopae* alone is preserved in the text.

VARRO

posteriora in coniunctis rebus vocabula ponuntur, sic bigae, sic quadrigae a coniunctu dictae. Itaque non dicitur, ut haec una lata et alba, sic una biga, sed unae bigae, neque[2] dicitur ut hae duae latae, albae, sic hae duae bigae et quadrigae, ⟨sed hae binae bigae et quadrigae⟩.[3]

25. Item figura verbi qualis sit refert, quod in figura vocis alias commutatio fit in *primo*[1] verbo sūit[2] modo sūit,[2] alias in medio, ut *curso*[3] cursito, alias in extremo, ut doceo docui, alias co⟨m⟩munis, ut lego legi.[4] Refert igitur ex quibus litteris quodque verbum constet, maxime extrema, quod ea in plerisque commutatur.[5]

26. Quare in his quoque partibus similitudines ab aliis male, ab aliis bene quod solent sumi in casibus conferendis, recte an perperam videndum ; sed ubicumque commoventur litterae, non solum eae sunt animadvertendae, sed etiam quae proxumae sunt neque moventur : haec enim vicinitas aliquantum potes⟨t⟩[1] in verborum declinationibus.

27. In quis figuris non ea similia dicemus quae

---

[2] *After* neque, *p and Sciop. deleted* ut.   [3] *Added by L. Sp.*, *cf.* ix. 64.

§ 25.   [1] *Mue., for* uno.   [2] *Mue. added the signs of quantity ; cf.* ix. 104.   [3] *Aug., for* cursu.   [4] *Aug., for* lege.   [5] *L. Sp. for* commutantur.

§ 26.   [1] *Aldus, for* potes.

---

[c] These are all lost.   [d] *Scopae*, as ' twigs ' done in a bundle ; *bigae* and *quadrigae*, because of the number of horses involved.   [e] The distributive numeral is used to multiply ideas whose singular is denoted by a plural form: *cf.* ix. 64.

§ 25.   [a] I have added the signs of quantity in *lego* and *legi*, to make clear Varro's point.

tioned [c] are set upon simple objects, and those mentioned later apply to compounded objects [d] ; thus *bigae* ' two-horse team ' and *quadrigae* ' four-horse team ' are employed in the plural because they denote a union of objects. Therefore we do not say one *biga*, like one *lata* ' broad ' and *alba* ' white,' but one *bigae*, with the numeral also in the plural ; nor do we say *duae* ' two ' with reference to *bigae* and *quadrigae*, as we say *duae* ' two ' with application to the plural forms *latae* and *albae*, but we say *binae* ' two sets ' of *bigae* and *quadrigae*.[e]

25. Likewise the character of the form of a word is important, because in the form of the spoken word a change is sometimes made in the first part of the word, as in *sŭit* ' sews ' and *sūit* ' sewed ' ; sometimes in the middle, as in *curso* ' I run to and fro,' and *cursito*, of the same meaning ; sometimes at the end, as in *doceo* ' I teach ' and *docui* ' I have taught ' ; sometimes the change is common to two parts, as in *lĕgo* ' I read,' *lēgi* ' I have read.'[a] It is important therefore to observe of what letters each word consists ; and the last letter is especially important, because it is changed in the greatest number of instances.

26. Because of this, since the likenesses in these parts also are wont to be used in the comparison of case-forms, and this is done ill by some and well by others, we must see whether this has been done rightly or wrongly. Yet wherever the letters are altered, not only the altered letters must be noted, but also those which are next to them and are not affected ; for this proximity has considerable influence in the inflections of words.

27. Among these forms we shall not call those

similis res significant, sed quae ea forma sint, ut
eius modi res simili*s*[1] ex instituto significare plerumque sole⟨a⟩nt,[2] ut tunicam virilem et muliebrem
dicimus non eam quam habet vir aut mulier, sed
quam habere ex instituto debet : potest enim muliebrem vir, virilem mulier habere, ut in sc*a*ena ab
actoribus haberi videmus, sed eam dicimus muliebrem,
quae de eo genere est quo indutui mulieres ut uteren-
tur est institutum.   Ut actor stolam muliebrem sic
Perpenna et C*a*ecina et ⟨S⟩purinna[3] figura muliebria
dicuntur habere nomina, non mulierum.

28.   Flexurae quoque similitudo videnda ideo
quod alia verba quam vi⟨a⟩m[1] habeant ex ipsis
verbis, unde declinantur, appar*e*t,[2] ut quemadmodum
oporteat ut*i*[3] praetor consul, praetori consuli ; alia
ex transitu intelleguntur, ut socer macer, quod
alterum fit socerum, alterum macrum, quorum utrumque in reliquis a transitu suam viam sequitur et in
singularibus et in multitudinis declinationibus.   Hoc
fit ideo quod naturarum genera sunt duo quae inter
se conferri possunt, unum quod per se videri potest,
ut homo et equus, alterum sine assumpta aliqua re

---

§ 27.   [1] *Mue.,* for similia.   [2] *Aldus,* for solent.
[3] *Aug., for* purinna.
§ 28.   [1] *Schoell (marginal note in his copy of A. Sp.'s ed.),*
for uim.   [2] *Pius, for* appellarit.   [3] *A. Sp., for* ut a.

---

§ 27.   [a] With *eius modi,* understand *figurae* ; *cf. in eius
modi,* v. 128.   [b] *Cf.* ix. 48.   [c] *Cf.* viii. 41, 81, ix. 41.
§ 28.   [a] That is, the nominative is the stem to which the
case-endings are added.   [b] That is, the stem is seen in an

words like which denote like things, but those which
are of such a stamp that such forms [a] are in most
instances wont by custom to denote like things, as
by a man's tunic or a woman's tunic we mean not a
tunic that a man or a woman is wearing, but one
which by custom a man or a woman ought to wear.[b]
For a man can wear a woman's tunic, and a woman
can wear a man's, as we see done on the stage by
actors ; but we say that that is a woman's tunic,
which is of the kind that women customarily use
to dress themselves in. As an actor may wear a
woman's dress, so *Perpenna* and *Caecina* and *Spurinna*
are said to have names that are feminine in form ;
they are not said to have women's names.[c]

28. The likeness of the inflection also must be
watched, because the way which some words take is
clear from the very words from which their inflection
starts,[a] as how it is proper to use *praetor* and *consul*,
dative *praetori* and *consuli*. Others are properly
appreciated only as a result of the change seen in the
inflections, as in *socer* ' father-in-law ' and *macer*
' lean,' because the one becomes *socerum* in the
accusative, and the other *macrum* ; after making
this change, each of them follows its own way in the
remaining forms,[b] both in the inflections of the
singular and in those of the plural. This method is
employed [c] because in the inflections there are two
kinds of natures which can be compared with each
other, one which can be seen in the word itself, such
as *homo* ' man ' and *equus* ' horse,' but the second
cannot be seen through without bringing in some-

oblique case rather than in the nominative ; *cf.* ix. 91-94.
[c] Varro's logical sequence is here at fault, for he brings in
derivative stems, after speaking only of noun declensions.

extrinsecus perspici non possit, ut eques et equiso ·
uterque enim dicitur ab equo.

29.   Quare hominem homini similem esse aut non
esse, si contuleris, ex ipsis homini⟨bus⟩[1] animadversis
scies ; at duo inter se similiterne sint longiores quam
sint eorum fratres, dicere non possis, si illos breviores
cum quibus conferuntur quam longi sint ignore*s*[2] ;
si⟨c⟩[3] latiorum atque altiorum, item cetera eiusdem
generis sine assumpto extrinsecus aliquo perspici
similitudines non possunt.   Sic igitur quidam casus
quod ex hoc genere sunt, non facile est dicere similis
esse, si eorum singulorum solum animadvertas voces,
nisi assumpseris alterum, quo flectitur in trans-
eundo[4] vox.

30.   Quod ad nominatuom[1] similitudines animadvertendas arbitratus sum satis es⟨se⟩ tangere,[2] haec
sunt.   Relinquitur de articulis, in quibus quaedam
eadem, quaedam alia.   De quinque enim generibus
duo prima habent eadem, quod sunt et virilia et
muliebria et neutra, et quod alia sunt ut significent
unum, ⟨alia⟩[3] ut plura, et de casibus quod habent
quinos : nam vocandi voce notatus non est.   Pro-
prium illud habent, quod partim sunt finita, et hic
haec, partim infinita, ut quis et quae,[4] quorum quod
adumbrata et tenuis analogia, in hoc libro plura
dicere ⟨non⟩[5] necesse est.

---

§ 29.   [1] *Canal, for* homini.   [2] *Aldus, for* ignorent.
[3] *Aug., for* si.   [4] *Aug., for* transeundum.
§ 30.   [1] *L. Sp. ;* -tuum *G, Aug., for* nominatiuom.
[2] *Aug., for* est angere.   [3] *Added by Aug.*   [4] *After* quae,
Aug. deleted et.   [5] *Added by Aug.*

thing from outside, as in *eques* ' horseman ' and *equiso* ' stable-boy '—for both are derived from *equus* ' horse.'[d]

29. By this method, you will, on making a comparison, know that of men observed in person one is or is not like the other; but you could not say that the two are in like fashion taller than their brothers, if you should not know how tall those shorter brothers are with whom they are compared. In this way the likenesses of things broader and higher, and others of the same kind, cannot be examined without bringing in some help from outside. So therefore, inasmuch as certain case-forms are of this kind, it is not easy to say that they are like, if you observe the spoken words in one case only ; to make a correct judgement, you will have to bring in another case-form to which the spoken word passes as it is inflected.

30. These considerations are what I have thought enough to touch upon, for observing the likenesses of nouns. It remains to speak of the articles, of which some are like nouns and others are different. For of the five classes the first two have the same properties, because they have forms for masculine, feminine, and neuter, they have some forms to denote the singular and others to denote the plural, and they have five cases ; the vocative is not indicated by a separate spoken form. They have this of their own, that some are definite, like *hic* ' this,' feminine *haec*, and others are indefinite, like *quis* ' which,' feminine *quae*. But since their system of Regularity is shadowy and thin, it is not necessary to speak further of it in this book.[a]

[d] *Cf.* viii. 14.
§ 30.   [a] *Cf.* x. 19-20.

VARRO

31. Secundum genus quae verba tempora habent neque casus, s*ed*[1] habent personas. Eorum declinatuum species sunt sex : una quae dicitur temporalis, ut legebam gemebam, l*ego*[2] gemo ; altera personarum, ut sero meto, seris metis ; tertia rogandi, ut scribone legone, scribisne legisne. Quarta respondendi, ut fingo pingo, fingis pingis ; quinta optandi, ut dicerem facerem, dicam faciam ; sexta imperandi, ut cape rape, capito rapito.

32. Item sunt declinatuum species quattuor quae tempora habent sine personis : in rogando, ut fodituren seriturne, et fodieturne sereturne. Ab respondendi specie eaedem figurae fiunt extremis syllabis demptis ; op⟨t⟩andi species, ut vivatur ametur, viveretur amaretur. Imperandi declinatus s*in*tne habet[1] dubitationem et eorum sitne[2] haec ratio : paretur pugnetur, para*tor* pugna*tor*.[3]

33. Accedunt ad has species a copulis divisionum quadrinis : ab infecti et perfecti, ⟨ut⟩[1] emo edo, emi

---

§ 31.   [1] *Aug., for* si.   [2] *For* logo.
§ 32.   [1] *Aug., for* sum ne habent.   [2] *Aug., for* sint ne.
[3] *Canal, for* parari pugnari.
§ 33.   [1] *Added by L. Sp.*

---

§ 31.   [a] *Cf.* x. 17.   [b] Respectively tense, person, interrogative (indicative), declarative indicative, subjunctive, imperative ; the technical vocabulary was not fully developed in Varro's time.
§ 32.   [a] Corresponding to the last four of the categories in § 31 ; Varro shows a good understanding of the impersonal passive.
§ 33.   [a] *Cf.* x. 14-17.

31. The second subdivision *a* consists of those words which have tenses but not cases, and have persons. The categories of their inflections are six *b* : one which is that of the tenses, as *legebam* ' I was reading,' *gemebam* ' I was groaning,' *lego* ' I read,' *gemo* ' I groan ' ; the second is that of the persons, as *sero* ' I sow,' *meto* ' I reap,' *seris* ' thou sowest,' *metis* ' thou reapest ' ; the third is the interrogative, as *scribone* ' do I write ? ', *legone* ' do I read ? ', *scribisne*, *legisne* ; the fourth is that of the answer, as *fingo* ' I form,' *pingo* ' I paint,' *fingis*, *pingis* ; the fifth that of the wish, as *dicerem* ' would I were saying,' *facerem* ' would I were making,' *dicam* ' may I say,' *faciam* ' may I make ' ; the sixth that of the command, as *cape* ' take,' *rape* ' seize,' *capito*, *rapito*.

32. Likewise there are four categories of inflections which have tenses without persons *a* : in the interrogative, as *foditurne* ' is digging going on ? ', *seriturne* ' is sowing going on ? ' and *fodieturne* ' will digging be done ? ', *sereturne* ' will sowing be done ? ' ; of the category for the answer the same forms are used, but without the last syllable *ne* ; the category for the wish, as *vivatur* ' may there be living,' *ametur* ' may there be loving,' *viveretur* ' would there were living,' *amaretur* ' would there were loving.' Whether the inflections for the impersonal command exist, is somewhat doubtful ; there is also doubt about the scheme of the forms, which is given as *paretur* ' let there be preparation,' *pugnetur* ' let there be fighting,' or *parator*, *pugnator*.

33. There are added to these categories those which proceed from the four sets of pairs *a* consisting of the divisions : from that of the incomplete and the completed, as *emo* ' I buy ' and *edo* ' I eat,' *emi* ' I

VARRO

edi ; ab semel et s*a*epius, ut scribo lego, scriptit*o* lectito[2] ; ⟨a⟩[3] faciendi et patiendi, ut uro ungo, uror ungor ; a singulari et multitudinis, ut laudo culpo, laudamus culpamus. Huius generis verborum cuius species exposui quam late quidque pateat et cuius modi efficiat figuras, in libris qui de formulis verborum erunt diligentius expedietur.

34. Tertii generis, quae declinantur cum temporibus ac casibus ac vocantur a multis ideo participalia, sunt hoc ge⟨nere⟩[1] . . .

HIC DESUNT FOLIA III IN EXEMPLARI[2]

35. . . . quemadmodum declinemus,[1] qu*a*erimus casus eius, etiamsi siqui[2] finxit poeta aliquod vocabulum et ab eo casu⟨m⟩[3] ipse aliquem perperam declinavit, potius eum reprehendimus quam sequimur. Igitur ratio quam dico utrubique, et in his verbis quae imponuntur et in his quae declinantur, neque non etiam tertia illa, quae ex utroque miscetur genere.

36. Quarum una qu*a*eque ratio collata cum altera

[2] *L. Sp., for* scriptitaui lectitaui.　　[3] *Added by L. Sp.*
§ 34.　[1] *Added by Rhol. ; F here leaves blank the rest of the page (a little more than 28 lines) and all the next page (39 lines).*　[2] *F¹, in margin.*
§ 35.　[1] *L. Sp., for* declinamus.　　[2] *L. Sp., for* is qui.
[3] *L. Sp., for* casu.

---

[b] Verbs.　[c] Not extant.
§ 34.　[a] Adjective to the more common term *participia* or participles ; both meaning ' taking part ' in the features of two sets of words (nouns and verbs). For the form *participalia* (in *F*) rather than *-pialia* (in *p*), *cf.* M. Niedermann, *Mnemosyne*, lxiii. 267-268 (1936).　[b] The lost text contained the discussion of participles, that of adverbs, and the beginning of that on *ratio*.
§ 35.　[a] This is perhaps the simplest way of giving a meaning to the incomplete sentence.　[b] Referring to the previous discussion, now almost entirely lost.　[c] The independent

have bought ' and *edi* ' I have eaten '; from that of the act done once and the act done more often, as *scribo* ' I write ' and *lego* ' I read,' *scriptito* ' I am busy with writing,' and *lectito* ' I read and reread '; from that of active and passive, as *uro* ' I burn ' and *ungo* ' I anoint,' *uror* ' I am burned ' and *ungor* ' I am anointed '; from that of singular and plural, as *laudo* ' I praise ' and *culpo* ' I blame,' *laudamus* ' we praise ' and *culpamus* ' we blame.' With regard to the words of this class [b] whose categories I have described, the matter of how full an equipment of forms each has, and what sort of forms it makes, will be set forth with more attention to detail in the books [c] which are to be on the paradigms of verbs.

34. The words of the third subdivision, which are inflected with tenses and cases and are by many therefore called participials,[a] are of this kind . . . [b]

HERE THREE LEAVES ARE LACKING IN THE MODEL
COPY

35. . . . When we meet a new word,[a] we ask about its case-forms, as to how we shall inflect them; and yet if some poet has made up some word and has himself formed from it some case-form in an incorrect way, we blame him rather than follow his example. Therefore *Ratio* or Relation, of which I am speaking, is present in both [b] : in the words which are imposed upon things,[c] and in those which are formed by inflection [d]; and then also there is that third kind of Relation, which combines the characteristics of the two.[e]

36. Among these, each and every relation, when

words.   [d] The paradigms.   [e] In derivatives formed by suffixes.

aut similis aut dissimilis, aut saepe verba alia, ratio
eadem, et nonnunquam ratio alia, verba eadem.
Quae ratio in amor amori, eadem in dolor dolori,
neque eadem in dolor dolorem, et cum eadem ratio
quae est in amor et[1] amoris sit in amores et amorum,
tamen ea, quod non in ea qua oportet confertur[2]
materia, per se solum efficere non potest analogias
propter disparilitatem vocis figurarum, quod verbum
copulatum singulare[3] cum multitudine : ita cum est
pro portione, ut eandem habeat rationem, tum
denique ea ratio conficit id quod postulat analogia ;
de qua deinceps dicam.

III. 37. Sequitur tertius locus, quae sit ratio
pro portione ; ⟨e⟩a Graece[1] vocatur[2] ἀνὰ λόγον ; ab
analogo dicta analogia. Ex eodem genere quae res
inter se aliqua parte dissimiles rationem habent
aliquam, si ad eas duas alterae duae res allatae sunt,
quae rationem habeant eandem, quod ea verba bina
habent eundem λόγον, dicitur utrumque separatim
ἀνάλογον, simul collata quattuor ἀναλογ⟨ί⟩α.[3]

38. Nam ut in geminis, cum simile⟨m⟩[1] dicimus
esse Menaechmum Menaechmo, de uno dicimus ;
cum similitudine⟨m⟩[2] esse in his, de utroque : sic
cum dicimus eandem rationem habere assem ad

---

§ 36. [1] *After* et, *a repeated* amor et *has been deleted.*
[2] *After* confertur, *Aug. deleted* a.   [3] *Aug., for* singularem.
§ 37. [1] *L. Sp., for* agrece.   [2] *Aug., for* uocantur.
[3] *GS. ;* analogia *Mue., with* G *; for* analoga.
§ 38. [1] *C. F. W. Mueller, for* simile.   [2] *Aug., for*
similitudine.

---

§ 36. [a] Because of the difference in number.
§ 37. [a] As in mathematics, two ratios of equal value make
a proportion.
§ 38. [a] In the comedy of Plautus.

compared with another, is either like or unlike ; and often the words are different but the relation is the same, and sometimes the relation is different but the words are the same. The same relation which is in *amor* ' love ' and dative *amori* is in *dolor* ' pain ' and dative *dolori*, but not in *dolor* and accusative *dolorem.* The same relation which is in *amor* and genitive *amoris* is in plural *amores* and genitive *amorum* ; and yet, because the subject-matter in it is not compared as it should be,[a] this relation cannot of itself effect Regularities, on account of the differences in the forms of the spoken word, because a singular word has been associated with a plural. So, when it is by a proportionate likeness that the word has the same relation, then and not until then does this relation achieve what is demanded by *Analogia* or Regularity ; of which I shall speak next.

III. 37. There follows the third topic : What is *Ratio* or Relation that is *pro portione* ' by proportionate likeness ' ? This is in Greek called ' according to *logos* ' ; and from analogue the term *Analogia* or Regularity is derived. If there are two things of the same class which belong to some relation though in some respect unlike each other, and if alongside these two things two other things which have the same relation are placed,[a] then because the two sets of words belong to the same *logos* each one is said separately to be an analogue and the comparison of the four constitutes an *Analogia.*

38. For it is as in a matter of twins : when we say that the one Menaechmus is like the other Menaechmus,[a] we are speaking of one only ; but when we say that a likeness is present in them, we are speaking of both. So, when we say that a copper *as* has the same

semissem quam habet in argento[3] libella ad si*mbell*am,[4] quid sit ἀνάλογον ostendimus ; cum utrubique dicimus et in aere et in argento esse eandem rationem, tum dicimus de analogia.

39. Ut sodalis et sodalitas, civis et civitas non est idem, sed utrumque ab eodem ac coniunctum, sic ἀνάλογον et ἀναλογία idem non est, sed item est congeneratum. Quare si homines sustuleris, sodalis sustuleris ; si sodalis, sodalitatem : sic item si sustuleris λόγον, sustuleris ἀνάλογον ; si id, ἀναλογίαν.

40. Quae cum inter se tanta sint cognatione, debebis suptilius audire quam dici expectare, id est cum dixero quid de utroque et erit co⟨m⟩mune, ⟨ne⟩[1] expectes, dum ego in scribendo transferam in reliquum, sed ut potius tu persequare animo.

41. Haec fiunt in dissimilibus rebus, ut in numeris si contuleris cum uno duo, sic cum decem viginti : nam ⟨quam⟩[1] rationem duo ad unum habent, eandem habent viginti ad decem ; in nummis in similibus sic est ad unum victoriatum denarius, si⟨cut⟩[2] ad alterum victoriatum alter denarius ; sic item in aliis rebus omnibus pro portione dicuntur ea, in quo est sic quadruplex natura, ut in progenie *quom*⟨odo⟩[3] est filius ad patrem, sic[4] est filia ad matrem, et ut est in

[3] *Pius, for* argumento.   [4] *Pius, for* singulas.
   § 40.   [1] *Added by Sciop.*
   § 41.   [1] *Added by Aldus.*   [2] *Aug., for* si.   [3] *Mue., for* cum.   [4] *After* sic, *Aug. deleted* si.

---

[b] A silver coin of the same value as the copper *as*.
   § 41.   [a] The *quinarius*, marked with a figure of Victory, and worth half a *denarius*.

relation to a half-*as* as a silver *libella* [b] has to a half-*libella*, then we are showing what an analogue is ; when we say that both in copper and in silver there is the same relation, then we are speaking of *Analogia* ' Regular Relation.'

39. As *sodalis* ' fellow ' and *sodalitas* ' fellowship,' *civis* ' citizen ' and *civitas* ' citizenship ' are not the same, but both come from the same origin and are connected, so analogue and *Analogia* are not the same, but are likewise congenitally connected. Therefore, if you take away men, you have taken away the *sodales* ; if you take away the *sodales*, you have taken away the *sodalitas* : just so, if you take away the *logos* or Relation, you have taken away the analogue, and if you have taken this away, you have taken away the *Analogia*.

40. Since these are of such close kinship to each other, you must listen with keen understanding rather than wait to be told, that is, when I have said something about either, it will be also of general application to both ; you should not wait for me to repeat it in writing in a later part of my work, but you should rather continue to follow up the line of thought.

41. These phenomena are produced in unlike things, as in numbers, if you compare two with one and so also twenty with ten ; for twenty has to ten the same relation which two has to one. It is found also in like things ; in coins, for example, one denarius is to one victoriate [a] as a second denarius is to a second victoriate. So likewise in all other things those are said to be in a status of comparative likeness, wherein there is a fourfold nature of such a kind as among children the daughter is to the mother as the son is to

te⟨m⟩poribus meridies ad diem, sic media nox ad noctem.

42. Hoc poetae genere in similitudinibus utuntur multum, hoc acutissime geometrae, hoc in oratione diligentius quam alii ab Aristarcho grammatici, ut cum dicuntur pro portione similia esse amorem amori, dolorem dolori, cum ita dissimile[1] esse videant amorem et *amori*,[2] quod est alio casu, item dolorem dolori, sed dicunt, quod ab similibus.

43. Nonnunquam rationes habet implicatas duas, ut sit[1] una derecta, altera transversa. Quod dico, apertius sic fiet. Esto sic expositos esse numeros, ut in primo versu sit unum duo quattuor, in secundo decem viginti quadraginta, in tertio centum ducenti quadringenti. In hac formula numerorum duo inerunt quos dixi logoe, qui diversas faciant analogias : unus duplex qui est in obliquis versibus, quod est ut unus ad duo, sic duo ad quattuor ; alter decemplex in directis ordinibus, quod est ut unum ad decem, sic decem ad centum.

44. Similiter in verborum declinationibus est bivium, quod et ab recto casu ⟨declinantur in obliquos et ab recto casu⟩[1] in rectu⟨m⟩,[2] ita ut formulam similiter efficiant, quod sit primo versu hic albus, huic albo, huius albi, secundo haec alba, huic albae, huius albae, tertio hoc album, huic albo, huius albi. Itaque

§ 42. [1] *For* dissimilem. [2] *Christ ;* amori *Canal, omitting* et *; for* et dolorem.
§ 43. [1] *For* sic.
§ 44. [1] *Added by* Mue. (obliquom *Mue. ;* obliquos *L. Sp.*). [2] *Mue., for* recto.

§ 42. [a] The rhetorical figure. [b] That is, proportionally.

the father, and in matters of time the midnight is to the night as the midday is to the day.

42. The poets make a great use of this kind of relationship in their similes,[a] and the geometricians use it with greatest keenness ; in reference to speech, Aristarchus and the grammarians of his school use it with more care than others do, as when acc. *amorem* and dat. *amori*, acc. *dolorem* and dat. *dolori* are said to be like by comparative likeness,[b] although they see that *amorem* is unlike *amori* because it is in another case, and likewise *dolorem* is unlike *dolori* ; but they say that the four are like, because they come from like words.

43. Sometimes it has two crossed relationships, in such a way that one is vertical and the other crosswise. What I mean will become clearer by this : Suppose that some numerals are so set down

that in the first line there are   1   2   4

     in the second line there are   10   20   40

     in the third line there are   100   200   400

In this scheme of numerals there will be two examples of what I have called *logos*, which make different systems of Regularity : one is the twofold which is in the crosswise lines, because two is to four as one is to two ; the other is the tenfold relation in the vertical lines, because ten is to one hundred as one is to ten.

44. Likewise the inflections of words may go in two directions, because from the nominative case they are inflected into the oblique cases, and from the nominative to the nominative, so that they make a similar scheme ; which is

in line 1 : masc. nom. *albus*, dat. *albo*, gen. *albi* ;

in line 2 : fem. nom. *alba*, dat. *albae*, gen. *albae* ;

in line 3 : neut. nom. *album*, dat. *albo*, gen. *albi*.

VARRO

fiunt per obliquas declinationes ex his analogiae hoc genus Albius Atrius, Albio Atrio, quae scilicet erit particula ex illa binaria,[3] per directas declinationes Albius Atrius, Albia Atria,[4] quae scilicet denaria[5] formula analogiarum, de qua supra dixi.

45. Analogia quae dicitur, eius genera sunt duo : unum deiunctum sic est : ut unum ad duo sic decem ad viginti ; alterum coniunctum sic : ut est unum ad duo, sic duo ad quattuor. In hoc quod duo bis dicuntur et tum ⟨cum⟩[1] conferimus ad unum et tunc cum ⟨ad⟩[2] quattuor,

46. hoc quoque natura dicitur quadruplex[1] ; sic e septem chordis[2] citharae tamen duo dicuntur habere tetrachorda,[2] quod quemadmodum crepat prima ad quartam chordam,[2] sic quarta ad septumam respondet, media est alterius prima, alterius extrema. Medici[3] in aegroto[4] septumos dies qui observant, quarto die ideo diligentius signa morbi advertunt, quod quam rationem habuit primus dies ad quartum eandem praesagit habiturum qui est futurus ab eo quartus, qui est septumus a primo.

47. Quadruplices deiunctae in casibus sunt vocabulorum, ut rex regi, ⟨lex legi⟩,[1] coniunctae sunt triplices in verborum tribus temporibus, ut legebam[2] lego legam, quod quam rationem habet legebam ad[3]

---

[3] quae . . . binaria *was transposed to this position by Mue., from its position after* albia atria ; binaria *Mue., for* vicenaria.   [4] *After the transposition (note* 3), albia atria atria quae *is left; the second* atria *is deleted.*   [5] *L. Sp., for* centenaria.

§ 45.   [1] *Added by L. Sp.*   [2] *Added by Sciop.*

§ 46.   [1] *For* quadriplex.   [2] *The* h *inserted by Aug.*   [3] *For* midici.   [4] *L. Sp., for* egrotos.

§ 47.   [1] *Added by Mue.*   [2] *After* legebam, *Aug. deleted* ab.   [3] *Aug., for* ab.

568

Therefore by the crosswise inflections there are made from these words systems of Regularity like *Albius* and *Atrius*, *Albio* and *Atrio*, which to be sure is only a small part of that binary scheme ; and by the vertical inflections are made *Albius* and *Atrius*, *Albia* and *Atria*, which is a part of the tenfold scheme of Regularities of which I have spoken above.

45. Of that which is called Regularity, there are two kinds. One is disjoined, thus : as one is to two, so ten is to twenty. The other is conjoined, thus : as one is to two, so two is to four. Because in it two is said twice, both when we compare it with one, and then when we compare it with four,

46. this kind also is said to be fourfold by nature. So the cithers, though with seven strings, are none the less said to have two sets of four strings, because just as the sound of the first string stands in a certain relation to that of the fourth, so the fourth stands in the same relation to the seventh ; the middle string is the first of the one set and the last of the other. The doctors who watch the seven days when a man is ill,[a] note the symptoms of the illness with greater care on the fourth day, for the reason that the relation which the first day had to the fourth, foretells that the day which will be fourth from it, that is, seventh from the first, will bear the same relation to the fourth.

47. The Regularities are disjoined and fourfold in the cases of nouns, such as *rex* ' king,' dative *regi*, and *lex* ' law,' dative *legi* ; they are conjoined and three-fold in the three tenses of verbs, such as *legebam* ' I was reading,' present *lego*, future *legam*, because the relation which *legebam* has to *lego*, this same relation *lego*

§ 46.　[a] In recurrent fevers ; specifically the quartan ague.

lego hanc habet lego ad legam. In hoc fere omnes homines peccant, quod perperam in tribus temporibus haec verba dicunt, cum proportione volunt pronuntiare.

48. Nam cum sint verba alia infecta, ut lego et legis, alia perfecta, ut legi et legisti, et debeant sui cuius⟨que⟩[1] generis in coniungendo copulari, et cum recte sit ideo lego ad[2] legebam, non recte est lego ad legi, quod legi significat quod perfectum : ut haec tutudi pupugi, tundo pungo, tundam pungam, item necatus[3] sum verberatus sum, ⟨necor verberor,[4] necabor[5]⟩ verberabor, iniuria reprehendant,[6] quod et infecti inter se similia sunt et perfecti inter se, ut tundebam tundo tundam et tutuderam tutudi tutudero ; sic amabar amor amabor, et amatus eram amatus sum amatus ero. Itaque ⟨inique⟩[7] reprehendunt qui contra analogias dicunt, cur dispariliter in tribus temporibus dicantur quaedam verba, natura cum quadruplex sit analogia.

49. Id nonnunquam, ut dixi, pauciores videtur habere partes, sic etiam alias pluris, ut cum est : quemadmodum ad tria unum et duo, sic ad sex duo et quattuor, quae tamen quadripertito[1] comprehenditur forma, quod bina ad singula conferuntur ; quod in oratione quoque nonnunquam reperietur sic :

§ 48.   [1] quoiusque *H*, *for* cuius *F, V, p.*   [2] *Aug.*, *for* et.
[3] *Aug.*, *for* haec catus.   [4] *Added by Mue.*   [5] *Added by Aug.*   [6] *Mue.*, *for* reprehendunt.   [7] *Added by Christ.*
§ 49.   [1] *GS.*, *for* quadripertita.

§ 47.   [a] That is, past action is to present action, as present is to future.

has to *legam.*[a] In this, almost all men make a mistake, because they cite these verbs wrongly in the three tenses, when they wish to express them in a proportion.

48. For since some verbs denote incomplete action, like *lego* ' I read ' and *legis* ' thou readest,' and others denote completed action, like *legi* ' I have read ' and *legisti* ' thou hast read,' and since in the conjoined form they ought to be connected with others of their own kind and by this principle *lego* is rightly related to *legebam*—*lego* is not rightly related to *legi*, because *legi* denotes something completed ; so that they are wrong in finding fault with *tutudi* ' I have pounded ' and *pupugi* ' I have pricked,' *tundo* and *pungo*, *tundam* and *pungam*, as well as *necatus sum* ' I have been killed ' and *verberatus sum* ' I have been beaten,' *necor* and *verberor*, *necabor* and *verberabor*, because the tenses of incomplete action are like one another, and those of completed action are like one another. Thus we should say *tundebam tundo tundam*, and *tutuderam tutudi tutudero*, and in the same way *amabar amor amabor*, and *amatus eram, amatus sum, amatus ero*. Therefore those who speak against the Regularities are unfair in finding fault on the ground that whereas Regularity is fourfold by nature certain words are cited in a different way, in three tense-forms merely.

49. This seems sometimes to have fewer parts, as I have said ; similarly it seems, at other times, to have more parts, as when it is thus : as one and two are to three, so two and four are to six. Yet this form is included in the fourfold type, because sets of two are compared with sets of one. In speech also, this will sometimes be found, thus : As nominative *Diomedes*

ut Diomedes confertur Diome⟨di et Diome⟩dis,[2] sic dicitur ab Hercules Herculi et Herculis.[3]

50. Et ut haec[1] ab uno capite ac recto casu in duo obliquos discedunt casus, sic contra multa ab duobus capitibus recti casu*is*[2] confluunt in obliquom unum. Nam ut ab his rectis hi ⟨B⟩a⟨e⟩biei, hae Baebiae fit his Baebieis, sic est ab his hi Caelii, hae Caeliae his Caeliis. A duobus similibus ⟨dis⟩similiter[3] declinantur, ut fit in his nemus *h*olus, nemora *h*olera. Alia ab dissimilibus similiter declinantur, ut in articulis ab hic iste, hunc istu*n*⟨c⟩.[4]

51. Analogia fundamenta habet aut a voluntate hominum aut a natura verborum aut ⟨a⟩[1] re utraque. Voluntatem dico impositionem vocabulorum, naturam declinationem vocabulorum, quo decurritur sine doctrina. Qui impositionem sequetur, dicet, si simile in recto casu dolus et malus, fore in obliquo dolo et malo ; qui naturam sequetur, si sit simile in obliquis Marco Quinto, fore ut sit Marcus Quintus[2] ; qui utrumque sequetur, dicet si sit simile, transitus ut est in servus serve, fore ut sit item cervus cerve. Co⟨m⟩mune omnium est, ut quattuor figurae vocis habeant proportione declinatus.

52. Primum genus est ortum ab similitudine in

[2] *L. Sp.*, *for* diomedibus.   [3] *L. Sp.*, *for* herculibus.
§ 50.   [1] *Mue.*, *for* he hic.   [2] *A. Sp.*, *for* casuum ; *cf. Gellius*, iv. 16. 1.   [3] *Christ*, *for* similiter.   [4] *Mue.*, *for* istum.
§ 51.   [1] *Added by G*, *H.*   [2] *Christ*, *for* marcum quintum.

§ 49.   [a] For the double genitive form, see viii. 26.
§ 50.   [a] The writing EI in these forms is historically correct, and was doubtless used by Varro himself ; but it rarely survives in the manuscript. *Caelii* and *Caeliis*, immediately following, have survived with I and not EI.

is compared with genitive *Diomedi* and *Diomedis*, so
from nominative *Hercules* are said the genitive forms
Herculi and *Herculis*.[a]

50. And as these move away from one starting-
point and nominative into two oblique case-forms,
so on the other hand from two starting-points of the
nominative many words unite in a single oblique
case-form. For as from the nominatives *Baebiei*
(masc.) and *Baebiae* (fem.) comes the dative *Baebieis*,[a]
so from the nominatives *Caelii* and *Caeliae* comes
Caeliis. From two like words forms are developed
in unlike fashion, as happens in *nemus* ' grove ' and
holus ' vegetable,' plural *nemora* and *holera*. Others
from unlike words are developed in like fashion, as in
the articles the accusatives *hunc* and *istunc* come from
hic ' this ' and *iste* ' that.'

51. Regularity has its foundations either in the
will of men or in the nature of the words, or in both.
By will I mean the imposition of the word-names :
by nature I mean the inflection of the words, through
which passage is made without special instruction.
He who starts from the imposition, will say that if
dolus ' guile ' and *malus* ' bad ' are alike in the nominative, there will be found in an oblique case *dolo* and
malo. He who starts from the nature of the words,
will say that if *Marco* and *Quinto* are alike in the
oblique cases, there will be nominatives *Marcus* and
Quintus. He who proceeds from both, will say that if
there is a likeness, then as the change is in *servus*
' slave ' and vocative *serve*, so also there will be *cervus*
' stag ' and vocative *cerve*. It is a common feature of
all, that the four word-forms have their inflectional
changes in a proportional relation.

52. The first kind starts from the likeness in the

rectis casibus, secundum ab similitudine quae est in obliquis, tertium ab similitudine quae est in transitibus de casu in casum. Primo genere ab imposito ad naturam proficiscimur, in secundo contra, in tertio ab utroque. Quocirca etiam hoc tertium potest bifariam divisum tertium et quartum dici, quod in eo vel prosus et rusus[1] potest dici.

53. Qui initia faciet analogiae impositiones, ab his obliquas figuras declinare debebit ; qui naturam, contra ; qui ab utraque, reliquas declinationes ab eiusmodi transitibus. Impositio est in nostro dominatu, nos in natura⟨e⟩[1] : quemadmodum enim quisque volt, imponit nomen, at declinat, quemadmodum volt natura.

54. Sed quoniam duobus modis imponitur vocabulum aut re singulari aut multitudine, singulari, ut cicer, multitudinis, ut scalae, nec dubium est, quin ordo declinatuum, in quo res singulares declinabuntur solae, ab singulari aliquo casu proficiscatur,[1] ut cicer ciceri ciceris, item contra in eo ordine, qui multitudinis erit solum, quin a multitudinis a⟨li⟩quo casu ordiri conveniat, ut scalae scalis scalas : aliud videndum est, cum duplex natura copulata ac declinatu⟨u⟩m bini fiant ordines, ut est Mars Martes, unde tum ratio analogiae debeat ordiri, utrum ab singulari re in multitudinem an contra.

55. Neque enim si natura ab uno ad duo pervenit,

§ 52.   [1] *For* rosus.
§ 53.   [1] *Stephanus, for* natura.
§ 54.   [1] *Stephanus, for* proficiscantur.

nominatives, the second from a likeness which is in oblique cases, the third from a likeness which is in the changes from case to case. In the first kind we set out from the imposed name to the nature, in the second we go in the other direction, in the third we go in both directions. Therefore in fact this third can be divided into two parts and called the third and the fourth, because in it the argument can actually go both forward and backward.

53. He who makes the imposed forms the starting-point for the Regularity, will have to develop the oblique forms from these ; he who makes the nature the starting-point, will have to work in the other direction; he who starts from both, will have to make the rest of the inflections from the changes of the same kind. The imposition is in our power, but we are under the control of the nature of the words: for each one imposes the name as he wishes, but he inflects it as its nature requires.

54. But since a noun is imposed in two ways, either on a singular thing or on a plural—singular like *cicer* ' chickpea,' plural like *scalae* ' stairs '—and there is no doubt that the line of the inflections wherein things which are singular only will be declined, proceeds from some case of the singular, as *cicer ciceri ciceris* ; and likewise that in the line of inflections which is in the plural only, it is proper to begin from some case of the plural, as *scalae scalis scalas* : another point must be examined, since their connected nature is twofold and two lines of inflections are made, like *Mars* and *Martes*, namely from what place the relation of Regularity ought to start, whether from the singular to the plural or *vice versa*.

55. For not even if nature does proceed from one

VARRO

i⟨d⟩circo non potest ap⟨er⟩*t*ius[1] esse in docendo
posterius, ut inde incipias, ut qu*i*d[2] sit prius ostendas.
Itaque et hi qui de omni natura disputant atque ideo
vocantur ph*y*sici, tamen ex his ab universa natura
profecti retro quae essent principia mundi ostendunt.
Oratio cum ex litteris conste*t*,[3] tamen ⟨ex⟩[4] ea grammatici de litteris ostenderunt.

56. Quare in demonstrando, quoniam potius pro-
fici*sci*[1] oportet ab eo quod apertius est quam ab eo
quod prius est et potius quam ⟨a corrupto⟩ principio
ab incorrupto,[2] ab natura rerum quam ab lubidine
hominum, et haec tria quae sequenda magis sunt
minus sunt in singularibus quam in ⟨multitudinis, a⟩
multitudine[3] commodius potest ordiri, quod in his
principi*is*[4] minus rationis[5] verbis fingendis. Verborum forma⟨s⟩[6] facilius ⟨ex multitudinis⟩[7] singulari*s*[8] videri posse quam ex singularibus multitudinis
haec ostendunt : trabes trabs, duces dux.

57. Videmus enim ex his verbis trabes duces de
extrema syllaba E litteram exclusam et ideo in singu-

§ 55. [1] *Canal, for* amplius *; cf.* § 56. [2] *For* quod.
[3] *L. Sp., for* constat. [4] *Added by L. Sp.*
§ 56. [1] *G, a, Sciop., for* proficisse *; after which Aug.
deleted* de litteris ostendunt, *repeated from above.* [2] *L.
Sp., for* potius quam ab incorrupto principio. [3] *GS.,
following Canal* (in multitudinis, multitudine) *and L. Sp.* (in
multitudine, a multitudine), *for* in multitudine. [4] *Aldus,
for* principibus. [5] *L. Sp., for* orationis. [6] *L. Sp., for*
forma. [7] *Added by GS. ; added before* videri *by Groth.*
[8] *Kent, for* singularia.

§ 55. [a] From Greek φύσις ' nature ' as an originating or
moving power. [b] Properly, of sounds.
§ 56. [a] *Principia* are the singular forms, in whichever
direction the argument is carried ; but perhaps *quam in
singulari* should be inserted between *ordiri* and *quod*.
[b] Because the B and the C ending the stems can be seen in the
576

to two, should the conclusion be drawn that in teaching the later thing cannot be the clearer, for the purpose of beginning from it, to show what the prior thing is. Therefore even those who deal with the nature of the universe and are on this account called *physici* [a] ' natural philosophers,' proceed from nature as a whole and show by backward reasoning from the later things, what the beginnings of the world were. Though speech consists of letters,[b] it is nevertheless from speech that the grammarians start in order to show the nature of the letters.

56. Therefore in the explanation, since one ought rather to set out from that which is clearer than from that which is prior, and rather from the uncorrupted than from a corrupt original, from the nature of things rather than from the fancy of men, and since these three factors which are more to be followed are less present in the singulars than in the plurals, one can more easily commence from the plural than from the singular, because in the latter as starting-points [a] there is less of a basis for relationship in the forming of words. That the singular forms of words can be more easily interpreted from plural forms than plural forms from the singular, is shown by these words [b] : plural *trabes* ' beams,' singular *trabs* ; plural *duces* ' leaders,' singular *dux*.

57. For we see that from the plural nominatives *trabes* and *duces* the letter E of the last syllable has been eliminated and thereby in the singular have been

plural, but cannot be inferred with certainty from the nominative singular, especially if we read not *trabs* but *traps* (Roth, *Philol.* xvii. 176, and Mueller's note to § 57), which represents the actual pronunciation. Yet Varro wrote *trabs* and not *traps*, according to Cassiodorus, *Gram. Lat.* vii. 159. 23 Keil.

lari factum esse trabs dux. Contra ex singularibus non tam videmus quemadmodum facta sint ex B et S trabs[1] et ex C et S dux.[2]

58. Si mul⟨t⟩itudinis[1] rectus casus forte figura corrupta erit, id quod accidit raro, prius id corrigemus quam inde ordiemur ; ⟨ab⟩[2] obliquis adsumere oportet[3] figuras eas quae non erunt ambiguae, sive singulares sive multitudinis,[4] ex quibus id, cuius modi debent esse, perspici possit.[5]

59. Nam nonnunquam alterum ex altero videtur, ut Chrysippus scribit, quemadmodum pater ex filio et filius ex patre, neque minus in fornicibus propter sinistram dextra stat quam propter dextram[1] sinistra. Quapropter et ex rectis casibus obliqui et ex obliquis recti et ex singularibus multitudinis[2] et ex multitudinis singulares nonnunquam recuperari possunt.

60. Principium id potissimum sequi debemus, ut in eo fundamentum sit[1] natura, quod in declinationibus ibi facilior ratio. Facile est enim animadvertere, peccatum magis cadere posse in impositiones eas quae fiunt plerumque in rectis casibus singularibus, quod homines imperiti et dispersi vocabula rebus imponunt, quocumque eos libido invitavit : natura

---

§ 57. [1] *Aug., for* trabes.   [2] *Aug., for* duces.
§ 58. [1] si multitudinis *Mue., for* similitudinis.   [2] *Added by Canal.*   [3] *L. Sp., for* oportere.   [4] *Aug., for* multitudines.   [5] *Sciop., for* possint.
§ 59. [1] *Laetus, for* dextras.   [2] *Vertranius, for* multitudines.
§ 60. [1] *After* sit, *L. Sp. deleted* in.

---

§ 59. [a] *Frag.* 155 von Arnim.

made the nominatives *trabs* and *dux*. But on the other hand, if we start from the singulars we do not so easily see how they have become *trabs*, from B and S, and *dux*, from C and S.

58. If the nominative plural is by any chance a corrupted form, which rarely occurs, we shall correct this before we make it our starting-point ; it is proper to take from the oblique cases, either singular or plural, some forms which are not ambiguous, from which can be seen the make-up which the other forms ought to have.

59. For sometimes the one is seen from the other and at other times the other is seen from the one, as Chrysippus writes,[a] as the father's qualities may be seen from the son, and the son's from the father, and in arches the right-hand side stands on account of the left-hand side, no less than the left on account of the right. Therefore the oblique forms can sometimes be regained from the nominatives, and sometimes the nominatives from the oblique forms ; sometimes the plural from the singular forms, and sometimes the singular forms from the plural.

60. The principle that we should most of all follow, is that in this the foundation be nature, because in nature [a] there is the easier relationship in inflections. For it is easy to note that error can more easily make its way into those impositions [b] which are mostly made in the nominative singular, because men, being unskilled and scattered,[c] set names on things just as their fancy has impelled them ; but nature [d] is of

§ 60. [a] Rather than in *voluntas*. [b] Or imposed word-names, characterized by *voluntas*. [c] For this point of the Stoic philosophy, *cf.* Cicero, *de Inventione*, i. 2. [d] The quality underlying the paradigms.

VARRO

incorrupta plerumque est suapte sponte, nisi qui
eam usu inscio depravabit.

61. Quare si quis principium analogiae potius
posuerit in naturalibus casibus quam in ⟨im⟩positiciis,[1]
non multa[2] ⟨inconcinna⟩[3] in consuetudine occurrent
et a natura libido humana corrigetur, non a libidine
natura, quod qui impositionem sequi voluerint
facient contra.[4]

62. Sin ab singulari quis potius proficisci volet,
initium[1] facere oportebit ab sexto casu, qui est pro-
prius Latinus : nam eius casuis[2] litterarum discriminibus facilius reliquorum varietate⟨m⟩[3] discernere poterit, quod ei habent exitus aut in A, ut hac
terra, aut in E, ut hac lance, aut in I, ut hac ⟨c⟩lavi,[4]
aut in O, ut hoc caelo, aut in U, ut hoc versu. Igitur
ad demonstrandas declinationes biceps via[5] haec.

63. Sed quoniam ubi analogia, tria,[1] unum quod
in rebus, alterum[2] quod in vocibus, tertium quod in
utroque, duo priora simplicia, tertium duplex, ani-
madvertendum haec quam inter se habeant rationem.

64. Primum ea quae sunt discrimina in rebus,
partim sunt quae ad orationem non attineant, partim
quae pertineant. Non pertinent ut ea quae observant in aedificiis et signis faciendis ceterisque rebus

---

§ 61. [1] *L. Sp.;* in impositivis *Aug.; for* in positiciis.
[2] *Aug., for* multae. [3] *Added by Christ.* [4] *Aug., for*
contraria.
§ 62. [1] *Groth, for* inillum. [2] *A. Sp.;* cassuis *Mue.;*
for casus his. [3] *Aug., for* uarietate. [4] *Groth, for* leui *;*
cf. Varro, R. R. i. 22. 6. [5] *Canal, for* una.
§ 63. [1] *Aldus, for* atria. [2] alterum *is repeated in* F.

---

[e] By making wrongly inflected forms.
§ 62. [a] The name ' ablative ' had not come into use in

ON THE LATIN LANGUAGE, X. 60-64

itself for the most part uncorrupted, unless somebody perverts it by ignorant use.[e]

61. Therefore, if one has founded the principle of Regularity on the natural cases rather than on the imposed case-forms, not many awkwardnesses will be his to face in usage ; human fancifulness will be corrected by nature, and not nature by fancy, because those who have wished to follow imposition will in reality act in the opposite way.

62. But if one should prefer to start from the singular, he ought to start from the sixth case,[a] which is a case peculiar to Latin ; for by the differences in the letters [b] of this case-form he will be more easily able to discern the variation in the remaining cases, because the ablative forms end either in A, like *terra* ' earth,' or in E,[c] like *lance* ' platter,' or in I, like *clavi* ' key,' or in O, like *caelo* ' sky,' or in U, like *versu* ' verse.' Therefore, for the explaining of the declensions, there is this way, which may proceed from either of two starting-points.

63. But where there is Regularity, there are three factors, one which is in the things, a second which is in the spoken words, a third which is in both ; the first two are simple, the third is twofold. In view of this, attention must be given to the relation which they have to one another.

64. First, of the differences which exist in the things, there are some which have no bearing on speech, others which are connected with it. Those which are not connected with it are like those which the artificers observe in making buildings and statues

Varro's time.   [b] That is, the endings.   [c] Varro does not list separately the ablative of the fifth declension, ending in long E.

artifices, e quis vocantur aliae *h*armonicae, sic item
aliae nominibus aliis : sed nulla harum fit ⟨in⟩[1]
loquendo pars.[2]

65. Ad orationem quae pertinent, res eae sunt
quae verbis dicuntur pro portione neque a similitudine
quoque vocum declinatus habent, ut Iupiter Marspiter, Iovi Marti. Haec enim gener*e*[1] nominum et
numero et casibus similia sunt inter se, quod utraque
et nomina sunt et virilia sunt et singularia et casu
nominandi et dandi.

66. Alterum genus vocale est, in quo voces modo
sunt pro portione similes, non res, ut biga bigae,
nuptia nuptiae : neque enim in his res singularis
subest una, cum dicitur biga quadriga, neque ab his
vocibus quae declinata sunt, multitudinis significant
quicquam, id[1] quod omnia multitudinis quae declinantur ab uno, ut a merula merulae : sunt ⟨enim⟩[2]
eius modi, ut singulari subiungatur, sic merulae duae,
catulae tres, faculae quattuor.

67. Quare cum idem non possit subiungi, quod[1]
⟨non⟩[2] dicimus biga una,[3] quadrigae duae, nuptiae
tres, sed pro eo unae bigae, binae quadrigae, trinae
nuptiae, apparet non esse a biga et quadriga[4] bigae
et quadrigae, sed ut est huius ordinis una[5] duae tres

§ 64. [1] *Added by L. Sp.* [2] *Sentence division of Boot.*
§ 65. [1] *Mue., for* genera.
§ 66. [1] *Fay, for* ideo. [2] *Added by Fay.*
§ 67. [1] *Sciop., for* cum. [2] *Added by Sciop.* [3] *L.
Sp. ;* una biga *Sciop. ; for* bigae unae. [4] *After* quadriga,
L. Sp. deleted et. [5] *Aug., for* unae.

§ 65. *a* The unlikeness is in the forms of the nominative :
but both words denote male deities.
§ 66. *a* The two words belong to the same declension and
both lack the singular forms ; but the objects denoted are
entirely unlike.

and other things, of which some are called harmonic, and others are called by other names ; but no one of these becomes an element in speaking.

65. The differences which pertain to speech, consist of those things which are expressed by the words in a proportionate way, and yet do not have a likeness of the spoken words also to help in forming the inflections : such as nominative *Iupiter* and *Marspiter*, dative *Iovi* and *Marti.*[a] For these are like one another in the gender of the nouns, and in the number, and in the cases ; because both are nouns, and are masculine, and singular, and nominative and dative in case.

66. The second kind has to do with the sounds, in which the spoken words only are similar in a proportionate way—and not the things—as in *biga* and *bigae*, *nuptia* and *nuptiae.*[a] For in these there is no underlying unit thing expressed by the singular when we say *biga* or *quadriga*, nor have the plural forms which are derived from these words any plural meaning. Yet all plurals which are derived from a unit singular, like *merulae* from *merula* ' blackbird,' do have such plural meaning ; for they are of such a sort that there is subordination to a singular form : thus two *merulae* ' blackbirds,' three *catulae* ' female puppies,' four *faculae* ' torches.'

67. Therefore since there cannot be the same subordinating relation because we do not say *una biga*, *duae quadrigae*, *tres nuptiae*, but instead *unae bigae* ' one two-horse team,' *binae quadrigae* ' two teams of four horses,' *trinae nuptiae* ' three sets of nuptials,' it is clear that *bigae* and *quadrigae* are not from *biga* and *quadriga*, but belong to another series : the usual

583

princip⟨i⟩um una, sic in hoc ordine altero unae binae trinae principium est unae.

68. Tertium genus est illud duplex quod dixi, in quo et res et voces similiter pro portione dicuntur ut bonus malus, boni mali, de quorum analogia et Aristophanes et alii scripserunt. Etenim haec denique perfecta ut in oratione, illae duae simplices inchoatae analogiae, de quibus tamen separatim dicam, quod his quoque utimur in loquendo.

69. Sed prius de perfecta, in qua et res et voces quadam similitudine continentur, cuius genera sunt tria : unum vernaculum ac domi natum, alterum adventicium, tertium nothum ex peregrino hic natum. Vernaculum est ut sutor et pistor, sutori pistori ; adventicium est ut Hectores Nestores, Hectoras Nestoras ; tertium illum nothum ut Achilles et Peles.

70. De ⟨his primo⟩[1] genere multi utuntur non modo poetae, sed etiam plerique omnes qui soluta oratione loquuntur. Haec primo[2] dicebant ut quaestorem praetorem, sic Hectorem Nestorem : itaque Ennius ait :

Hectoris natum de muro iactari⟨er⟩.[3]

§ 70. [1] *Added by A. Sp.* [2] *Lachmann transferred* haec primo *from its position after* plerique. [3] *So Scaliger* (moero) *for* Hectoris natum de Troiano muro lactari *F : the misquoted line must be made metrical to establish the long* o *in* Hectoris.

§ 68. [a] Page 267 Nauck ; the grammarian of Byzantium, see v. 9, note *a*.

§ 69. [a] The type is marked by the ō in the stem. [b] The type is marked by the ŏ in the stem, and the short vowels in the case endings -es and -as, for both of which native Latin had -ēs. [c] With -ēs replacing the normal -ευς of the Greek nominatives (though Arcadian and some other dialects had -ης) ; the standardized Latin had Achilles, but Peleus.

series *una, duae, tres,* has *una* as its beginning, but in this second series *unae, binae, trinae,* the beginning is *unae.*

68. The third kind of Regularity is that which has two elements, which I mentioned, in which both the things and the spoken words are uttered with a similarity in a proportionate way, like *bonus* ' good ' and *malus* 'bad,' plural *boni* and *mali*; Aristophanes [a] and others have written about the Regularity in such words. And indeed this is a perfected Regularity in speech, but those two simple forms of Regularity are only incomplete beginnings; yet I shall speak of them separately, because we use them also in speaking.

69. But first I shall speak of the perfected Regularity, in which both the things and the spoken words are held together by a certain likeness; of this there are three kinds : one native, born here among us ; the second coming from abroad ; the third hybrid, born here of foreign paternity. The native type is such as *sutor* ' cobbler ' and *pistor* ' baker,' dative *sutori* and *pistori* [a] ; the foreign type is such as *Hectŏrĕs* ' men like Hector ' and *Nestŏrĕs* ' men like Nestor,' accusative *Hectŏrăs* and *Nestŏrăs* [b] ; that third type, the hybrid, consists of such words as *Achilles* and *Peles.* [c]

70. Of these, many use the first type, not merely poets, but also almost all who speak in prose. At first they used to say *Hectōrem* and *Nestōrem* like *quaestōrem* and *praetōrem* ; so Ennius says [a] :

That Hector's [b] son be hurlèd from the Trojan wall.

<hr/>

§ 70. [a] *Andromache Aechmalotis, Trag. Rom. Frag.* 93 Ribbeck[3] ; *Scen.* 82 Vahlen[2] ; *R.O.L.* i. 248-249 Warmington.   [b] *Hectōris,* as the scansion shows,

VARRO

Accius haec in tragoediis largius a prisca consuetudine movere coepit[4] et ad formas Graecas verborum magis revocare,[5] a quo Valerius ait :

Accius He⟨c⟩torem[6] nollet facere, Hectora mallet.

Quod adventicia pleraque habemus Graeca, secutum ut de nothis Graecanicos quoque nominat*us*[7] plurimos[8] haberemus. Itaque ut hic alia Graeca, alia Graecanica, sic analogiae.

71. E quis quae hic not*h*ae fiunt declinationes, de his aliae sunt priscae, ut Ba⟨c⟩chidēs et Chr*y*sidēs,[1] aliae *iu*niores,[2] ut Chr*y*sidĕs et Ba⟨c⟩chidĕs,[1] aliae recentes,[3] ut Chr*y*sidas et Ba⟨c⟩chidas ; cum his omnibus tribus utantur nostri, maxime qui sequontur media in loquendo offendunt minimum, quod prima parum similia videntur esse Gra*e*cis, unde sint tralata, tertia parum similia nostris.

IV. 72. Omnis analogiae fundamentum similitudo quaedam, ea, ut dixi, quae solet esse in rebus et in vocibus et in utroque ; in qua⟨m⟩ harum parte⟨m⟩ *quod*que[1] sit inferend*u*⟨m⟩[2] et cuius modi, videndum. Nam, ut dixi, neque rerum neque vocis similitudo ad has duplicis qua*s*[3] in loquendo qu*a*erimus analogias

---

[4] *For* caepit.   [5] *After* revocare, *L. Sp. deleted* et.   [6] *For* haetorem.   [7] *V, for* nominatos.   [8] *A. Sp., with a, for* plurimus.

§ 71.   [1] *The quantities of the vowels were added by Christ ; cf. Charisius, G. L. i. 148. 38 Keil, and Diomedes, G. L. i. 305. 13 Keil.*   [2] *Sciop., for* minores.   [3] *Aldus, for* regentes.

§ 72.   [1] *Kent, for* in qua harum parte cumque.   [2] *GS., for* inferendo.   [3] *Mue., for* quae.

---

[c] *Trag. Rom. Frag., inc. fab.* XXXVI Ribbeck[3] ; *R.O.L.* ii. xxiii, 364-365, 556-557, 599 Warmington.   [d] Page 78 Funaioli ; page 40 Morel.

586

Accius in his tragedies ^{c} began to take these words away from the early usage and rather to restore them to their Greek forms ; hence Valerius says ^{d} :

> Accius would not use *Hectōrem*, but *Hectŏra* rather.

Because most of our foreign words are Greek, it has followed that the greatest number of the hybrid nouns which we have are also Greek in origin. Therefore, as in these types some words are Greek and others are Greek in origin, so also are the systems of Regularity.

71. Of the hybrid inflectional forms which are made from these materials in our country, some are early, like *Bacchidēs* and *Chrysidēs*,^{a} others are younger, like *Chrysidĕs* and *Bacchidĕs*,^{b} and still others are recent, like *Chrysidăs* and *Bacchidăs* ^{c} ; our fellow-countrymen use all three, but those who follow the middle forms in speaking give the least offence, because those of the first set seem insufficiently like the Greek forms from which they are taken, and those of the third seem insufficiently like our own forms.

IV. 72. The basis of all Regularity is a certain likeness, that, as I have said, which is wont to be in things and in spoken words and in both ; we must see in which one of these sections each word should be entered,^{a} and of what sort it is. For, as I have said, neither the likeness of the things nor that of the spoken words is separately sufficient to express these double Regularities of the words, which we seek in

§ 71. ^{a} Nom.-acc., with Latin ending. ^{b} Nom., with Greek ending, but differing from Latin only in the quantity of the vowel. ^{c} Acc., with Greek ending.
§ 72. ^{a} A bookkeeping idiom.

verborum exprimendas[4] separatim satis est, quod
utraque parte opus est simili.   Quas ad loquendum
ut perducas accedere debet usus : alia enim ratio qua
facias vestimentum, alia quemadmodum utare vesti-
mento.

73.   Usui⟨s⟩[1] species videntur esse tres : una consuetudinis veteris, altera consuetudinis huius, tertia
neutra⟨e⟩.[2]   Vetera, ut cascus casci, surus suri[3];
huius consuetudinis, ut albus caldus, albo caldo ;
neutrae, ut scala scalam, phalera phaleram.[4]   Ad
quas accedere potest quarta mixta, ut amicitia inimicitia, amicitiam inimicitiam.   Prima est qua usi antiqui et nos reliquimus, secunda qua nunc utimur,
tertia qua utuntur poetae.

74.   Analogia[1] non item ea definienda quae de-
rigitur ad naturam verborum atque illa quae ad usum
loquendi.   Nam prior definienda sic : analogia est
verborum similium declinatio similis, posterior sic :
analogia est verborum similium declinatio similis
non repugnante consuetudine co⟨m⟩muni.   At quom[2]
harum duarum ad extremum additum erit hoc " ex

[4] analogias verborum exprimendas, *after* simili *in F, was set
here by A. Sp. (after* duplicis, *by Mue.*).

§ 73.   [1] *L. Sp.* ; usus *Aug.* ; *for* usui.   [2] *Canal, for*
neutra.   [3] *Scaliger, for* furus furi.   [4] *For* falera faleram.
§ 74.   [1] *Aug., for* analogiae.   [2] *Sciop., for* ad quam.

[b] That is, the ' regular ' form may be constructed, but it must
also be found in use to have any value.

speaking, because there must be a likeness in both
respects. To introduce them into speech there must
be also actual use ; for the method by which you
make a garment is quite different from that in which
you wear it.[b]

73. The categories of use appear to be three :
one that of old usage, the second that of to-day's usage,
the third that of neither. Old words are such as
cascus casci ' old,' *surus suri* ' stake ' ; words of to-day's
usage, such as *albus* ' white,' *caldus* [a] ' hot,' datives *albo*
and *caldo* ; words of neither usage, such as *scala* and
acc. *scalam* ' stair,' *phalera* and *phaleram* ' trapping.'[b]
To these there can be added a fourth kind which does
not belong exclusively to one category, like *amicitia*
' friendship ' and *inimicitia* ' enmity,' accusatives
amicitiam and *inimicitiam*.[c] The first is that which
the ancients used and we have abandoned ; the second
is that which we now use ; the third is that which the
poets use.

74. That *Analogia* or Regularity which is directed
toward the nature of the words [a] is not to be defined
in the same way as that which is directed toward the
actual use in speaking. For the former should be
defined thus : *Analogia* is the like inflection of like
words ; and the latter thus : *Analogia* is the like
inflection of like words, not inconsistent with common
usage. But when to the end of these two there has
been added " within a certain range," then poetic

§ 73. [a] The syncopated form of *calidus*, current in Varro's
time. [b] Normally used only in the plural ; the forms
cited are not ambiguous with any plural cases. [c] Composition by prefixes yielded words belonging to each of the
three categories.
§ 74. [a] As evidenced in their paradigms.

VARRO

quadam parte," poetica analogia erit definita. Harum
primam sequi debet populus, secundam omnes[3]
singuli e populo, tertiam poetae.

75. Haec diligentius quam apertius dicta esse
arbitror, sed non obscurius quam de re simili definitiones grammaticorum sunt, ut Aristeae, Aristodemi,
Aristocli, item aliorum, quorum obscuritates eo minus
reprehendendae, quod pleraeque definitiones re in-
cognita propter summam brevitatem non facile
perspiciuntur, nisi articulatim sunt explicata⟨e⟩.[1]

76. Quare magis apparebit, si erit aperte de
singulis partibus, quid dicatur verbum, quid similitudo
verbi, quid declinatio, quid similitudo declinationis
non repugnante consuetudine co⟨m⟩muni, quid ex
quadam parte.

77. Verbum dico orationis vocalis[1] partem, quae
sit indivisa et[2] minima. Si declinationem naturalem
habeat, simile[3] verbum verbo tum quom[4] et re[5] quam
significat et voce[6] qua significat et[7] in figura e transitu
declinationis parile. Declinatio est, cum ex verbo
in verbum aut ex verbi discrimine, ut transeat mens,
vocis commutatio fit aliqua. Similitudo declinationis,

---

[3] *Aug., for* omnem.
   § 75. [1] *Sciop., for* explicata.
   § 77. [1] *Aug., for* vocabulis. [2] *For* eo. [3] *Sciop., for*
similem. [4] *Aug., for* quoniam. [5] *Mue., for* rem.
[6] *Mue., for* vocem. [7] *Aug., for* est.

---

[b] *Cf.* § 78; the poets, while having certain privileges, are yet
under some restrictions.
   § 75. [a] Apparently followers of Aristarchus. Varro
seems to have had a book containing a collection of definitions of *analogia*, arranged according to an alphabetical list
of their authors.

Analogia will be defined.[b] The first of these is that which the people ought to follow ; the second is that which all the individuals in the people ought to follow ; and the third is that which the poets ought to follow.

75. I think that these things have been said with more care than clarity, but not more obscurely than are the definitions of the same subject given by the grammarians, such as Aristeas, Aristodemus, Aristocles, and others,[a] whose obscurities are the less to be found fault with, because most definitions, being on an unknown theme and being expressed with extreme brevity, are not easily understood unless they are expounded point by point.

76. Therefore the matter will be more apparent if there is a clear exposition of the parts one by one, as to what is meant by a word, what is meant by the likeness of the word, by inflection, by likeness of inflection not inconsistent with common usage, and by " within a certain range."

77. By word I mean that part of spoken speech which is the smallest indivisible unit. If a word has natural inflection,[a] then a word is like another word when it is similar to the other word in the thing which it denotes and in the spoken word by which it denotes the thing and in the form which it has after an inflectional change has taken place. Inflection [b] is that which takes place when some change of the spoken word is made from word-form to word-form or to a new word-stem by derivation, in order to express a change of the thought. Likeness of in-

§ 77. [a] That is, inflection rather than stem-derivation ; both these ideas are included under *declinatio*.   [b] Including derivation.

cum item ex aliqua figura in figuram transit, ut id
transit, cum quo confertur.

78. Adiectum est " non repugnante consuetudine
co⟨m⟩muni," quod quaedam verba contra usum
veterem inclinata patietur, ut passa Hortensium
dicere pro hae[1] cervices cervix, quaedam non, ut si
dicas pro fauces faux. Ubi additur " ex quadam
parte," significat non esse in consuetudine in his
verbis omnis partis, ut declinatum ab amo[2] vivo amor
⟨sed non⟩[3] vivor.

V. 79. Quid videretur analogia in oratione et quas
haberet species et quae de his sequenda⟨e⟩[1] vide-
re⟨n⟩tur,[2] ut brevi potui informavi ; nunc, in quibus
non debeat esse ac proinde ac debeat soleat quaeri,
dicam. Ea fere sunt quattuor genera : primum in
id genus verbis quae non declinantur analogia non
debet quaeri, ut in his nequam mox vix.

80. De his magis in alio quam in alio erratur
verbo. Dant enim non habere casus mox et vix,
nequam habere, quod dicamus hic nequam et huius
nequam et huic nequam. Cum enim dicimus hic
nequam et huius nequam, tum hominis eius, que⟨m⟩[1]
volumus ostendere esse nequam, dicimus casus, et ei
proponimus tum hic no⟨me⟩n,[2] cuius putamus
nequitiam.

§ 78. [1] *Stephanus, for* hac si.   [2] *L. Sp., for* amabo.
[3] *Added by Kent.*
§ 79. [1] *Kent, for* sequenda.   [2] *Aug., for* videretur.
§ 80. [1] *For* quae.   [2] *Sciop., for* non.

§ 78. [a] *Frag. Poet. Lat.*, page 91 Morel ; cf. viii. 14.
§ 79. [a] *Cf.* viii. 9.

flection exists, when it passes from some form to another form in the same way in which that other word passes with which it is being compared.

78. There is the addition " not inconsistent with common usage," because usage tolerates some words inflected contrary to the old practice, as it suffered Hortensius [a] to say *cervix* 'neck' instead of the plural *cervices*, but does not tolerate certain others, as when you should say *faux* 'throat' instead of the plural *fauces*. When the addition " within a certain range " is made, it means that in the relevant words not all the forms are in use, as, for example, there is derived from *amo* 'I love' and *vivo* 'I live' the passive *amor* but not the passive *vivor*.

V. 79. What *Analogia* or Regularity in speech is seen to be and what categories it has, and which of these seem essential to follow, I have set forth as briefly as I could. Now I shall speak of the categories in which it ought not to exist and yet it is usually looked for just as if it ought to be there ; these are in general of four kinds. First, Regularity ought not to be looked for in such words as are not inflected, for example *nequam* 'worthless,' *mox* 'soon,' *vix* 'hardly.'[a]

80. Among these, a greater error is made in one word than in another. For they grant that *mox* and *vix* have no cases, but assert that *nequam* has, because we use it with nominative *hic* 'this,' with genitive *huius*, with dative *huic*. For when we say *hic nequam* and *huius nequam*, then we are uttering the cases of this man whom we wish to show as worthless, and before the word we then set *hic* to represent the name of him whose worthlessness we are considering.

81. Quod vocabulum factum ut ex non et volo nolo sic ex ne et quicquam item media extrita syllaba coactum est nequam. Itaque ut eum quem putamus esse non hili dicimus n⟨i⟩hili,[1] sic in quo putamus esse ne quicquam dicimus nequam.

82. Secundo, si unum solum habent casum in voce, quod non decline⟨n⟩tur,[1] ut litterae omnes. Tertio, si singularis est vocabuli series neque habet cum qua comparari possit, ut esse putant caput capiti capitis capite. Quartum, si ea vocabula quattuor quae conferuntur inter se rationem ⟨non⟩[2] habent quam oportet, ut socer socrus, soceros socrus.[3]

VI. 83. Contra in quibus debeat quaeri analogia, fere totidem gradus debent esse coniuncti : primum ut sint res,[1] secundum ut earum sit usus, tertium uti hae res vocabula habeant, quartum ut habeant de-clinatus naturalis. De primo gradu, quod natura subest et multitudinis et singularis, dicimus hi asses hosce asses,[2] hic as hunc assem ; contra quod in numeris finitis multitudinis natura singularis non est, dicitur hi duo et hi tres, his duobus et his tribus.

84. Secundo gradu si est natura neque est usus,

§ 81.   [1] *For* anhili.
§ 82.   [1] *Laetus,* *for* declinetur.   [2] *Added* *by* *Mue.*
[3] *Mue., for* socerum.
§ 83.   [1] *Aug., for* tres.   [2] *For* asces.

§ 81.   [a] From *ně* and *volo.*   [b] From *nē* and *quam.*
[c] From *ně* and *hili ;* *cf.* ix. 54.
§ 82.   [a] *Cf.* ix. 51-52.   [b] *Cf.* ix. 53.

81. This word is made like *nolo*[a] ' I do not wish ' from *non* 'not' and *volo* 'I wish'; thus from *ne* 'not' and *quicquam* ' anything,' with loss of the middle syllable, is likewise compounded *nequam*.[b] So as him whom we think to be *non hili* 'worth not a whit' we call *nihili*,[c] him in whom we think that there is *ne quicquam* ' not anything ' we call *nequam*.

82. Second, Regularity is not to be looked for if the words have only one case in their spoken form, because they are not inflected, like all names of letters.[a] Third, it is not to be looked for if the series of forms which the noun has is unique and has nothing with which it can be compared, as they consider true of *caput* ' head,' dat. *capiti*, gen. *capitis*, abl. *capite*.[b] Fourth, it is not to be sought if those four noun-forms which are compared with one another fail to have the mutual relation which they should have, as in *socer* ' father-in-law ' and *socrus* ' mother-in-law,' accusative plural *soceros* and *socrus*.

VI. 83. On the other hand, in words in which Regularity ought to be looked for, in general the same number of stages should be found in conjunction : first, the things should exist ; second, the things should be in use ; third, these things should have names ; fourth, they should have natural inflection. As for the first stage, because the nature of plural and singular is basic, we say plural nom. *asses*, acc. *asses*, singular nom. *as*, acc. *assem* ; on the other hand, because in definite plural numerals the singular nature does not exist, only plural forms are used, such as nominative *duo* ' two ' and *tres* 'three,' dative *duobus* and *tribus*.

84. In the second stage, if the nature exists but

id genus ut sit discriminandum, ut fit in faba et id
genus, quae item et ex parte et universa nominamus :
non enim opu⟨s⟩ fuit ut in servis. . . .[1]

§ 84.   [1] *The rest of the page in F, and five further pages,
are blank ; after which Cicero's Oration pro Cluentio is
written.*

---

§ 84.   [a] *Cf.* viii. 48, ix. 38 ; the Romans seem to have used
names of materials and foodstuffs freely in the singular, with

there is no practice of making this kind of distinction, as happens in *faba* [a] ' bean ' and in that class of words which we use for one and for all collectively, without change of form : for there was no need, as in the matter of slaves . . . [b]

collective meaning.   [b] The thought seems to have been, that as one name was sufficient for a slave since he had no family name (*cf.* ix. 59), so one form was adequate for such words as *faba*, whether denoting an individual thing or many as a collective unit.

M. TERENTI VARRONIS
DE LINGUA LATINA

III

Fr. 1.[1] DEUS autem vel dea generale nomen est omnibus. . . . Varro ad Ciceronem tertio : " Ita respondeant cur dicant deos, cum ⟨de⟩[2] omnibus antiqui dixerint divos."

Fr. 2.[1] Figor ambigue declinatur apud veteres tempore perfecto. Reperimus enim fictus et fixus : . . . Varro ad Ciceronem tertio " fixum."

Fr. 3.[1] Hoc nomen licet veteres Latinum negent, auctoritate tamen valet. Dicebant enim leonem masculum et feminam. . . . Leam vero Varro ad Ciceronem dicit libro III : " Sicut no*n* est[2] panthera et lea."

Fr. 1.   [1] *Serv. Dan. in Aen.* xii. 139.   [2] *Added by Thilo.*
Fr. 2.   [1] *Diomedes, Ars Grammatica,* i. 377. 11-13 *Keil.*
Fr. 3.   [1] *Philarg. in Buc.* ii. 63.   [2] *For* nocest.

II.-IV.   [a] *Cf.* also v. 1 ; v. 6 ; vii. 109-110 ; viii. 1 ; Frag. 21.

Fr. 1.   [a] The word split into two paradigms, as a result of extensions from *deus, divi, divo, deum,* etc., which has come about by regular phonetic development.

M. TERENTIUS VARRO'S
ON THE LATIN LANGUAGE

FRAGMENTS OF BOOKS II–IV [a]

III

Fr. 1. *Deus* 'god' or *dea* 'goddess' is in fact a general name for all. . . . Varro, in the third book of the treatise addressed to Cicero, says: "So let them give answer why they say *dei* 'gods,' when in reference to all of them the old-time Romans used to say *divi*.[a]"

Fr. 2. *Figor* 'I am transfixed' is by the old writers inflected in two ways in the perfect tense. For we find both *fictus* and *fixus*; . . . Varro in the third book of the treatise addressed to Cicero has "*fixum.*"

Fr. 3. Though the old writers say that the name *leaena* 'lioness' is not good Latin, still it has the force of authority. For they used to say *leo* 'lion' both as masculine and as feminine. . . . But *lea* 'lioness' Varro has, in the third book of the treatise addressed to Cicero: "Just as *panthera* 'panther' and *lea* 'lioness' are not." [a]

Fr. 3. "That is, are not similarly formed from a corresponding masculine; *cf.* v. 100, ix. 55.

VARRO

IV

Fr. 4.[1] Varro de Lingua Latina lib. IIII : " Pro-
lubi*um*[2] et lubidinem[3] dici ab eo quod lubeat : unde
etiam lucus Veneris Lubentina⟨e⟩ dicatur."

LIBRI VIII FRAGMENTUM

Fr. 5.[1] (5) M. Varronis liber ad Ciceronem de
Lingua Latina octavus nullam esse observationem
similium docet inque omnibus paene verbis consuetudinem dominari ostendit : (6) " Sicuti cum dicimus,"
inquit, " lupus lupi, probus probi et lepus leporis, item
paro paravi et lavo lavi, pungo pupugi, tundo tutudi
et pingo pinxi. (7) Cumque," inquit, " a ceno et
prandeo et poto et cenatus sum et pransus sum et
potus sum dicamus, a destringor tamen et extergeor
et lavor destrinxi et extersi et lavi dicimus.

(8) " Item cum dicamus ab Osco Tusco Graeco

Fr. 4. [1] *Nonius Marcellus*, 64. 15-17 *M.*   [2] *Guiet, for*
proluuiem.   [3] *Quicherat, for* prolubidinem.
Fr. 5. [1] *Aulus Gellius, Noct. Att.* ii. 25. 5-10 ; *the text
follows Rolfe's, in the Loeb Classical Library.*

Fr. 4. [a] *Cf.* vi. 47.
VIII. [a] See also vii. 90, ix. 53, 66, 79, 80, 81, 89, 90, 96,
97, 100, 101, 104, 105, 108, 111, which refer to passages in
VIII. that are not extant.
Fr. 5. [a] The translation is essentially Rolfe's, in the Loeb
Classical Library.   [b] *Cf.* especially viii. 25.   [c] *Cf.* viii.
34, ix. 91.   [d] *Cf.* ix. 106.   [e] *Cf.* ix. 99, x. 48.   [f] Per-
fect passives of active verbs, yet with active meaning.

IV

Fr. 4.   Varro in the fourth book of the treatise *On the Latin Language* : " *Prolubium* and *lubido* ' desire ' are derived from *lubet* ' it is pleasing ' ; whence also the grove of Venus *Lubentina* gets its name.[a] "

FRAGMENT OF BOOK VIII [a]

Fr. 5.[a]   (5) The eighth book of Marcus Varro's treatise *On the Latin Language*, addressed to Cicero, maintains that no regard is paid to Regularity, and points out that in almost all words usage rules.[b]   (6) " As when we decline," says he, " *lupus* ' wolf,' gen. *lupi*, *probus* ' honest,' gen. *probi*, but *lepus* ' hare,' gen. *leporis* [c] ; again, *paro* ' I prepare,' perf. *paravi*, and *lavo* ' I wash,' perf. *lavi*,[d] *pungo* ' I prick,' perf. *pupugi*, *tundo* ' I pound,' perf. *tutudi*,[e] and *pingo* ' I paint,' perf. *pinxi*.   (7) And although," he continues, " from *ceno* ' I dine ' and *prandeo* ' I lunch ' and *poto* ' I drink ' we form the perfects *cenatus sum*, *pransus sum*, and *potus sum*,[f] yet from *destringor* ' I scrape myself ' and *extergeor* ' I wipe myself dry ' and *lavor* ' I bathe myself ' we make the perfects *destrinxi* ' I am scraped ' and *extersi* ' I am dried ' and *lavi* ' I have had a bath.'[g]

(8) " Furthermore, although from *Oscus* ' Oscan,' *Tuscus* ' Etruscan,' and *Graecus* ' Greek ' we derive the adverbs *Osce* ' in Oscan,' *Tusce* ' in Etruscan,'

[g] Active perfects of passive verbs, yet with passive (intransitive, reflexive) meaning : this meaning of the perfect *lavi* is regular in Plautus, but is nowhere attested for *destrinxi* and *extersi*.

Osce Tusce Graece, a Gallo tamen et Mauro Gallice
et Maurice dicimus ; item a probus probe, a doctus
docte, sed a rarus non dicitur rare, sed alii raro dicunt,
alii rarenter."

(9) Idem M. Varro in eodem libro : " Sentior,"
inquit, " nemo dicit et id per se nihil est, adsentior
tamen fere omnes dicunt. Sisenna unus adsentio
in senatu dicebat et eum postea multi secuti, neque
tamen vincere consuetudinem potuerunt."

(10) Sed idem Varro in aliis libris multa pro ἀνα-
λογίᾳ tuenda scribit.

Librorum XI-XXIV Fragmenta

XI

Fr. 6.[1] Et ubi auctoritas maiorum genus tibi non de-
monstraverit, quid ibi faciendum est? Scripsit Varro
ad Ciceronem : " Potestatis nostrae est illis rebus
dare genera, quae ex natura genus non habent."

Fr. 7a.[1] Nunc de generibus dicamus. Varro dicit
" genera dicta a generando. Quicquid enim gignit
aut gignitur, hoc potest genus dici et genus facere."

Fr. 6. [1] *Julianus Toletanus, Commentarius in Donatum,*
v. 318. 31-34 *Keil.*
Fr. 7. [1] *[Sergii] Explanat. in Donatum,* iv. 492. 37-493. 3
Keil.

---

[h] Charisius, i. 217. 8 Keil, cites *rare* as used by Cicero,
Cato, and Plautus (*Rudens* 995) ; but editors usually replace
it by *raro.*   [i] That is, not a deponent unless compounded ;
even in a passive meaning, the passive form of the un-
compounded verb is rare, though occasionally found, as in
Caesar, *Bellum Civile* i. 67 (*sentiretur*), where it is however
impersonal.   [j] Notably in ix.

and *Graece* ' in Greek,' yet from *Gallus* ' Gaul ' and *Maurus* ' Moor ' we have *Gallice* ' in Gallic ' and *Maurice* ' in Moorish ' ; also from *probus* ' honest ' comes *probe* ' honestly,' from *doctus* ' learned ' *docte* ' learnedly,' but from *rarus* ' rare ' there is no adverb *rare*, but some say *raro*, others *rarenter*." [h]

(9) In the same book Varro goes on to say : " No one uses the passive *sentior*,[i] and that form by itself is naught, but almost every one says *adsentior* ' I agree.' Sisenna alone used to say *adsentio* in the senate, and later many followed his example, yet could not prevail over usage."

(10) But this same Varro in other books [j] wrote a great deal in defence of Regularity.

XI

Fr. 6. Where the authority of our ancestors has not shown you the gender of a word, what in this instance must be done ? Varro wrote, in the treatise addressed to Cicero : " We men have the right and power to give genders to the names of those things which by nature have no gender." [a]

Fr. 7a. Now let us speak of genders. Varro says : " *Genera* ' genders ' are named from *generare* ' to generate.' For whatever *gignit* ' begets ' or *gignitur* ' is begotten,' that can be called a *genus* and can

XI.-XXIV. [a] On Books XI.-XIII., see also vii. 110, viii. 2, 20, 34, x. 33 ; and on Books XIV.-XXV., see vii. 110.
Fr. 6. [a] Varro uses *genus* both for grammatical gender and for natural sex ; each is a ' kind ' or ' class,' *cf.* Frag. 7, note *a*.

VARRO

Quod si verum est, nulla potest res integrum genus habere nisi masculinum et femininum.

Fr. 7b.[2] Tractat de generibus. Varro ait "genera tantum illa esse quae generant : illa proprie dicuntur genera." Quodsi sequemur auctoritatem ipsius, non erunt genera nisi duo, masculinum et femininum. Nulla enim genera creare possunt nisi haec duo.

Fr. 8.[1] Ostrea[2] si primae declinationis fuerit, sicut Musa, feminino genere declinabitur, ut ad animal[3] referamus ; si[4] ad testam, ostreum[5] dicendum est neutro genere et ad secundam declinationem, ut sit huius ostrei, *huic* ostre*o*,[6] quia dicit[7] Varro "nullam rem animalem neutro genere declinari."

Fr. 9.[1] Ait Plinius Secundus secutus Varronem : "Quando dubitamus principale genus, redeamus ad diminutionem, et ex diminutivo cognoscimus principale genus. Puta arbor ignoro cuius generis sit : fac diminutivum arbuscula, ecce hinc intellegis et principale genus quale sit. Item si dicas columna,

---

[2] *Pompeius, Commentum Artis Donati,* v. 159. 23-26 *Keil.*

Fr. 8. [1] *Cledonius, Ars Grammatica,* v. 41. 24-28 *Keil.*
[2] *For* ostria.   [3] *Keil, for* animam.   [4] *For* sic.   [5] *For* ostrium.   [6] *Keil, for* sicui ostri.   [7] *For* dicitur.

Fr. 9. [1] *Pompeius, Commentum Artis Donati,* v. 164. 13-18 *Keil.*

Fr. 7. [a] The root *gen-* lies at the basis of all these words : but *genus* has the weakened meaning ' kind, class,' from which the idea of ' begetting ' has faded out.   [b] Donatus, the eminent grammarian who flourished about 350 A.D.   [c] That is, ' kinds ' ; *cf.* Frag. 6, note *a*.

Fr. 8. [a] This distinction is not borne out by the use of the words in the Latin authors.   [b] Almost precisely true for Latin, though there are many exceptions in Greek and in the Germanic languages (*cf.* τέκνον, German *das Kind*, and the neuter diminutives in -ιον, *-chen, -lein*).

produce a *genus*." [a]   If this is true, then the *genus*
that a thing has is not perfect unless it is masculine
or feminine.

Fr. 7b.   He [b] treats of genders.   Varro says: " Only
those are *genera* ' genders ' which *generant* ' generate ';
those are properly called *genera*."   But if we follow
his authority, there will be only two genders, masculine and feminine.   For no genders [c] can procreate
except these two.

Fr. 8.   If *ostrea* ' oyster ' is of the first declension,
like *Musa* ' Muse,' it will be declined in the feminine
gender, so that we refer the word to the living being ;
if we use it for the shell, then the word must be
ostreum, inflected in the neuter and according to
the second declension, so that it is genitive *ostrei*,
dative *ostreo* [a] : because Varro says :   " No living
creature has a name which is inflected in the neuter
gender." [b]

Fr. 9.   Plinius Secundus [a] says, following Varro :
" When we are in doubt about the gender of a main
word, let us turn to the diminutive form, and from
the diminutive we learn the gender of the main word. [b]
Suppose that I do not know the gender of *arbor*
' tree ' ;   form the diminutive *arbuscula*, and lo !
from this you observe as well the gender of the word
from which it comes.   Again, if you say, What is the

Fr. 9.   [a] This and subsequent citations from Pliny are
taken from the Elder Pliny's *Dubius Sermo*, a work in eight
books, mentioned by the Younger Pliny, *Epist.* iii. 5. 5.
[b] Diminutives have in Latin the gender of the words from
which they are derived ; the exceptions are very few.   In
Greek and in the Germanic languages, however, diminutives
are commonly neuter without regard to their primitives ; *cf.*
Frag. 8, note *b*.

cuius generis est ? facis inde diminutivum, id est
columella, et inde intellegis quoniam principale
feminini generis est."

Fr. 10.[1] " *H*ypocorismata semper generibus suis
und⟨e oriuntur consonant, pauca dissonant, velut
haec rana⟩ hic ranunculus, hic ung⟨u⟩is haec ungula,
h⟨oc glandium haec glandula, hic panis hic pastillus
et⟩ hoc pastillum," ut Varro dixit : " haec beta hic
betace⟨us, haec malva hic malvaceus⟩, hoc pistrinum
haec pistrilla, ut Terentius in Ad⟨elphis, hic ensis
haec ensicula et hic ensiculus⟩ : sic in Rudente
Plautus."

Fr. 11.[1] Dies communis generis est. Qui masculino genere dicendum putaverunt, has causas reddi-
derunt, quod dies festos auctores dixerunt, non festas,
et[2] quartum et quintum Kalendas, non quartam nec
quintam, et cum hodie dicimus, nihil aliud quam hoc
die intelligitur.[3] Qui vero feminino, catholico utuntur, quod ablativo casu E non nisi producta finiatur,

Fr. 10. [1] *Charisius, Instit. Gram.* i. 37. 13-18 *Keil. The
right-hand edge of the manuscript is destroyed, but the restora-
tions are made with certainty from almost verbatim repetitions
Charisius i. 90. 10-12, 155. 14-17, 535. 21-25, 551. 36-38 Keil,
in which Varro is not mentioned as the source.* Hic pastillus,
required by the space, was added by Keil from i. 90. 11, i.
94. 4.
Fr. 11. [1] *Charisius, Instit. Gram.* i. 110. 8-16 *Keil.*
[2] *For* ut. [3] *For* intellegatur.

Fr. 10. [a] As substantive, for *pes betaceus* : but *betaceus* is
an adjective, not a diminutive. [b] Also an adjective ; its
application as substantive is not known. [c] *Adelphoe* 584.
[d] *Rudens* 1156-1157.
Fr. 11. [a] *Dies* was by origin a masculine ; in Latin,
because it was declined like the feminines of the fifth declension, possibly also because its counterpart *nox* was

gender of *columna* ' column ' ?, make from it the diminutive, that is, *columella*, and therefrom you understand that the word from which it comes is of the feminine gender."

Fr. 10. " Diminutives always agree in gender with the words from which they come : a few differ, such as fem. *rana* ' frog,' diminutive masc. *ranunculus* 'tadpole' ; masc. *unguis* ' nail (of finger or toe),' fem. *ungula* ' hoof, talon ' ; neut. *glandium* ' kernel of pork ', fem. *glandula* ' tonsil ' ; masc. *panis* ' loaf of bread,' masc. *pastillus* and neut. *pastillum* ' roll,' " as Varro said ; " fem. *beta* ' beet,' masc. *betaceus* [a] 'beet-root'; fem. *malva* 'mallow,' masc. *malvaceus* [b] ' mallow-like vegetable '; neut. *pistrinum* ' pounding-mill,' fem. *pistrilla* ' small mill,' as Terence says in *The Brothers* [c] ; masc. *ensis* ' sword,' fem. *ensicula* and masc. *ensiculus* ' toy-sword ' : so Plautus in *The Rope*.[d] "

Fr. 11. *Dies* ' day ' is of common gender.[a] Those who thought that it must be used as a masculine, offered these reasons : that their authorities said *dies festi* 'holidays,' with the masculine adjective, not the fem. *festae* ; that they said the fourth and the fifth day before the Kalends,[b] with the masculine and not the feminine form of the adjective ; and that when we say *hodie* ' to-day,' it is understood as *hoc die* ' on this day,' with the masculine article,[c] and nothing else. On the other hand, those who regard *dies* as feminine, use the general argument, that in the ablative the

feminine, it acquired use as a feminine in some meanings.
[b] Full phrase : *ante diem quartum* (*quintum*) *Kalendas*.
[c] The demonstrative was an ' article,' in the grammatical terminology of the Romans ; *cf.* viii. 45.

et quod deminutio eius diecula sit, non dieculus, ut
ait Terentius :

> Quod tibi addo dieculam.

Varro autem distinxit, ut[4] masculino genere unius
diei cursum significare⟨t⟩, feminino autem temporis
spatium ; quod nemo servavit.

Fr. 12.[1] Catinus masculino genere dicitur . . . et
hinc deminutive catillus fit. . . . Sed Varro ad
Ciceronem XI " catinuli " dixit, non catilli.

Fr. 13.[1] Naevus generis neutri, sed Varro ad
Ciceronem " hic naevus."

Fr. 14a.[1] Antiquissimi tamen et hic gausapes et
haec gausapa et hoc gausape et plurale neutri haec
gausapa quasi a nominativo hoc gausapum protulisse
inveniuntur, . . . Varro vero de Lingua Latina ait,
" talia ex Graeco sumpta ex masculino in femininum
transire et A litera finiri : ὁ κοχλίας haec cochlea,
ὁ χάρτης haec charta, ὁ γαυσάπης haec gausapa."

Fr. 14b.[2] Varro autem ait " vocabula ex Graeco
sumpta, si suum genus non retineant, ex masculino
in femininum Latine transire et A littera terminari

---

[4] For et.
  Fr. 12. [1] *Charisius, Instit. Gram.* i. 79. 23-80. 4 *Keil.*
  Fr. 13. [1] *De Dubiis Nominibus,* v. 584. 27 *Keil.*
  Fr. 14. [1] *Priscian, Inst. Gram.* ii. 333. 9-14 *Keil.*
[2] *Charisius, Inst. Gram.* i. 104. 13-16 *Keil.*

---

[d] But this masculine diminutive was used in Oscan.
[e] *Andria* 710.   [f] That is, a short space of time, as a
respite.

word ends in a long E, never in a short E ; and that
its diminutive is the feminine *diecula* (not the masculine *dieculus* [d]), as Terence has it [e] :

> That to you I give a daytime.[f]

But Varro made the distinction, that in the masculine
it means the course of one day, in the feminine a
space of time : a distinction to which nobody has
conformed in practice.

Fr. 12. *Catinus* ' bowl ' is used in the masculine
gender . . . and from it is made the diminutive *catillus*.
. . . But Varro, in the eleventh book of his treatise
addressed to Cicero, sponsored the form *catinuli*, and
not *catilli*.

Fr. 13. *Naevus* ' mole, wart,' is of the neuter
gender [a] ; but Varro in the treatise addressed to
Cicero uses it as a masculine.

Fr. 14a. Yet the oldest writers are found to have
employed masculine *gausapes* ' cloth,' and feminine
gausapa, and neuter *gausape*, and a neuter plural
gausapa as if from a neuter nominative singular *gausapum*. . . . But Varro in his treatise *On the Latin
Language* says : " Such words, when taken from
Greek, pass from the masculine to the feminine, and
end in the letter A : fem. *cochlea* ' snail ' from masc.
κοχλίας, fem. charta ' paper ' from masc. χάρτης,
fem. *gausapa* from masc. γαυσάπης."

Fr. 14b. But Varro says : " Words taken from
Greek, if they do not keep their own gender, pass
from the masculine to the feminine in Latin and end
in the letter A, like *cochlea* from κοχλίας, *herma* ' pillar-

Fr. 13. [a] Apparently an error ; *naevus* is always
masculine.

velut κοχλίας cochlea, Ἑρμῆς herma, χάρτης charta,
ergo γαυσάπης gausapa."

Fr. 14c.[3] Margarita feminini generis est, quia
Graeca nomina -ης terminata in A transeunt et fiunt
feminina, ut ὁ χάρτης haec charta, μαργαρίτης margarita, aut communia, ut ἀθλητής athleta. Ergo
neutraliter hoc margaritum dicere vitiosum est ; et
tamen multi dixerunt, ut Valgius . . . et Varro
Epistularum[4] VIII "margaritum unum, margarita
plura." Sed idem Varro saepe et alii plures margarita feminine dixerunt ; in genetivo tamen plurali
non nisi feminino genere margaritarum.

Fr. 15.[1] VAS terminata et SIS faciunt genitivo et
DIS, hoc vas huius vasis ; utrumque Varro ait de
Lingua Latina : hic vas huius vadis.

Fr. 16.[1] VIS et ipsa tertiae sunt declinationis et
similem nominativo faciunt genetivum, ⟨hic⟩[2] civis
huius civis, haec vis huius vis et plurali hae vis, sicut
⟨Luc⟩retius[2] et Varro : nam hae vires numero semper
plurali declinantur.

Fr. 17.[1] M. Varronem et P. Nigidium, viros
Romani generis doctissimos, comperimus non aliter

---

[3] *Charisius, Inst. Gram.* i. 108. 4-12 *Keil.*   [4] *Or* Epistu-
licarum ; *cf. Charisius,* i. 104. 21 *Keil.*
  Fr. 15. [1] *Probus, Catholica* iv. 30. 26-27 *Keil.*
  Fr. 16. [1] *Probus, Catholica* iv. 30. 30–31. 2 *Keil.*   [2] *Additions from Priscian,* ii. 249. 9-10 *Keil.*
  Fr. 17. [1] *Aulus Gellius, Noct. Att.* iv. 16. 1 ; *Rolfe's text,
in the Loeb Classical Library.*

  Fr. 14. [a] A sculptured head, originally of a bearded
Hermes, at the top of a rectangular pillar.   [b] On the title

bust ' [a] from Ἑρμῆς, *charta* from χάρτης, therefore *gausapa* from γαυσάπης."

Fr. 14c. *Margarita* ' pearl ' is of the feminine gender, because Greek nouns ending in -ης change to A and become feminine, like fem. *charta* from masc. χάρτης, *margarita* from μαργαρίτης, or else they are of common gender, like *athleta* ' athlete ' from ἀθλητής. Therefore to use *margaritum* as a neuter is wrong ; and yet many have done so, like Valgius . . . and Varro in the eighth book of his *Letters* [b] : " One *margaritum*, several *margarita*." But Varro likewise often used *margarita* in the feminine, and so did many others ; and in the genitive plural they never used any form except the feminine *margaritarum*.

Fr. 15. Nouns ending in VAS [a] make the genitive in -SIS and -DIS : neuter nom. *vas* ' vessel,' gen. *vasis*. Varro mentions both in his tratise *On the Latin Language*, the other being masc. *vas* ' bondsman,' gen. *vadis*.

Fr. 16. Nouns ending in VIS are also of the third declension and make the genitive like the nominative : *civis* ' citizen,' gen. *civis* ; nom. *vis* ' force,' gen. *vis*, and also nom. plural *vis*, used by Lucretius [a] and Varro ; for the plural *vires* is always inflected in the plural number.

Fr. 17.[a] I learn that Marcus Varro and Publius Nigidius,[b] the most learned of all the Romans, always

of this work, see the critical note, and F. Ritschl, *Rhein. Mus.* vi. 537.

Fr. 15.   [a] The only word with this ' ending ' is the word *vas*, which is in reality two distinct words.

Fr. 16.   [a] iii. 265 ; also acc. pl. *vis*, ii. 586.

Fr. 17.   [a] Rolfe's translation, in the Loeb Classical Library, with modifications.   [b] *Operum Rell.*, frag. 63 Swoboda.

elocutos esse et scripsisse quam senatuis et domuis et
fluctuis, qui est patrius casus ab eo quod est senatus,
domus, fluctus ; huic senatui, domui, fluctui, ce-
teraque is consimilia pariter dixisse.

Fr. 18.[1]   Amni Maro,

Secundo defluit amni.

Ubi Plinius eodem libro " Ab antiquis " inquit " quos
Varro reprehendit, observatio omnis illa damnata est,
non quidem in totum.   Dicimus enim," inquit, " ab
hoc canali siti tussi febri.   Maiore tamen ex parte
forma mutata est.   Ab hoc enim cane orbe carbone
turre falce igne veste fine monte fonte ponte strig⟨i⟩le
tegete ave asse axe nave classe dicimus."

Fr. 19.[1]   Quem Plinius ad eundem XI " rure
ordinatum arbustum "[2] dixisse laudat.

Fr. 20.[1]   Fonteis[2] : " Quorum nominum genetivi
pluralis ante UM syllabam I litteram merebuntur,

Fr. 18.   [1] *Charisius, Inst. Gram.* i. 122. 23-29 *Keil.*
Fr. 19.   [1] *Charisius, Inst. Gram.* i. 142. 20-21 *Keil.*
[2] *For* ambustum.
Fr. 20.   [1] *Charisius, Inst. Gram.* i. 129. 19-24 *Keil.*
[2] *For* fontis.

Fr. 18.   [a] *Georg.* iii. 447.   [b] The rule, stated at i. 120.
19-24 Keil, is that nouns with genitives ending in *is* have the
ablative in *e*, unless the genitive is identical with the nominative, when the ablative ends in *i* ; an adjective also has the
ablative in *i* if it stands before a noun which it modifies. The
scientific formulation is that consonant-stems should have
short *e* in the ablative, and *i*-stems should have long *i* : a
status much disturbed by the encroachment of the *e*-ending
on the *i*-ending.   [c] Not all these should, by the ' rule,'
end in *i* ; for *carbo, falx, mons, fons, pons, teges* do not have
identical nom. and gen. ; and the nom. of *asse* is *as*, very
rarely *assis*.   As to the actual forms of the ablative, *igni* is
commoner than *igne* ; *orbi, turri, fini, strigili, avi, axi, navi,*

said and wrote *senatuis*, *domuis*, and *fluctuis* as the genitive case of the words *senatus* ' senate,' *domus* ' house,' and *fluctus* ' wave,' and used *senatui*, *domui*, *fluctui* as the dative ; and that they used other similar words with the corresponding endings.

Fr. 18.   *Amni* was used by Vergil [a] as ablative of *amnis* ' river,' as in

He drifts with the stream of the river.

On this point, Pliny in the same book says : " By the old writers, whom Varro criticizes adversely, all observance of the rule [b] is disregarded, yet not utterly.   For we still say," says he, " *canali* ' canal,' *siti* ' thirst,' *tussi* ' cough,' *febri* ' fever ' as the ablative forms.   But in most words the form has been changed, and uses the ablative which ends in E : *cane* ' dog,' *orbe* ' circle,' *carbone* ' charcoal,' *turre* ' tower,' *falce* ' sickle,' *igne* ' fire,' *veste* ' garment,' *fine* ' limit,' *monte* ' mountain,' *fonte* ' spring,' *ponte* ' bridge,' *strigile* ' scraper,' *tegete* ' mat,' *ave* ' bird,' *asse* ' as,' *axe* ' axle,' *nave* ' ship,' *classe* ' fleet.' " [c]

Fr. 19.   Varro, whom Pliny mentions as having said, in the eleventh book of his treatise addressed to Cicero " a plantation of trees set in rows *rure* [a] ' in the country.' "

Fr. 20.   *Fonteis* ' springs,' accusative plural spelled with EIS : " The nouns which gain an I in the genitive plural before the ending UM," says Pliny, " have the

classi are found in authors of the first century B.C., but are less common than the forms with *e*, or are used to satisfy metrical requirements ; *ponti* is found once in older Latin ; *monti* and *fonti* are cited by Varro, ix. 112.

Fr. 19.   [a] Instead of the usual locative form *ruri*.

VARRO

accusativus," inquit Plinius, "per EIS loquetur,
montium monteis ; licet Varro," inquit, " exemplis
hanc regulam confutare temptarit istius modi, falcium
falces, non falceis facit, nec has merceis, nec hos axeis
lintreis ventreis stirpeis urbeis *corbeis*[3] vecteis *menteis*.[4] Et tamen manus dat praemissae regulae
ridicule, ut exceptis his nominibus valeat regula."

Fr. 21.[1] Poematorum et in II et in III idem Varro
adsidue dicit et his poematis, tam quam nominativo
hoc poematum sit et non hoc poema. Nam et ad
Ciceronem XI, horum poematorum et his poematis
oportere dici.

Fr. 22.[1] Git : Varro ad Ciceronem XI per omnes
casus id nomen ire debere conmeminit ; vulgo autem
hoc gitti dicunt.

XIII

Fr. 23.[1] Palpetras per T Varro ad Ciceronem
XIII dixit. Sed Fabianus de Animalibus primo palpebras per B. Alii dicunt palpetras genas, palpebras
autem ipsos pilos.

[3] *For* curueis.　　[4] *GS., for* inepteis, *cf.* viii. 67.
　Fr. 21.　[1] *Charisius, Inst. Gram.* i. 141. 29-31 *Keil.*
　Fr. 22.　[1] *Charisius, Inst. Gram.* i. 131. 7-8 *Keil.*
　Fr. 23.　[1] *Charisius, Inst. Gram.* i. 105. 14-16 *Keil.*

　Fr. 20.　[a] This EI does not represent an earlier diphthong,
but was often written for a long *i* after the original diphthong
had become identical in sound with the long *i*. There are
scattered examples of the ending EIS in the accusative, found
in inscriptions and manuscripts.

614

accusative in EIS,[a] like genitive *montium* ' mountains,'
accusative *monteis* ; although Varro," he continues,
" tried to refute this rule by examples of the following
sort : to the genitive *falcium* ' sickles ' the accusative
is *falces* and not *falceis*, nor is the proper spelling
merceis ' wares,' nor *axeis* ' axles,' *lintreis* ' skiffs,'
ventreis ' bellies,' *stirpeis* ' stocks,' *urbeis* ' cities,'
corbeis ' baskets,' *vecteis* ' levers,' *menteis* ' minds.'
And yet he gives up the fight against the aforesaid
rule in a ridiculous fashion, saying that apart from
these nouns the rule holds."

Fr. 21.   In the second and the third books Varro
constantly uses the genitive *poematorum* ' poems ' and
the dative *poematis*, as though the word were *poematum* in the nominative and not *poema*.   For in the
eleventh book of the treatise addressed to Cicero he
says that genitive *poematorum* and dative *poematis* are
the proper forms to be used.

Fr. 22.   *Git* ' fennel ' [a] :   Varro in the eleventh
book of the treatise addressed to Cicero states that
this form ought to be used in all the cases ; but
people quite commonly say *gitti* in the ablative.

XIII

Fr. 23.   Varro in the thirteenth book of the treatise
addressed to Cicero used *palpetrae*, with T.   But
Fabianus,[a] in the first book *On Animals*, wrote *palpebrae* with B.   Others say that *palpetrae* means the
eyelids, and *palpebrae* the eyelashes.

Fr. 22.   [a] *Nigella sativa.*
Fr. 23.   [a] Papirius Fabianus, who wrote on philosophy
and on natural history in the time of Augustus.

Fr. 24.[1]   Oxo : " Varro ad Ciceronem XIII olivo et oxo putat fieri," inquit Plinius Sermonis Dubii libro VI.

XVIII

Fr. 25.[1]   Indiscriminatim, indifferenter.   Varro de Lingua Latina lib. XVIII : " Quibus nos in hoc libro, proinde ut nihil intersit, utemur indiscriminatim, promisce."

XXII

Fr. 26.[1]   Rure Terentius in Eunucho :

Ex meo propinquo rure hoc capio commodi.

Itaque et Varro ad Ciceronem XXII " rure veni."

XXIII

Fr. 27.[1]   Varro ad Ciceronem in libro XXIII : " ingluvies tori," inquit, " sunt circa gulam, qui propter pinguedinem fiunt atque interiectas habent rugas."   Sed nunc pro gula positum.

Fr. 24.   [1] *Charisius, Inst. Gram.* i. 139. 15-16 *Keil.*
Fr. 25.   [1] *Nonius Marcellus, de Compendiosa Doctrina,* 127. 24-26 *M.*
Fr. 26.   [1] *Charisius, Inst. Gram.* i. 142. 18-20 *Keil.*
Fr. 27.   [1] *Serv. Dan. in Georg.* iii. 431.

Fr. 24.   [a] Antecedent unknown.   [b] Greek ὄξος (neuter, third decl.), denoting sour wine, and vinegar made therefrom.
Fr. 25.   [a] Antecedent unknown.
Fr. 26.   [a] 971.   [b] These are examples of *rure* as a pure ablative.   The continuation is our Fragment 19, in which examples of *rure* as a locative are discussed.
Fr. 27.   [a] That is, double chins.

Fr. 24. *Oxo*, ablative : " Varro, in the thirteenth book of the treatise addressed to Cicero, expresses the opinion that it [a] is composed of olive-oil and *oxos* [b] ' vinegar,' " says Pliny in the sixth book of the treatise entitled *Variations in Speech.*

XVIII

Fr. 25. *Indiscriminatim* means ' without difference.' Varro in the eighteenth book of the treatise *On the Latin Language* says : " Which [a] in this book we shall use *indiscriminatim* ' without distinction,' promiscuously, just as if there were no difference between them."

XXII

Fr. 26. The ablative *rure* is used by Terence in the *Eunuchus* [a] :

I get this comfort from my near-by country-seat.

So also Varro, in the twenty-second book of the treatise addressed to Cicero, says : " I have come *rure* ' from the country.' " [b]

XXIII

Fr. 27. Varro, in the twenty-third book of the treatise addressed to Cicero, says : " The *ingluvies* is the bulging muscles around the throat, which are produced by fatness and have creases between them." [a] But now the word is used merely for the throat.

VARRO

Fr. 28.[1] (1) Cum in disciplinas dialecticas induci atque imbui vellemus, necessus fuit adire atque cognoscere quas vocant dialectici εἰσαγωγάς. (2) Tum, quia in primo περὶ ἀξιωμάτων discendum, quae M. Varro alias profata, alias proloquia appellat, Commentarium de Proloquiis L. Aelii, docti hominis, qui magister Varronis fuit, studiose quaesivimus eumque in Pacis Bibliotheca repertum legimus. (3) Sed in eo nihil edocenter neque ad instituendum explanate scriptum est, fecisseque videtur eum librum Aelius sui magis admonendi quam aliorum docendi gratia.

(4) Redimus igitur necessario ad Graecos libros. Ex quibus accepimus ἀξίωμα esse his verbis ⟨definitum⟩: λεκτὸν αὐτοτελὲς ἀπόφαντον ὅσον ἐφ᾽ αὐτῷ. (5) Hoc ego supersedi vertere, quia novis et inconditis vocibus utendum fuit, quas pati aures per insolentiam vix possent. (6) Sed M. Varro in libro de Lingua Latina ad Ciceronem quarto vicesimo expeditissime ita finit : " Proloquium est sententia in qua nihil desideratur."

(7) Erit autem planius quid istud sit, si exemplum eius dixerimus. Ἀξίωμα igitur, sive id proloquium dicere placet, huiuscemodi est : Hannibal Poenus fuit ; Scipio Numantiam delevit ; Milo caedis damnatus est ; Neque bonum est voluptas neque malum ; (8) et omnino quicquid ita dicitur plena atque perfecta verborum sententia, ut id necesse sit aut verum aut falsum esse, id a dialecticis ἀξίωμα

Fr. 28. [1] *Aulus Gellius, Noctes Atticae*, xvi. 8. 1-14 ; Rolfe's text, in the Loeb Classical Library.

Fr. 28. [a] Rolfe's translation, in the Loeb Classical Library, with modifications. [b] In Vespasian's Temple of Peace, in the *Forum Pacis*. [c] Page 75 Funaioli.

Fr. 28.[a] (1) When I wished to be introduced to the science of logic and instructed in it, it was necessary to take up and learn what the logicians call εἰσαγωγαί, or 'introductory exercises.' (2) Then because at first I had to learn about axioms, which Marcus Varro calls, now *profata* or 'propositions,' and now *proloquia* or 'forthright statements,' I sought diligently for the *Commentary on Proloquia* of Lucius Aelius, a learned man, who was the teacher of Varro; and finding it in the Library of Peace,[b] I read it. (3) But I found in it nothing that was written to instruct or to make the matter clear; Aelius[c] seems to have made that book rather as suggestions for his own use than for the purpose of teaching others.

(4) I therefore of necessity returned to my Greek books. From these I obtained this definition of an axiom : " a proposition complete in itself, declared with reference to itself only." (5) This I have forborne to turn into Latin, since it would have been necessary to use new and as yet uncoined words, such as, from their strangeness, the ear could hardly endure. (6) But Marcus Varro, in the twenty-fourth book of his treatise *On the Latin Language*, dedicated to Cicero, thus defines the word very briefly : " A *proloquium* is a statement in which nothing is lacking."

(7) But his definition will be clearer if I give an example. An axiom, then, or a forthright statement, if you prefer, is of this kind : " Hannibal was a Carthaginian " ; " Scipio destroyed Numantia " ; " Milo was found guilty of murder " ; " Pleasure is neither a good nor an evil " ; (8) and in general any saying which is a full and perfect thought, so expressed in words that it is necessarily either true or false, is called by the logicians an axiom ; by Marcus Varro,

appellatum est, a M. Varrone, sicuti dixi, proloquium,
a M. autem Cicerone pronuntiatum, quo ille tamen
vocabulo tantisper uti se adtestatus est, " quoad
melius," inquit, " invenero."

(9) Sed quod Graeci συνημμένον ἀξίωμα dicunt, id
alii nostrorum adiunctum, alii conexum dixerunt.
Id conexum tale est : Si Plato ambulat, Plato move-
tur ; Si dies est, sol super terras est.   (10) Item quod
illi συμπεπλεγμένον, nos vel coniunctum vel copulatum dicimus, quod est eiusdemmodi : P. Scipio,
Pauli filius, et bis consul fuit et triumphavit et censura
functus est et collega in censura L. Mummi fuit.
(11) In omni autem coniuncto si unum est mendacium,
etiamsi cetera vera sunt, totum esse mendacium
dicitur. Nam si ad ea omnia quae de Scipione illo vera
dixi addidero Et Hannibalem in Africa superavit,
quod est falsum, universa quoque illa quae coniuncte
dicta sunt, propter hoc unum quod falsum accesserit,
quia simul dicentur, vera non erunt.

(12) Est item aliud quod Graeci διεζευγμένον ἀξίωμα,
nos disiunctum dicimus. Id huiuscemodi est : Aut
malum est voluptas aut bonum, aut neque bonum
neque malum est. (13) Omnia autem quae disiun-
guntur pugnantia esse inter sese oportet, eorumque
opposita, quae ἀντικείμενα Graeci dicunt, ea quoque
ipsa inter se adversa esse. Ex omnibus quae dis-

---

[d] *Tusc. Disp.* i. 7. 14.   [e] Two connected statements, of
which the second follows as the result of the first.   [f] This
is the younger Africanus, who destroyed Carthage in 146 B.C.;
it was the older Africanus who defeated Hannibal at Zama
in 202 B.C.

as I have said, a *proloquium* or 'forthright statement'; but by Marcus Cicero [d] a *pronuntiatum*
or 'pronouncement,' a word however which he
declared that he used "only until I can find a better
one."

(9) But what the Greeks call a συνημμένον ἀξίωμα
or 'connected axiom,'[e] some of our countrymen
call *adiunctum* 'adjoined,' others call *conexum* 'connected.' The following are examples of this: "If
Plato is walking, Plato is moving"; "If it is day,
the sun is above the earth." (10) Also what they
call συμπεπλεγμένον or a 'compound axiom,' we call
coniunctum 'conjoined' or *copulatum* 'coupled'; for
example: "Publius Scipio, son of Paulus, was twice
consul and celebrated a triumph, and held the
censorship, and was the colleague of Lucius Mummius
in his consulship." (11) But if in the whole of a proposition of this kind one member is false, even if the
others are true, the whole is said to be false. For if
to all those true statements which I have made about
that Scipio [f] I add "and he worsted Hannibal in
Africa," which is false, all those other statements
which have been made in conjunction will not be
true, on account of this one false statement which
has been added to them, because they will now all
be spoken of together as one statement of fact.

(12) There is also another form, which the Greeks
call a διεζευγμένον ἀξίωμα or 'disjunctive proposition,' and we call *disiunctum* 'separated.' For
example: "Pleasure is either good or evil, or it is
neither good nor evil." (13) Now all statements
which are contrasted ought to be opposed to each
other, and their opposites, which the Greeks call
ἀντικείμενα, ought also to be opposed. Of all state-

iunguntur unum esse verum debet, falsa cetera.
(14) Quod si aut nihil omnium verum aut omnia
plurave quam unum vera erunt, aut quae disiuncta
sunt non pugnabunt, aut quae opposita eorum sunt contraria inter sese non erunt, tunc id disiunctum mendacium est et appellatur παραδιεζευγμένον, sicuti hoc
est, in quo quae opposita non sunt contraria : Aut
curris aut ambulas aut stas. Nam ipsa quidem
inter se adversa sunt, sed opposita eorum non pugnant : non ambulare enim et non stare et non currere
contraria inter sese non sunt, quoniam contraria ea
dicuntur quae simul vera esse non queunt ; possis
simul eodemque tempore neque ambulare neque
stare neque currere.

Fr. 29.[1] Excipiuntur haurio hausi (invenitur tamen
etiam haurivi vel haurii ; Varro in XXIIII ad
Ciceronem : " Cum indidem haurierint "), saepio
saepsi, . . .

INCERTAE SEDIS FRAGMENTA

Fr. 30a.[1] Proceres : Varro ad Ciceronem dixit
" proceres qui processerunt ante alios, unde et proceres tigna quae alia tigna porro excesserunt."

Fr. 30b.[2] Proceres autem ideo secundum Varronem principes civitatis dicuntur, quia eminent in

---

Fr. 29.   [1] *Priscian, Inst. Gram.* ii. 540. 3-5 *Keil.*
Fr. 30.   [1] *Schol. cod. Ambr. in Aen.* iii. 58.   [2] *Serv. in*
Aen. i. 740.

Fr. 29.   [a] To the rule that in the fourth conjugation the
perfect is formed by changing the *is* of the second person
singular of the present, to *ivi* or *ii*; *cf.* Priscian, ii. 539. 8-11
Keil.

ments which are contrasted, one ought to be true and the rest false. (14) But if none at all of them is true, or if all, or more than one, are true, or if the contrasted things are not at odds, or if those which are opposed to each other are not contrary, then that is a false contrast, and is called παραδιεζευγμένον or 'wrong-disjunctive.' For instance, this case, in which the things which are opposed are not contraries : " Either you run or you walk or you stand." These acts are indeed contrasted, but their opposites are not contrary ; for 'not to walk' and 'not to stand' and 'not to run' are not contrary to one another, since those things are called 'contraries' which cannot be true at the same time. But you may together and at the same time neither walk nor stand nor run.

Fr. 29. Exceptions [a] are *haurio* 'I draw off,' perfect *hausi* (yet *haurivi* or *haurii* also is found ; Varro, in the twenty-fourth book of the treatise addressed to Cicero, says " when they *haurierint* 'have drained' from the same "), *saepio* 'I fence in,' perfect *saepsi*, . . .

FRAGMENTS OF UNDETERMINABLE POSITION

Fr. 30a. *Proceres* : Varro in the treatise addressed to Cicero said that *proceres* are those who *processerunt* 'have advanced' ahead of others,[a] whence also those beams are called *proceres* which project beyond the other beams.[b]

Fr. 30b. *Proceres* however, according to Varro, is a name applied to leaders of the state, because they

Fr. 30. [a] Wrong etymology. [b] The ends of the rafters project beyond the line of the wall on which they rest.

VARRO

ea, sicut in aedificiis mutuli quidam, hoc est capita trabium, quae proceres nominantur.

Fr. 31a.[1] Senior: secundum Varronem senior et iunior comparativi sunt per inminutionem. . . . Ergo senior non satis senex, sicut iunior non satis iuvenis, intra iuvenem, sicut pauperior intra pauperem. Dicit autem hoc Varro in libris ad Ciceronem.

Fr. 31b.[2] Iam senior: aut pro positivo posuit, id est senex, aut, ut diximus, senior est virens senex, ut iunior intra iuvenem est: quam rem a Varrone tractatam confirmat et Plinius.

Fr. 32.[1] In summo vero constructionis eius, quam similem navali carinae diximus, caput conlocavit, in quo esset regimen totius animantis, datumque illi hoc nomen est, ut quidem Varro ad Ciceronem scribit, quod hinc capiant initium sensus ac nervi.

Fr. 33.[1] Non nulli proprie calamos lupinorum alas dici putant, ut Aelius: alae ex lupino, s⟨urculi sine fo⟩liis; Cato in Originibus: alae ex lup⟨ino⟩ leg⟨umine; Varro⟩ de Lingua Latina alam culmum fabae dic⟨i docet⟩.

Fr. 34.[1] Haec de quattuor coniugationibus quae

Fr. 31. [1] *Serv. in Aen.* v. 409. [2] *Serv. in Aen.* vi. 304.
Fr. 32. [1] *Lactantius, de Opificio Dei*, v. 6.
Fr. 33. [1] *Serv. Dan. in Georg.* i. 75.
Fr. 34. [1] *Diomedes, Ars Gram.* i. 371. 23-26 *Keil.*

Fr. 31. [a] Such a comparative expresses something which is not even as great as the positive: *smaller* is a typical example; but this feature of *senior* is not clear. [b] In both passages of the *Aeneid* the *senior* is still physically vigorous: the boxer Entellus, the ferryman Charon.
Fr. 32. [a] The backbone of man. [b] Wrong etymology.

stand out in it, just as in buildings certain mutules, that is, heads of beams, stand out, which are called *proceres*.

Fr. 31a. *Senior*: according to Varro, *senior* and *iunior* are comparatives of diminution.[a] . . . Therefore *senior* is not a man who is completely old, just as a *iunior* is not an entirely youthful person, but one not quite as much as a *iuvenis* ' young man,' as a *pauperior* ' poorer ' person is not even as much as *pauper* ' poor.' Varro says this in the books addressed to Cicero.

Fr. 31b. *Iam senior* ' now older ' : either he set this as a positive, namely *senex*, or, as we have said, a *senior* is a vigorous old man,[b] as a *iunior* is one not yet a youth. The matter is mentioned by Varro, and is confirmed by Pliny.

Fr. 32. But at the top of this edifice,[a] which we have said was like a ship's keel, he set the *caput* ' head,' in which there was to be the guidance of the whole creature, and the name *caput* was given to it, as indeed Varro writes in the treatise addressed to Cicero, because from it the senses and the nerves *capiunt* ' take ' their start.[b]

Fr. 33. Some think that the stems of lupines are properly called *alae*[a] ' wings '; thus Aelius[b] : " *alae* of lupine, shoots without leaves "; Cato in the *Origins*[c] : " *alae* of lupine pulse "; Varro in the treatise *On the Latin Language* instructs us that the stalk of the bean is called an *ala*.

Fr. 34. With regard to the four conjugations, these

Fr. 33.   [a] Properly, the places where the branches or shoots start from the stem.   [b] Page 59 Funaioli.   [c] Frag. 122 Peter.

VARRO

pertinent ad verba quae analogiae parent, quarum
exempla passim perscripta sunt et sunt nota. Quae
siquis conceperit animo, non facile labetur. Sunt
enim evidenter exposita et Varroni Menippeo.

Fr. 35.[1] Sapio tam sapui vel sapii quam sapivi
protulisse auctores inveniuntur ; Probo tamen sapui
placet dici, Charisio sapui vel sapivi, Aspro sapivi et
sapii secundum Varronem, quod Diomedes etiam
approbat.

Fr. 36.[1] Sunt alia verba, quibus desunt diversa
tempora, usu deficiente, non ratione significationis.
Et quibusdam deest praeteritum perfectum et omnia,
quae ex eo nascuntur, ut ferio sisto tollo fero aio furo,
quod Varro ponit. Ergo aliorum verborum perfectis,
quae videntur eandem significationem habere, pro
his utimur.

Fr. 37.[1] Puer et in feminino sexu antiqui dicebant,
ut Graeci ὁ παῖς καὶ ἡ παῖς ; ut in Odyssia vetere,
quod est antiquissimum carmen :

Mea puer,[2] quid verbi ex tuo ore audio ?

Fr. 35.   [1] *Priscian, Inst. Gram.* ii. 499. 17-19 *Keil.*
Fr. 36.   [1] *Priscian, Inst. Gram.* ii. 418. 27–419. 2 *Keil.*
Fr. 37.   [1] *Charisius, Inst. Gram.* i. 84. 5-11 *Keil.*   [2] *The verse is quoted with* mea puera *and* supra fugit (*for* audio) *by Priscian,* ii. 231. 10 *Keil.*

Fr. 34.   [a] The rules for the formation of the perfect active.
[b] Varro, as author of the *Menippean Satires*, is sometimes called *Varro Menippeus*, as here ; but the present passage may be textually corrupt.

are the principles [a] applying to the verbs which obey Regularity ; examples are set down everywhere and are well known. Anyone who has mastered them will easily avoid error. For they are set forth clearly also by Varro of the Menippean Satire.[b]

Fr. 35. To *sapio* ' I am wise,' authors are found to have employed as perfect *sapui* or *sapii* as well as *sapivi* ; yet Probus [a] prefers *sapui*, Charisius [b] *sapui* or *sapivi*, Asper *sapivi* or *sapii* in reliance on Varro, a view which Diomedes [c] also approves.

Fr. 36. There are other verbs, which lack different tenses ; it is the use of a form that is lacking, the reason for the meaning exists. Certain verbs lack the perfect and all the forms made from it ; such are *ferio* ' I strike,' *sisto* ' I put,' *tollo* ' I pick up,' *fero* ' I bear,' *aio* ' I say,' *furo* ' I am mad '—a list which Varro sets down. Therefore for the perfects of these verbs we use the perfects of other verbs which seem to have the same meaning.[a]

Fr. 37. *Puer* ' boy ' the ancients used to use also as a feminine, like the Greek παῖς, masc. meaning ' boy ' and fem. meaning ' girl ' ; as in the old *Odyssey*,[a] a very ancient poem :

My child, what word is this I hear fall from your lips ?

Fr. 35. [a] *Cf.* iv. 36. 12 Keil. [b] i. 246. 11 Keil. [c] i. 369. 25 Keil. All these four grammarians belong to the fourth century A.D.

Fr. 36. [a] The text then cites *ferio percussi, sisto statui, tollo sustuli, fero tuli, furo insanivi*. After Varro's time, a perfect *furui* was occasionally used.

Fr. 37. [a] Livius Andronicus, frag. 3 Baehrens; *R.O.L.* ii. 24-25 Warmington.

VARRO

Et in Nelei Carmine, *a*eque[3] prisco :

Saucia puer filia sumam ;

ubi tamen Varro cum A puera putat dictum, sed Aelius ⟨S⟩*t*ilo,[4] magister eius, et Asinius contra.

Fr. 38.[1] Leontion et *C*hrysion et *P*hanion[2] ex neutris Graecis feminina n*o*str*i*[3] fecere, et Plautus quod dixit haec *P*hronesium et Caecilius ⟨haec⟩[4] Leontium. Varroni autem placet talia nomina dativo tantum casu et ablativo declinari, *in*[5] ceteris vero sic efferri ut nominativo.

---

[3] *Keil, for* eoque.   [4] *For* aedilius cilo.
    Fr. 38. [1] *Charisius, Inst. Gram.* i. 104. 1-4 *Keil.*   [2] *For* thyrusion et faunion.   [3] *For* neutra.   [4] *Added by Fabricius.*   [5] *For* de.

---

[b] *Trag. Rom. Frag.*, page 271 Ribbeck [3]; *R.O.L.* ii. 628-629 Warmington.   [c] The verse is incomplete in sense; perhaps the text is corrupt.   [d] Page 69 Funaioli.   [e] Page 499 Funaioli.

And in the *Song of Neleus*,[b] which is equally old :

> A wounded child, a daughter, I'll take [c] . . .

In this however Varro thinks that *puera*, with A, was used, but his teacher Aelius Stilo [d] and Asinius [e] take the opposite view.

Fr. 38. *Leontion* and *Chrysion* and *Phanion* [a] are neuters in Greek, but when we took them into Latin we made feminines of them ; Plautus [b] used *Phronesium* [c] as a feminine, and Caecilius [d] used *Leontium* in the same way. But Varro thinks that such nouns are inflected only for the dative and the ablative, and that in the other cases the same form as the nominative is used.[e]

Fr. 38. [a] Neuter diminutives, as women's names. [b] *Truculentus* 323. [c] This and *Leontium*, with Latin *-um* replacing the Greek *-on*. [d] *Comic. Rom. Frag.*, page 93 Ribbeck³. [e] That is, nom. acc. voc. in *-um*, dat. abl. in *-o*, gen. lacking.

COMPARATIVE TABLE OF THE FRAGMENT NUMBERS

K = the present edition.
GS = Goetz and Schoell, edition of 1910.
F = Funaioli, *Grammaticae Romanae Fragmenta*, 1907.
W = Wilmanns, *de M. Terenti Varronis libris grammaticis*, 1864.

K	GS	F	W	K	GS	F	W
1	2	6	4	20	21	255	20
2	3	7	5	21	22	14	21
3	4	8	6	22	23	15	23
4	5	9	7	23	24	17	30
5	p. 146 {11 / 12}		..	24	25	18	31
6	7	24	..	25	26	19	33
7	8	245	8	26	27	20	34
8	9	246	9	27	28	21	35
9	10	247	10	28	29	22	36
10	11	248	11	29	30	23	37
11	12	249	12	30	31	32	..
12	13	16	25	31	32	28	24
13	14	25	13	32	33	30	38
14	15	26	14	33	34	31	39
15	16	27	16	34	35	261	26
16	17	253	15	35	36	262	27
17	18	..	..	36	37	263	..
18	19	254	18	37	38	250	28
19	20	13	19	38	39	258	29

INDEX OF AUTHORS AND WORKS

References are to Book (Roman numeral) and Section (Arabic number), and to Fragment (F.) and serial number (Arabic), with subdivisions.

631

INDEX

632

INDEX

INDEX OF LATIN WORDS AND PHRASES

INDEX

635

INDEX

636

INDEX

INDEX

INDEX

INDEX

INDEX

INDEX

643

INDEX

decuriones, **v.** 91
decussis, v. 170 ; ix. 81
dedicat dedicatur, vi. 61
definitiones grammaticorum, x. 75
deierare sub tecto, v. 66
Dei Penates, *v.* deus
deiunctum, *v.* analogia
Deli, vii. 16
Deliadae, vii. 16
delicuum, deliquare, vii. 106
Delphi, vii. 17
delubra, *v.* Cabirum
Demetrius rex, vii. 52
demptio litterarum, v. 6 ; vii. 1
denarius denarii, v. 170, 173, 174 ;
    viii. 71 ; ix. 85 ; x. 41 ; denarium
    (non -orum), viii. 71, ix. 82, 85 ;
    v. formula, gradus, numeri
denasci, v.70
dens, v. 135 ; viii. 67 ; dentum
    dentes, viii. 67
densum, v. 113
deorsum, v. 161 ; deorsum versus,
    ix. 86
depsere, vi. 96
derectae declinationes, x. 44
derectus, *v.* ordo, ratio
des, *v.* bes
despicio, vi. 82
despondet, vi. 69 ; desponsa, vi. 70 ;
    despondisse, vi. 71 ; despondisse
    animum, filiam, vi. 71
desponsor, vi. 69
destringor destrinxi, F. 5. 7
detrectio (syllabarum), v. 6
detrimentum, v. 176
detritum, *v.* E, S
deunx, v. 172
deus deei, viii. 70 ; dei, v. 57, 65,
    66, 71 ; deos, F. 1 ; dei contrarii,
    v. 71 ; deo principe, vi. 34 ; dei
    principes, v. 57 ; Dei Consentes,
    viii. 70 ; Deum (non Deorum)
    Consentium aedem, viii. 71 ; dei
    magni, v. 58, vii. 34 ; diis inferis,
    vi. 34 ; Dii Penates nostri, v. 144 ;
    Dei Penates, viii. 70 ; aedes Deum
    Penatium, v. 54 ; Di Manes ser-
    viles, vi. 24 ; ara deum, v. 38 ;
    arae deorum, v. 52 ; liberorum
    dei nomina, ix. 55, 59 ; *v.* Samo-
    thraces ; *cf.* Novensides
dextans, v. 172
dextra, *v.* propter

diabathra, vii. 53
Dialis flamen, v. 84 ; vi. 16
Diana, v. 68 (Diviana), 74 ; vii. 16 ;
    Dianae templum, v. 43 ; *v.* Titanis,
    Trivia
dibalare, vii. 103
dicare, vi. 61
dicendi pars, viii. 44
dicis causa, vi. 61, 95
dico, vi. 30, 61, 62 ; dicit, vi. 78 ;
    dicere, vi. 42 ; dico dicebam dixe-
    ram, ix. 34 ; dicerem dicam, x.
    31 ; *v.* do
dictata in ludo, vi. 61
dictator, v. 82 ; vi. 61, 93 ; *v.* Poe-
    telius
dictiosus, vi. 61
dictum in mimo, vi. 61 ; dicta in
    manipulis castrensibus, vi. 61
dies, v. 68 ; vi. 4 ; ix. 73 ; x. 41 ; F.
    11 ; Dies Agonales, vi. 12 ; die
    auspicato, v. 143 ; dies concepti-
    vus, vi. 25 ; dies fasti, vi. 29, 53 ;
    dies Fortis Fortunae, vi. 17 ; dies
    nefasti, vi. 30, 53 ; dies sacri
    Sabini, v. 123 ; dies et nox, v. 11 ;
    dierum nomina, vi. 10-32 ; dierum
    singulorum vocabula, vi. 33 ; *v.*
    Alliensis, atri, civilia, comitiales,
    februatus, intercisi, Iupiter,
    Larentinae, prodixit, quando,
    quartus, septumus, statuti, Venus
Diespiter, v. 66 ; Diespiter Dies-
    pitri Diespitrem, ix. 75, 77
dilectus, vi. 65
diligens, vi. 65 ; diligentior dili-
    gentissimus -ma, viii. 78
Di Manes, *v.* deus, Manes
diminutio, F. 9
diminutivum, F. 9
diobolares, vii. 64
Diomedes -di -dis, x. 49
Dionem, vi. 2 ; Diona, viii. 41, ix. 42
Diores, ix. 12
Diovis, v. 66, 84
directus, *v.* derectus
discere, vi. 62 ; discebam disco dis-
    cam, didiceram didici didicero,
    ix. 96
discerniculum, v. 129
discessit, vi. 38
disciplina, vi. 62 ; loquendi, x. 1
discordia verborum novorum ac
    veterum, v. 6

644

INDEX

discrimen, vi. 12 (naturale), 81 ; ix.
56 ; x. 20, 77 (verbi) ; discrimina
verborum, rerum, vi. 36, 38, viii.
1, 2, 10, 14, 16, 17 (*cf.* 51), ix. 32,
x. 64 (in rebus) ; discrimina litterarum, x. 62 ; discriminum
numerus, x. 10
disertus, vi. 64
disparilitas vocis figurarum, x. 36
Dis pater, v. 66
dispendium, v. 183 ; ix. 54
dispensator, v. 183
disputare, disputatio, vi. 63
disserit, vi. 64
dissimilia, viii. 34, etc. ; *v.* simile
dissimilitudo, viii. 23, 24, 29, 31, 32,
etc. ; ix. 46, etc. ; x. 1, 3, etc.
distractio doloris, vii. 60
distrahuntur, vii. 60
dius, v. 66 ; vii. 34
Dius Fidius, v. 66 ; aedes Dei Fidi,
v. 52
diva, *v.* Palatua
dives, v. 92 ; viii. 17
Diviana, *v.* Diana
dividia, vii. 60
divisio, vii. 60 ; ix. 97 ; x. 14, 15,
17, 33 ; divisiones, viii. 14, ix.
95, 101 ; ex eodem genere et ex
divisione, ix. 96, 97
divum, v. 66 ; vii. 27, 50 ; divos,
F. 1 ; sub divo, v. 66 ; divi potes,
v. 58 ; *v.* deus
do dico addico, vi. 30
do, *v.* ollus
doceo, vi. 62 ; docet, x. 17 ; doceo
docui, x. 25 ; docentur inducun-
tur, vi. 62 ; docens, x. 17 ; doctus,
F. 5. 8
docilis, x. 17
docte, viii. 12, 44 ; x. 17 ; F. 5. 8
doctiloqui, vii. 41
doctor, vi. 62
doctus -a -um, viii. 46 ; ix. 57 ;
doctus -a doctissimus -a, viii. 77 ;
doctus docte, viii. 12
documenta, vi. 62
dodrans, v. 172
dolia, *v.* sirpata
doliola, v. 157
dolo dolas dolavi, ix. 108
dolor dolori dolorem, x. 36, 42 ; *v.*
distractio
dolus malus, dolo malo, x. 51

domare, vi. 96
domus, v. 160 ; domus domuis
domui, F. 17 ; *v.* hibernum, Maelius, video
donum, v. 175
dos, v. 175
Dossennus, vii. 95
drachmae, ix. 85
ducenti, v. 170 ; x. 43
ducere ductor, vi. 62
Duellona Bellona, v. 73, vii. 49
duellum, v. 73 ; vii. 49
duigae, *v.* bigae
duini, *v.* bini
dulcis dulcior dulcissimus, viii. 76
duo duae, ix. 64, 65, 87 ; x. 24, 41,
43, 45, 49, 67, 83
duodenarius numerus, v. 34
duonus, vii. 26
duplex verbum, ix. 97 ; duplicia
vocabula, ix. 63 ; *v.* logoe
duplicarii, v. 90
dupondium dupondius, v. 169, 173 ;
ix. 81 (-um), 83, 84
dux, vi. 62 ; duces dux, x. 56, 57

E, viii. 68 ; ix. 52 ; E : AE. v. 97,
vii. 96 ; EI : US, ix. 89 ; E : A, v.
114, vii. 94 ; E : I, vi. 95 ; E : U,
v. 91 ; E detritum, vii. 74 ; E ex-
clusum, x. 57 ; E exemptum, ix.
44 ; E exitus, x. 62
ecbolicas aulas, v. 108
echinus, v. 77
ecurria, vi. 13
edictum, vi. 92
edo, vi. 84 ; edo edi, x. 33
edulium, vii. 61 ; edulia, vi. 84
edus, *v.* hedus
effari, templa effantur, fines effantur, vi. 53
effata, vi. 53
effutitum, vii. 93
Egeria, vii. 42
elegantia, viii. 31
elephans, elephantos, vii. 39
Elicii Iovis ara, vi. 94
eliquatum, vii. 106
elixum, v. 109
eloquens, vi. 57
eloqui, vi. 57
eminisci, vi. 44
emo emi, x. 33 ; *v.* homo
em pa, vii. 27

645

INDEX

INDEX

filius, x. 59 ; filius -a, ix. 55, x. 41

filum, v. 113

fimbriae, v. 79

fingo, v. 7 ; vi. 78 ; fingo fingis, x. 31

finis fine, F. 18 ; v. copulae, effari

finitum et infinitum, v. 11 ; viii. 45 ; ix. 31, 64, 85 ; x. 18, 20, 30 ; v. infinitei, numerus ; cf. templum

fircus, v. 97

fiscina, v. 139

fistula, v. 123

fixum, F. 2

Flaccus flamen Martialis, vi. 21

flamen vinum legit, vi. 16 ; flamines, v. 84, vii. 45 ; v. Dialis, Falacer, Flaccus, Floralis, Furinalis, Martialis, Palatualis, Pomonalis, Quirinalis, Volcanalis, Volturnalis

Flaminius circus, campus, v. 154

flexura, x. 28

Flora, v. 74, 158 ; vii. 45

Floralis flamen, vii. 45

fluctus fluctuis fluctui, F. 17

flumen, v. 27, 28

fluvius, v. 27

fodari, vii. 100

foditurne fodieturne, x. 32

foedus, v. 86 ; fidus, v. 86 ; foedesum, vii. 27

Fons, v. 74 ; vi. 22 ; fons, v. 123 ; fonte, F. 18 ; fonti et fonte, ix. 112 ; fontis fontes, viii. 66 ; v. corona

Fontanalia, vi. 22

forda (quae fert in ventre), vi. 15

Fordicidia, vi. 15

forma, vi. 78 ; viii. 9, 47 ; ix. 21, 39-41, 82 ; x. 1 (vocabulorum), 22, 27, 49 ; forma etymologiae, vii. 109 ; forma'in declinando, ix. 37 ; formae verborum, ix. 101, 102, 109, 115, x. 56 ; formae Graecae verborum, x. 70 ; v. similitudinum

formido, vi. 48

formo, vi. 78

formula, ix. 103 ; x. 44 ; formula numerorum, x. 43 ; formulae verborum, x. 33 ; analogiarum formula binaria, denaria, x. 44

fornices, v. 19 (caeli) ; x. 59

Fortis Fortunae fanum, vi. 17 ; v. dies

Fortuna, v. 74 ; vii. 93 ; v. vocabula

fortunatum, v. quod bonum

forum, v. 47, 145, 148, 149 ; vi. 59 ; vii. 94 ; ix. 17 ; v. Bovarium, Cupidinis, Holitorium, Piscarium, vetus

fossa, v. 143 ; vii. 100

Fratres, v. Arvales

fratria, v. 85

fremere, vi. 67 ; vii. 104

fremor oritur, vi. 67

frendit, vii. 104

frequens, vii. 99

frequentare, vii. 99

fretum fretu, vii. 22

frigidum, v. 59 ; v. aquae

frigus, v. 60

fringuillae vox, vii. 104

fringuttis, vii. 104

fritinnit, vii. 104

frondenti coma, vii. 24

fructus, v. 37, 40, 104

fruges, v. 37, 104 ; frugis frux (haec), ix. 76 ; frugis -i -em, ix. 75

frugi (non frugalus -a) frugalissumus -ima, viii. 77

frumentum, v. 104

fruor, v. 37, 104

fugitiva, v. 5

fulgur, v. 70

fulguritum, v. 70, 150

fullo, vi. 43

fulmen, v. 70

fulmentum, viii. 10

Fulvia, v. Basilica

fumificus, vii. 38

fundolus, v. 111

fundula, v. 145

fundus, v. 37

funesta familia, v. 23

funus, v. indicit, indictivum

Furinalis flamen, v. 84 ; vi. 19 ; vii. 45 ; Furinales feriae, v. 84

Furnacalia, vi. 13

furo, F. 36

Furrina, v. 84 ; vi. 19 ; vii. 45

Furrinalia, vi. 19

fustes, v. 137

futis, v. 119

futurum, viii. 20, 58

G, v. C ; GL, v. 134 ; GS : X, ix 44

Gabii, v. 33

648

INDEX

INDEX

illicit, vi. 95 ; *v.* inlicere
immortales, v. 75 ; immortalia in
   locis, v. 57
impendium, v. 183 ; vi. 65
imperandi (facies), x. 31, 32 ; in imperando, x. 32 ; cum imperamus,
   ix. 101 ; *v.* declinatus
imperator, **v.** 87 ; vi. 77 ; vii. 37
impius, vi. 30
impluium, v. 161
imponenda (vocabula), vi. 3
impos, *v.* inpos
imposticia nomina, viii. 5 ; imposi-
   ticii casus, x. 61
impositio verborum (vocabulorum),
   v. 1, 3 ; vi. 3 ; vii. 32, 109, 110 ;
   viii. 5, 7 ; x. 15, 16, 34, 51, 53,
   60, 61
impositor, v. 18 ; vii. 1, 2
impositum (verbum, vocabulum,
   nomen), v. 1-3 ; viii. 1, 9, 10, 22,
   27 ; ix. 34, 52
impurro, *v.* amburvom
inaequabilitas, viii. 28, 30 ; ix. 1
incertus ager, v. 33
incessit, vi. 38
inchoata (=infecta) res, ix. 96 ; *v.*
   analogia
incircum, v. 25
inclinanda verba, x. 13
inclinatio inclinationes, ix. 1, 113 ;
   cf. x. 13
incommutabilia, ix. 99
incrementum, viii. 17
increpitare, vi. 67
incultus, *v.* ager
incurvicervicum, v. 7
indagabilis ambitus, v. 28
indagare, v. 5
indeclinabilia, x. 14, 79, 80, 82 ;
   viii. 9
indicandi, ix. 101
indicit bellum, vi. 61 ; indixit funus,
   vi. 61
indicium, vi. 61
indictivum funus, v. 160 ; vii. 42
indiscriminatim, F. 25
indoctus, viii. 62 ; indocti, ix. 22
indusiatam, v. 131
indusium, v. 131
indutui, v. 131 ; x. 27
infantes, vi. 52
infecta (verba), ix. 97, 100, 101 ; x.
   48 ; infecti verba, ix. 99, 101, x.

33, 48 ; infecti tempora, ix. 96 ;
   infectae res, ix. 32 ; *cf.* inchoata
infeineitei, *v.* infinitei
inferi, vii. 37, *v.* deus ; infera loca,
   v. terra
inficientem esse, vi. 78
infima Nova Via, v. 43
infinitei articuli, viii. 50 ; infinita
   natura articulorum, viii. 52 ; infinitae naturae verborum, viii. 3 ;
   infinitum, v. 11, viii. 45, ix. 84 ;
   v. finitum
infrequens, vii. 99
infulae, vii. 24
infulatae hostiae, vii. 24
ingeniosi, viii. 15
ingluvies, F. 27
inhumatus, v. 23
inimicitia -am, x. 73
initia, v. 60 ; rerum initia, v. 11 ;
   initiorum quadrigae, v. 12 ; initia
   regis, v. 8 ; initia analogiae, x.
   53 ; *v.* nascendi, Samothraces
inlex inlicis, *v.* illex
inlicere populum, vi. 90 ; inliciatur
   ad magistratus conspectum, **vi.**
   94
inlicium vocare, visere, vi. 86-88,
   93-95 ; *v.* illicit
inlocabilem, v. 14
inminutio, F. 31 a
inops, v. 92
inpos, v. 4
insane, vii. 86
insicia, v. 110
insidiae, vi. 90
insignia militaria, vii. 37
insipitur, v. 105
Insteianus Vicus, v. 52
institutum, x. 27
instrumentum, v. 105 ; instrumentum mulieris, ix. 22 ; *v.* rustica
insulsus, viii. 62
intempesta nox, vi. 7 ; vii. 72
Interamna, v. 28
intercisi dies, vi. 31
interduo, vii. 91
intermestris, vi. 10
interpolata (verba), v. 3
interrex, vi. 93
interrogando, ix. 32
intertrigo, v. 176
intertrimentum, v. 176

651

INDEX

intervallum mundi motus, vi. 3, *cf.* v. 12
intuiti, vii. 7
intusium, *v.* indusium
inumbravit, vi. 4
invident, vi. 80 ; invidit invidendum, vi. 80
Ion, viii. 21, 22
Iones, v. 146 ; vi. 9
Ionia, v. 16 ; viii. 21
ircus, *v.* hircus
irpices, v. 136
irundo, *v.* hirundo
is ea id, ea eae, eius eaius, ei eae, ieis eais, viii. 51 ; eius viri, eius mulieris, eius pabuli, viii. 51
Isis, v. 57
iste istunc, x. 50
Italia, vii. 86
ite (*imperat.*), vi. 96
iter, v. 22, 35
Itus (Tuscorum), vi. 28

iactarier, x. 70
iaculum, v. 115
iam, viii. 9
ianeus, vii. 26
ianitor ianitos, vii. 27
Ianualis Porta, v. 165
Ianuarius, vi. 34 ; Kalendae Ianuariae, vi. 28
Ianus, v. 165 ; Ianus geminus, v. 156, *cf.* vii. 26 ; Iani signum, v. 165
Ioum Ioverum, *v.* Iupiter
iuba, vii. 76, *cf.* vi. 6
iubar, vi. 6, 7 ; vii. 76
iubilare, vi. 68
iucunditas, ix. 46
iudex, vi. 61 ; iudices, vi. 88
iudicare, vi. 61
iudicium, *v.* addixit, censorium, decemvirum
iugerum, v. 35
inglans, v. 102
Iugula, vii. 50
iugum, v. 135
iumentum, v. 135
iungendi pars, viii. 44
Iuniae Idus, vi. 17 ; Iunius mensis, vi. 17, 33
iuniores, vi. 33, (declinationes) x. 71 ; *v.* iuvenis
Iuno, v, 65, 67 ; Iunonis, viii. 49 ;

Iuno Covella, vi. 27 ; aedes Iunonis Lanuvi, v. 162 ; Iuno Lucina, v. 69, 74 ; aedes Iunonis Lucinae, v. 50 ; lucus Iunonis Lucinae, v. 49 ; Iuno Regina, v. 67 ; *v.* Caprotina, Iupiter, terra
Iupiter, v. 65, 67, 84 ; vi. 4 ; vii. 12, 16, 85 ; Iupiter non Ious, viii. 74 ; Iupiter Iovi, viii. 34, x. 65 ; Iuppitri, viii. 33 ; Iupiter Iovis Iovem, viii. 49 ; Iovis Iovem Iovi, viii. 74 ; Ioum Ioverum, viii. 74 ; aedes Iovis, v. 41 ; aedes (Iovis) in Capitolio, v. 158 ; ara Iovis Vimini, v. 51 ; sacellum Iovis Iunonis Minervae, v. 158 ; dies Iovis non Veneris, vi. 16 ; Iovis Iuno coniunx, v. 67 ; Iovis filium et filiam (non) Iovem et Iovam, ix. 55 ; antiquius Iovis nomen, v. 66 ; *v.* Elicii, Fagutal
iurgare, iurgium, vii. 93
ius, *v.* ex iure, praetorium
Iuturna lympha, v. 71
iuvencus, v. 96 ; *v.* Hercules
iuvenis iunior, F. 31 a, F. 31 b

Kalendae, vi. 20, 27-29 ; *v.* Ianuariae
kalo, vi. 16, 27

L, *v.* G ; L : S, v. 138
Lacedaemonii, v. 146
lact, v. 104
lactuca, v. 104
lacus, v. 26 ; *v.* Curtius, Cutiliensis, Velini
laena, v. 133
laeta, vi. 50
laetari, vi. 50
laetitia, vi. 50
lana, v. 113, 130, *cf.* 133 ; vii. 24 ; ix. 92 ; lana Gallicana et Apula, ix. 39 ; *v.* carere, vellere
lanea, v. 130
langula, v. 120
laniena, viii. 55
Lanuvium, v. 162
lanx lance, x. 62
lapathium, v. 103
lapicidae, viii. 62
lapidicinae, v. 151
Larentalia, vi. 23
Larentia, *v.* Acca

INDEX

INDEX

viii. 83 ; orti a publicis servis Romani, viii. 83
Libethrides, vii. 20
libidinosus, vi. 47
libido, vi. 47 ; x. 60, 61 ; *v.* lubido
Libitina, *v.* Venus
Libo, *v.* Poetelius
libra, v. 169, 174, 182 ; vii. 14 ; *v.* aes
librarii, viii. 51 ; ix. 106
libum, v. 106 ; libum libo, ix. 54 ; liba, vii. 44
Libya, vii. 40 ; viii. 56
Libyatici non dicitur, viii. 56
Libyci, vii. 39
lictores, vii. 37
ligna, vi. 66
lignicidae non dicitur, viii. 62
ligo, v. 134
lilium, v. 103
lima, vii. 68 ; limae, x. 14
limax, vii. 64
lingere, vi. 96
lingua Latina, v. 1, 29 ; vii. 55, 110 ; viii. 58 ; ix. 113 ; lingua nostra, v. 3, 29 ; *v.* Armenia, Graecus, Osca, Sabinus
lingula, vii. 107
lingulaca, v. 77
lintres non lintreis, F. 20
linum lino, ix. 54
liquidum, vii. 106
liquitur, vii. 106
lis, vii. 93
liticines, v. 91 ; vi. 75
litora, *v.* Lemnia
litterae, v. 30 ; vi. 2, 66 ; vii. 2 ; viii. 63 ; ix. 52 ; x. 25, 26, 55, 82 ; antiquae litterae, vii. 143, vi. 33 ; litterae Latinae, v. 73, vii. 2, ix. 51 ; litterae Graecae, viii. 64, 65 ; interpretationem exili littera expeditam, vii. 2 ; littera praeterita, vii. 2 ; littera extrema, ix. 44, x. 21, 25 ; littera extrita, v. 96 ; litteram adicere, vii. 1 ; litteras assumere, vi. 2 ; litteras mittere, vi. 2 ; litterarum vocabula, ix. 51 ; *v.* additio, commutatio, demptio, discrimina, productio, traiectio
lixulae, v. 107
locare, v. 14, 15
locarium, v. 15
locatum, v. 14

locus, v. 11-15, 57 ; viii. 12 ; loca, vi. 97, vii. 5 ; loca agrestia, vii. 10 ; loca Europae, **v.** 32 ; loci muliebres, v. 15 ; loca naturae, v. 16 ; loca urbis, v. 45 ; origines locorum, vii. 110 ; vocabula *vel* verba locorum, v. 10, 184, vi. 1 ; *v.* animalia, caelum. Caeriolensis, terra, Tutilinae, urbs
Loebeso (=Libero), vi. 2
logoe, x. 43 (duplex, decemplex), *cf.* x. 2, 37, 39
lolligo, v. 79
longavo, v. 111
longus, viii. 17 ; longiores, x. 29
loquax, vi. 57
loquela, vi. 57
loquor, viii. 59 ; loquontur, vi. 1 ; loqui, vi. 56 ; loquens locuturus locutus, viii. 59 ; *v.* concinne, disciplina
lorica, v. 116
Lua Saturni, viii. 36
Lubentina, *v.* Venus
lubere, vi. 47
lubido hominum, x. 56 ; lubidinem, F. 4 ; *v.* libido
Luca bos, vii. 39, 40 ; Lucana bos, vii. 39
Lucani, v. 32, 111 ; vii. 39, 40 ; Lucana origo, v. 100
Lucanica, v. 111
lucere, vi. 79
Luceres, v. 55, 81, 89, 91
lucerna, v. 9, 119
Lucia, ix. 61 ; Lucia Volumnia, ix. 61
Lucienus, vi. 2
Lucina, *v.* Iuno
lucifer (stella), vii. 76
Lucius, ix. 60 ; Lucii, vi. 5 ; *v.* Aelius ; *cf.* Lucia
Lucretia, vi. 7
lucrum, v. 176
Lucumo, v. 55
lucus, *v.* Esquilina, Facutalis, Iuno, Mefitis, Poetelius, Venus
ludens, vi. 35
ludus, ix. 15 ; ludi quibus virgines Sabinae raptae, vi. 20 ; *v.* Apollinares, dictata, Taurii
lumariae falces, v. 137
lumecta, v. 137
lumen facere, vi. 79

INDEX

655

INDEX

Martialis (flamen), v. 84 ; vii. 45 ;
    v. Flaccus
Martius (mensis), vi. 33 ; Martius
    campus, v. 28, vi. 13, 92
mas femina, v. 58, 61 ; viii. 7, 40 ;
    ix. 38 ; mas femina neutrum, ix.
    55, 57, 59, 62, cf. viii. 36, 47, 78,
    x. 22 ; v. genus ; cf. virilia
masculinum, F. 14 a, F. 14 b ; mas-
    culino genere, F. 11
Maspiter, v. Mars
matellio, v. 119
mater, x. 41 ; matres familias, vii.
    44 ; v. Mania, Ops, terra
materia, x. 11, 36
Matralia, v. 106
mattea, v. 112
matula, v. 119
Maurus Maurice, F. 5. 8
maximus, v. Circus, Cluaca
Mecinus, v. maximus
media, v. 118 ; media nox, x. 41 ;
    media vocabula, viii. 79
medicina ars, v. 93 ; vii. 4 ; ix. 111
medicus, v. 8, 93 ; ix. 11 ; x. 46
Meditrinalia, vi. 21
Mefitis lucus, v. 49
Megalesion, vi. 15 ; Megalesia, vi. 15
mel mellis melli melle, viii. 63
melander, v. 76
Melicertes Melicerta, viii. 68 ; ix. 91
melios, vii. 26 ; meliosem, vii. 27 ;
    v. bonus
melius, v. bonus
Melius, v. Maelius
meminisse, vi. 44, 49
memoria, vi. 44, 49
Menaechmum -mo, x. 38 ; Me-
    naechmi gemini, viii. 43
mendicus, v. 92
mens, v. 59 ; vi. 43-45, 48, 49 ; mens
    mentium mentes, viii. 67 ; mentes
    non menteis, F. 20 ; v. agitatus
mensa, v. 118 ; vii. 43 ; v. escaria,
    urnarium, vasaria, vinaria
mensis, v. 69 ; vi. 10, 33 ; mensium
    nomina, vi. 33 ; v. novus, Ianu-
    arius, Februarius, Martius,
    Aprilis, Maius, Iunius, Quintilis,
    Septembres, October, December
menstruae, v. feriae
mensura, ix. 67 ; mensura ac pon-
    dera, ix. 66
menta, v. 103

meo meas, ix. 109
mera (=sola), v. 76
merces, v. 44, 175, 178 ; vii. 52 ;
    viii. 19 ; merces non merceis,
    F. 20
mergus, v. 78
meridies, vi. 4 ; vii. 7 ; x. 41
merula, v. 76 ; ix. 28, 55 (non meru-
    lus) ; merula merulae, x. 66 ;
    merulae vox, vii. 104
Mesium rustici, non Maesium, vii.
    96
messor, viii. 57
Metellus Metella, ix. 55
meto metis, x. 31 ; meto metam
    metebam, ix. 89 ; metendo, viii.
    57
Meto Metonis Metonem, ix. 89
Mettius, v. Curtius
metuere, vi. 48 ; metuit (non
    sperat), vi. 73 ; metuisti, vi. 45
metus, vi. 45
Mico, ix. 12
miliariae (aves), v. 76
miliariae (decuriae numerorum), ix.
    87 ; miliaria (vocabula), ix. 85
miliens, ix. 88
militare aes, v. 181 ; v. raudus ;
    militaria, v. insignia, ornamenta
milites, v. 89 ; milites aerarii, v.
    181 ; militis stipendia, v. 182 ; v.
    legio, tribuni
milium, v. 76, 106
mille milia, ix. 82, 85, 88 ; mille
    aeris, ix. 83 ; hi, hoc, huius,
    horum mille, ix. 87, 88 ; haec duo
    milia, ix. 87
Minervae, v. 74 ; aedes Minervae,
    vi. 17 ; v. Iupiter
Minervium, v. 47
minima vocabula, viii. 79
minores, ix. 87
minuendi (genus declinationis), vii.
    52
minusculae, v. Quinquatrus
minuta opera, v. Myrmecidis
miraculae, vii. 64
miriones, vii. 64
miser, v. 92
mitra, v. 130
moenere, v. 141
moenia, v. 141
moerus, v. 141 ; moeri, vi. 87 ; v.
    murus

656

INDEX

mola (sale et farre), v. 104; molae, v. 138
monere, vi. 49; monerint, vii. 102
monimenta, vi. 49
monitor, v. 94
montes (Romae), v. 41; vi. 24; monte, F. 18; monti monte, ix. 112; montes montis, viii. 66; v. Albanus, Caelius, Cespius, Oppius, Ripaei, Saturnius, Tarpeius
morbus, v. quartus, septumus
mors, v. vita
mortales, v. 75; mortalia in locis, v. 57
morticinum, vii. 84
mortui lectus, v. lectus
motacilla, v. 76
motus, v. 11, 12; vi. 3, 4, 8; ix. 34 (caeli); motus in mari, ix. 25; v. sol
mox, x. 14, 79, 80
Mucialis collis, v. 52
Mucionis porta, v. 164
Mucius, Q., vi. 30; viii. 81; Muci et Bruti sedulitas, v. 5; Mucia, viii. 81
Mugionis, v. Mucionis
mugit, vii. 104
mulgere, vi. 96
muliebre, viii. 46, 51; muliebria, ix. 41, 48, 110, x. 30; nomina muliebria, viii. 36; v. locus, mundus, stola, tunica
mulier, viii. 80; x. 4; mulieris, mulieribus, viii. 51; praenomina mulierum antiqua, ix. 61; v. antiqua, cum muliere
multa, v. 95, 177
multitudo multitudinis, viii. 7, 14, 36, 46, 48, 60, 66, 67; ix. 64-66, 68, 69, 76, 81, 82, 84, 85, 87; x. 28, 33, 36, 54, 56, 58, 59, 66, 83; multitudinis solum, ix. 63, x. 54, 66; multitudinis vocabula, ix. 64, 65; multitudo verborum, vi. 35, 40; v. copulae
mulus mula, ix. 28; v. mutuum
mundus, vi. 3; (=ornatus muliebris), v. 129; v. intervallum, terra
municipes, v. 179
municipium, viii. 83
munus, v. 141, 179
muraena, v. 77; ix. 28, 113
Murciae, v. Circus

Murmecidis, v. Myrmecidis
murmurantia litora, vi. 67
murmurari, vi. 67
murtatum, v. 110
Murteae Veneris sacellum, v. 154
murtetum, v. 154
murus, v. 143; v. circum, moerus, postici, Saturnii, terreus
Musa, ix. 63; Musae, vii. 20, 26, ix. 64
musica, ix. 111
mussare, vii. 101
mustela, ix. 113
muti, vii. 101
Muti, v. Mucius
mutuum, v. 179; mutua muli, vii. 28
Myrmecidis opera minuta, ix. 108; obscuram operam Myrmecidis, vii. 1
mysteria, vii. 11, 19, 34
mystica vada, vii. 19

N, cf. M
Naevia Porta, v. 163; Naevia nemora, v. 163
naevius, F. 13
nanus, v. 119
narratio, vi. 51
narro, vi. 51
narus, vi. 51
nascendi initia, v. 15; causa, v. 61; cf. v. 60, 70
natare, viii. 74; ix. 71
natator, v. 94
natura, ix. 37, 38, 58, 62, 63, 70, 72, 76, 78, 94, 101; x. 15, 17, 24, 41 (quadruplex), 51-53, 55, 56, 60, 61, 83, 84, F. 6; natura novenaria, octonaria, ix. 86; natura sermonis, viii. 25; natura verborum, viii. 43, x. 51, 74; naturae verbi, v. 2; naturarum genera, x. 28; v. copulae, gentilicia, infinitei, locus
naturalis, v. casus, declinatio, discrimen, genus
naviculae ratariae, vii. 23
navis longa, vii. 23; nave, F. 18
Neapolis (Novapolis), v. 85; vi. 58
necatus sum necor necabor, x. 48
necessitas, viii. 31
nefas, vi. 30, 31
nefasti, v. dies

657

INDEX

659

INDEX

pa (= patrem), vii. 27
pabulum, viii. 51
Paganalia, vi. 24
paganicae (feriae), vi. 26
pagus, vi. 26; v. Succusanus
pala, v. 134
Palanto, v. 53
Palatina tribus, v. 56; regio, v. 45;
Palatini, v. 53, 54; Palatinum, v.
antiqua
Palatium, v. 21, 53, 68 (Bal-), 164
Palatua diva, vii. 45
Palatualis flamen, vii. 45
Pales, v. 74; vi. 15
Palilia, vi. 15
palla, v. 131
Pallantes, v. 53
pallium, v. 133, 167; viii. 28; ix. 48
palma, v. 62
palpetras, non palpebras, F. 23
Paluda, vii. 37
paludamenta, vii. 37
paludatus, vii. 37
palus, v. 26
panarium, v. 105
Pandana Porta, v. 42
pandura, viii. 61
panificium, v. 105
panis, v. 105; panis pastillus pastillum, F. 10
pannus, v. 114
panther, v. 100; panthera, v. 100,
(non pantherus) ix. 55, F. 3;
pantherae, vii. 40
Pantheris, v. 100
panuvellium, v. 114
Pappus, vii. 29, 96
parapechia, v. 133
Parcae, vi. 52
Parentalia, vi. 23
parentant, vi. 23; parentare, vi.
13, 34
parentum parentium, viii. 66
paries, ix. 41
Paris, vii. 82; viii. 80; Paris Pari,
viii. 34
parma, v. 115
Parma (urbs), viii. 56
Parmenses (non Parmani), viii. 56
paro paretur parator, x. 32; paro
paravi, F. 5. 6
partes animae, ix. 30; partes orationis, viii. 11, 38, 44, 53, x. 7,
cf. vi. 36, viii. 48, ix. 31, x. 17;

v. casuale, ex quadam, scaena,
templum, urbs
participalia, x. 34
participia, viii. 58; ix. 110
patella, v. 120
patena, v. 120
pater, v. 65; x. 41, 59; pater
patres, viii. 48; pater familias,
patres familias familiarum, viii.
73; patres (=senatores), vi. 91;
v. Dis, Falacer
paterae, v. 122
patiendi, v. faciendi
patricus (casus), viii. 66, 67; ix. 54,
76, 85; cf. viii. 16
patrius casus, v. 17
Patulcium, vii. 26
pauper, v. 92; pauper (sed non
paupera) pauperrumus pauperrima, viii. 77; pauper pauperior,
F. 31 a
pavet, vi. 48
pavo, v. 75
pavor, vi. 48
pecten, v. 129
pectere, vi. 96
pectunculi, v. 77
peculatus, v. 95
peculiariae oves, v. 95
peculium, v. 95
pecunia, v. 92, 95, 175, 177, 180,
181; vi. 65, 70; pecunia debita,
vii. 105; pecuniae signatae vocabula, v. 169; v. nuncupatae
pecuniosus, v. 92; viii. 15, 18
pecus (pecoris), v. 80, 95, 110; vii.
14; ix. 74; pecudem, v. 95;
pecudis caro, v. 109; pecus ovil-
lum, v. 99; v. ago
pedem posuisse, v. 96
pedica, v. 96
pedisequus, v. 96
peius, v. malum
pelagus sermonis, ix. 33
Peles, x. 69
Pelium, vii. 33
pellesuina, viii. 55
pellexit, vi. 94
pelliaria taberna non dicitur, viii. 55
pellicula, vii. 84
peloris, v. 77
pelvis, v. 119
penaria, v. 162
Penates, v. deus

660

INDEX

pensio prima, secunda, etc., v. 183
Percelnus Percelna, viii. 81
percubuit, ix. 49
percutio percussi percutiam, ix. 98
perduellis, v. 3; vii. 49
peregrinus, v. 3; peregrinus ager, v. 33; peregrina vocabula, v. 77, 100, 103, 167
perfectum, ix. 100, 101; x. 48; perfecti (verba), ix. 96, 101, x. 33, 48; perfecta, ix. 97, 99, x. 48; perfectae res, ix. 32, 96; v. analogia, similitudo
Pergama, vi. 15; Pergamum, viii. 56
Pergamenus (non Pergamus -a), viii. 56
pergendo (= progrediendo), v. 33
periacuit, ix. 49
peripetasmata, v. 168
peristromata, v. 168
perna, v. 110
perorat, vi. 76
Perpenna, viii. 41, 81 (non Perpennus), ix. 41; x. 27; Marcus Perpenna, viii. 81
Persarum nomina, viii. 64
persedit, ix. 49
perseverantia, v. 2
persibus, vii. 107
personae, verbi, viii. 20 (qui loqueretur, ad quem, de quo); ix. 32, 95, 100-102, 108, 109; x. 31, 32; v. copulae, secunda
perstitit, ix. 49
pertinacia, v. 2
pervade, v. polum
pes, v. 95; pes lecti ac betae, vi. 55; pes magnus, v. 95; v. pedem
pessimum, v. malus
phalera -am, x. 74
phanclas, v. zanclas
Phanion, F. 38
Philippi caput, ix. 79
Philolacho, ix. 54
Philomedēs -dēs, viii. 68; ix. 91
philosophia, v. 8
Phoenice, v. 31
Phoenicum, v. Poenicum
Phryx Phryge Phryges, ix. 44
physici, v. 69; x. 55
piacularis hostia, vi. 30
piaculum, vi. 29, 53

pila terrae, vii. 17; pila aequa, vii. 19
pilani, v. 89
pili in corpore, vi. 45
pilum, v. 116, 138
pingo pingis, x. 31; pingo pinxi, F. 5. 6
pinnae, v. 142
pinus, v. 102
pipatus pullorum, vii. 103
Pipleides, vii. 20
pipulo, vii. 103
Piscarium Forum, v. 146
pisces, viii. 61; ix. 28, 113; piscium nomina, vii. 47; piscium vocabula, v. 77
pisciceps non dicitur, viii. 61
piscina (non dicuntur piscinula piscinilla), ix. 74
pistor pistori, x. 69
pistrinum pistrina, v. 138; pistrinum pistrilla, F. 10
pistrix, v. 138
placenta, v. 107
platanus platani, ix. 80
plaustrum, v. 140
Plautius Plauti, viii. 36
Plautus Plauti, viii. 36
plebs, v. tribuni
pluit, ix. 104
plumbea, ix. 66
plumbum (non plumba), ix. 66
plura, ix. 32; x. 31
plusima, vii. 27
pocillum, ix. 66
poculum, vi. 84; viii. 31; pocula, v. 122
poema non poematum, F. 21; poemata, vii. 2; poematorum, F. 21; poematis, vii. 2, 36, viii. 14, F. 21; poematibus, vii. 34
poena, v. 177
Poeni, v. 113, 182
Poenicum, v. 113; Poenicum vocabula, viii. 65
poeta poetae, v. 22, 88; vi. 52, 58, 67, 77, 83; vii. 36, 110; ix. 5, 17, 65, 78, 115; x. 35, 42, 70, 73, 74; vocabula apud poetas, v. 1; vocabula a poetis comprehensa, v. 10; vocabula poetarum, vii. 1; poetarum verba, v. 7, 9; verba a poetis posita, vii. 5; verba apud poetas, vii. 107; cf. poetica, vetus

INDEX

INDEX

pro (=ante), vi. 58
probus probi, F. 5. 6; probus probe, F. 5. 8
procare, vii. 80
procedere, vii. 81; processit, vi. 38
proceres, F. 30 a, F. 30 b
prodire, vii. 81
prodixit diem, vi. 61
productio syllabarum (vel litterarum), v. 6; ix. 104
profanatum, vi. 54
profanum, vi. 54
profata, F. 28. 2
professi, vi. 55
Progne, v. 76
proiecta, v. porrecta
prolabitur, vi. 47
prolocutus, vi. 56
proloquium proloquia, F. 28. 2, 6, 7, 8
prolubium, F. 4
proludit, vi. 58
Prometheus, v. 31
promisce, F. 25
pronomen, viii. 45; ix. 94
pronuntiare, vi. 42, 58
Propontis, vii. 21
proportione vel pro portione, v. 170, 181; viii. 50, 68, 78, 80, 83; ix. 27, 29, 30, 33, 48, 61, 62, 83, 103, 110; x. 2, 9, 36, 37, 41, 42, 47, 51, 65, 66, 68; proportionem, viii. 57; cf. ratio
propositio, vi. 63, 76; v. putari
proprio nomine, vi. 55, 78
propter dextram sinistra, propter sinistram dextra, x. 59
prosapia, vii. 71
proscaenium, vi. 58
prosectum, v. 110
proserpere, v. 68
Proserpina, v. 68
prosicium, v. 110
prosus et rusus, x. 52
protinam, vii. 107
Protogenes, ix. 12
proversus, vii. 81
providere, vi. 96
provincia nostra, v. 16
provocabula, viii. 45
proximus a Flora clivus, v. 158
prudens, viii. 15, 17
psalterium, viii. 61
publici servi, v. libertini

Publicius Clivos, v. 158; Publicii aediles, v. 158
publicus, v. honor
Publius, v. Scipio
puer, vii. 28; viii. 41; x. 4; puer puella, viii. 25, ix. 29; pueri, vi. 56, ix. 10, 11, 15, 16
puera, F. 37
pugil, v. 94; pugiles, viii. 15
pugnetur pugnator, x. 32; v. volsillis
pulli, ix. 93; v. pipatus
Pullius Clivus, v. 158; Pullius viocurus, v. 158
pulmentarium, v. 108
pulmentum, v. 108
puls, v. 105, 107, 108, 127
pulvinar, v. 167
pulvini, ix. 48
pungo pupugi pungam, ix. 99; x. 48; pungo pupugi, F. 5. 6; pungebam pungo pungam, pupugeram pupugi pupugero, ix. 99
Punicum bellum, v. 159; Punicum malum, vii. 39
puppis puppes, viii. 66
purgamentum, v. februm
purgare (familiam), v. 23
purpura, v. 113
pusus pusa, vii. 28
putari, propositio putandi, vi. 63
putator, vi. 63
Puteoli, v. 25; Puteolis, ix. 69
putere, v. 96
puteus, v. 25; vi. 84; v. corona
puticuli, v. 25
putidus, v. 25
putiluci, v. 25
putor, v. 25
putum, vi. 63
Pyrrhi bellum, vii. 39
Pythagoras (artifex), v. 31
Pythonos tumulus, vii. 17

quadraginta, x. 43
quadrans, v. 44, 171, 172, 174
quadrigae, viii. 55; x. 24, 67; quadriga, x. 66; v. agitantur, initia
quadringenti, x. 43
quadrini, viii. 55
quadripertitio, v. 11; vii. 5; cf. v. 6, 12, viii. 50, ix. 31, x. 49
quadruplex fons, x. 22; natura, x. 41; analogia, x. 47, 48

663

INDEX

664

INDEX

respondendi, x. 31, 32 ; (species), x. 31, 32
respondet, vi. 69 ; respondere, vi. 72 ; respondere ad spontem, vi. 72 ; *v.* species
restibilis ager, v. 39
restipulari, v. 182
restis restes, viii. 66
rete, v. 130
reticulum, v. 130
reus, vi. 90 ; reus reei, viii. 70
rex regi, vi. 12, 13, 28, 31 ; x. 47 ; ad regem conveniebat populus, vi. 28 ; ferias rex edicit populo, vi. 28 ; *v.* Attalus, Aventinus, Demetrius, Hostilius, initia, Latinus, Pompilius, quando, recum, Romulus, Tatius, Tiberinus, Tullius
Rhea, v. 144
Rhodius ab Rhodo, viii. 81
rica, v. 130
ricinium, v. 132, 133
Ripaei montes, vii. 71
rite, vii. 88
ritu, vii. 88 ; *v.* Alcyonis, Etrusco, Graecus, Romanus
Robigalia, vi. 16
Robigo, vi. 16
rogandi (species), x. 31, 32
Roma, v. 33, 41, 45, 51, 56, 74, 101, 143, 144, 157, 164 ; vi. 15-17, 32 ; vii. 10 ; viii. 18, 56, 83 ; ix. 34 ; x. 15, 16, 20 ; Roma non Romula, viii. 80, ix. 50 ; Romae -am -a, x. 15
Romanula Porta, v. 164 ; vi. 24
Romanus, viii. 18, 83 ; x. 16 ; Romanus ager, v. 33, 55, 123 ; Romanus populus, vi. 86 ; Romano ritu, v. 130, vii. 88 ; Romani, vi. 25, vii. 3, viii. 56 (non Romenses), 83 ; Romanorum liberti, viii. 83 ; Romana stirps, v. 144
Romilia tribus, v. 56
Romulus, v. 9, 33, 46, 54, 55, 144, 149 ; viii. 18, 45, 80 ; ix. 34, 50 ; x. 15 ; Romulo -i -um, ix. 34 ; Romulus et Remus, v. 54 ; aedes Romuli, vi. 54
Romus, *v.* Romulus, v. 33
rorarii, vii. 58
rosa, v. 103
Rostra, v. 155 ; vi. 91
rosus, *v.* rusus

rudentum sibilus, **v. 7**
rudet, vii. 103
rufae (mulieres), vii. 83
ruminalis ficus, v. 54 '
runcina, vi. 96
runcinare, vi. 96
ruo ruis, ix. 109
rura, v. 40 ; rure, (*loc.*) F. 19, (*abl.*) F. 26
rustici, v. 177 ; vi. 68 ; vii. 73, 84, 96 ; rustica instrumenta, v. 134 ; *v.* pretor, Vinalia
rusus, *v.* prosus
ruta, v. 103
ruta caesa, ix. 104
rutilare, vii. 83
rutili rutilae, vii. 83
rutrum, v. 134
rutunda stagna, v. 26

S : R, vii. 26 ; S demptum, ix. 44 ; S detritum, v. 136 ; S extritum, vii. 97 ; *v.* C, G, L
Sabine, v. 159
Sabinus (ager), v. 123 ; Sabina lingua, v. 66, *cf.* 74 ; origo Sabina, vii. 28 ; Sabinum bellum, v. 149 ; Sabinum vocabulum, v. 107 ; Sabini cives, v. 159 ; Sabini, v. 32, 41, 68, 73, 74, 97, 107, vi. 5, 13, 28, vii. 29, 46, 77 ; Sabinae virgines, vi. 20 ; fana Sabina, vi. 57 ; *v.* Curtius, dies
sacellum, v. 152 ; *v.* Argei, Iupiter, Lares, Murtea, Strenia, Velabrum, Volupia ; aliquot sacra et sacella, vii. 84
sacer, vii. 10 ; *v.* dies, sacra, vas
sacerdos, sacerdotes, v. 83 ; vi. 16, 20, 21, 23 (nostri), 24 ; vii. 44 ; *v.* Liber
sacerdotulae, v. 130
sacra nostra, vi. 13 ; *v.* Argei, Bacchus, carnem, Nonalia, sacellum, tubae, tubicines
Sacra Via, v. 47, 152 ; *v.* caput
sacrae aedes, vii. 10
sacramentum, v. 180
sacraria, *v.* Argei, Ops Consiva
sacrificia, v. 98, 124 ; *v.* Argei
sacrifico sacrificor, sacrificabo, sacrificaturus aut sacrificatus sum, ix. 105 ; in sacrificando deis v. 122

665

INDEX

666

INDEX

667

INDEX

lare vocabulum, ix. 57, 69; *v.* gradus

singuli (homines), ix. 5, 6, 18, 114, 115; x. 74; singula, ix. 32

sinistra, *v.* auspicium, propter

sinum, v. 123; ix. 21

sirpando (=alligando), v. 137; sirpatur, v. 139

sirpata dolia, v. 137

sirpea, v. 139

sirpices, v. 136

sirpiculae, v. 137

siser, viii. 48

sisto, F. 36

sisymbrium, v. 103

siti, F. 18

socer soceri, ix. 91; socer socerum, x. 28; socer socrus soceros socrus, x. 82

societas verborum, v. 13; vi. 40; societatum servi, viii. 83

sodalis et sodalitas, x. 39; Sodales, *v.* Titii

Sol, v. 68(=Apollo), 74; ix. 24, 25; de sole, **v.** 59; solis motus, vi. 4, 8; *v.* novus, occasus

sola terrae, v. 22

solarium, vi. 4

solea, ix. 113

soleo solitus sum solui, ix. 107

solium, v. 128

solstitium, vi. 8; ix. 24, 25; *cf.* circulus

solu solum, vi. 2

soluta, *v.* oratio

solvunt (=luunt), **v.** 137; *v.* luo, trutina

sonant (arma), vi. 67

sonitus, vi. 84; *v.* similitudo

sonus vocis, vi. 84

sorbeo, vi. 84

sors, v. 183; vi. 65; sortes, 65, vii. 48

sortilegi, vi. 65

species, vi. 36; viii. 57; x. 13, 18, 79; species animalium, x. 4; nominatus, x. 21; usuis, x. 73; declinatuum (imperandi, optandi, personarum, respondendi, rogandi, temporalis), x. 31-33, *cf.* ix. 32; *v.* declinatus

specillum, vi. 82

specio, vi. 82; x. 18, 21, 79; specere, v. 129, vi. 82, *v.* avis

spectare, vi. 82

spectio, vi. 82

specula, vi. 82

speculator, vi. 82

speculor, vi. 82

speculum, v. 129; vi. 82

sperat, vi. 73; sperata, vi. 73

spes, vi. 73; *cf.* v. 37

spica, vi. 45; spicae, v. 37

spiceret, vii. 12

spondere, vi. 69-72

sponsa, vi. 69, 70

sponsalis, vi. 70

sponsio, vi. 70

sponsor, vi. 69, 74

sponsu, vi. 69, 70, 73; *v.* ago; sponsu alligatus, vi. 71

sponsus, vi. 70; vii. 107

sponte, vi. 69, 71-73; *v.* respondere, sine sponte

spumae, v. 63

Spurinna, x. 27

stadium, v. 11

stagnum, v. 26

stamen, v. 113

status, v. 11

statuti dies, vi. 25

stercum stercus, vi. 32

sternere, vi. 96

stillicidium, v. 27

stipare, v. 182

stipatores, vii. 52

stipendium, v. 182; *v.*|milites

stips, v. 182

stipulari, v. 182

stirps, *v.* Romanus; stirpes non stirpeis, F. 20

stiva, v. 135

sto, vi. 37

stola muliebris, viii. 28; x. 27; *cf.* ix. 48

stragulum, v. 167

strangulare, vi. 96

Streniae sacellum, v. 47

strenuitas, viii. 15

strenuus, viii. 17; strenui, viii. 15

strettillare, vii. 65

stribula, vii. 67

strigile, F. 18

stringere, vi. 96

strittabillae, vii. 65

strittare, vii. 65

strues (non strus), struis -em -i, viii. 74; ix. 79

INDEX

INDEX

670

INDEX

INDEX

INDEX

vesper, vi. 6; vii. 50; vesperi, ix. 73; vespere, ix. 73; *v.* novus
Vesperugo, vi. 6, 7; vii. 50
Vesta, v. 74; vi. 17; Vestae aedes, vi. 32
Vestales virgines, vi. 17, 21; virgo Vestalis Tarpeia, v. 41
Vestalia, vi. 17
vestibulum, vii. 81
vestigator, v. 94
vestimentum -ta, ix. 20, 48; x. 72
vestis, v. 130; veste, F. 18
vestispica, vii. 12
vestitus, v. 105; viii. 28, 30; *cf.* viii. 31, ix. 45
Veturi, *v.* Mamuri
Veturii Cicurini, vii. 91
vetus vetustius veterrimum, vi. 59; vetus consuetudo, v. 2, ix. 13, 20, 21, x. 73; Forum Vetus, vii. 29; veteres leges abrogatae, ix. 20; veteres, v. 14, 52 (poetae), 98 (nostri), vii. 32; vetera, x. 73; vetera vocabula, ix. 20; *v.* Aesculapii, Capitolium, Curia, verbum
vetustas, v. 3, 5; vi. 2
vexillum, vi. 93
via, v. 8, 22, 35; vii. 15; *v.* nova, sacra
viales, *v.* Lares
Vibenna, *v.* Caeles
vibices, vii. 63
vicessis, v. 170
Victoria, v. 62; caeligena, v. 62
victoriatus, ix. 85; x. 41
victrix Venus, v. 62
victus, v. 105
vicus, v. 8, 160; vici, v. 145; *v.* Africus, Cyprius, Insteianus, Sceleratus, Tuscus
video, vi. 80; tu domi videbis, vii. 12; vide, vii. 12
vieri (=vinciri), v. 62; versibus viendis, vii. 36
vigilant, vi. 80
vigilium, vi. 80
viginti, x. 41, 43, 45
villae, v. 35
villi, *v.* velli
Viminalis Collis, v. 51
Viminius Iupiter, v. 51
Vinalia, v. 13; vi. 16; rustica, vi. 20
vinaria mensa, v. 121; taberna,

viii. 55; vasa, v. 123; vinarium truleum, v. 118
vinciri, v. 62
vinclum, v. 62
vinctio, v. 61
vinctura, v. 62
vindemia, v. 37; vi. 16
vindemiator, v. 94
vineae, v. 37, 117
vineta, v. 37
vinum, v. 13, 37; vi. 16; vinum vina, ix. 66, 67; *v.* Chio, flamen, Lesbo
viocurus, v. 7, 158
violavit virginem, vi. 80
violentia, v. 70
vir, viii. 80; ix. 85; x. 4; vireis, viii. 36; *v.* centumvirum, decemvirum, quindecimviri, triumviri
virago, vii. 37
virgo virgines, *v.* Sabinus, Tarpeius, Vestales, violavit
virgultum, v. 102
viride, v. 102
virile virilia, viii. 46, 51; ix. 41, 48, 81, 110; x. 8, 21, 30; nomina virilia, viii. 36, x. 65; nomen virile, viii. 81, ix. 40, x. 65; *v.* tunica; *cf.* genus
virtus, v. 73
vis, v. 37, 61, 63, 70, 102; vi. 80; viii. 7; haec vis, huius vis, hae vis, F. 16; *v.* Venus, vita
visenda, vi. 82
visere, *v.* inlicium
Visolus, *v.* Poetelius
visus, vi. 80
vita a vi, v. 63; vita et mors, v 11; *v.* decernunt
vitio manumissus, creatus magistratus, vi. 30
vitis, v. 37, 102
Vitula, vii. 107
vitulantes, vii. 107
vitulus, v. 96; vituli, ix. 28; vituli vox, vii. 104
vivices, *v.* vibices
vivo non vivor, x. 78; vivatur viveretur, x. 32
vix, viii. 9; x. 14, 79, 80
vocabulum vocabula, vi. 56; viii. 11, 12, 40, 45, 52, 53, 56-59, 61, 64, 71, 75, 78, 79, 80; ix. 1, 9, 21, 34, 41, 50-52, 54, 55, 57, 58, 62, 63,

INDEX

INDEX OF GREEK WORDS

References are to Book (Roman numeral) and Section (Arabic number),
and to Fragment (F.) and serial number (Arabic), with subdivisions.

ἀγαθόν, v. φῶς
ἀγρόν, v. 34
ἀγών, vi. 12
ἀεὶ ὄν, vi. 11
αἴθεσθαι, vi. 9
αἰῶνα, vi. 11
ἀλεξίκακον, vii. 82
ἀλκυών, v. 79 ; vii. 88
ἄμαξαν, vii. 74
ἄμβωνες, v. 115
ἀμέλγειν, vi. 96
ἀμφίβια, v. 78
ἀναγαργαρίζεσθαι, vi. 96
ἀναλογία, x. 37, 39 ; ἀναλογίαν,
    x. 39 ; ἀναλογίας, viii. 23
ἀνὰ λόγον, viii. 32, 55 ; x. 2, 37
ἀνάλογον x. 37, 38, 39
ἀνδρὶ μάχεται, vii. 82
ἀνταρκτικόν, ix. 24
ἀντικείμενα, F. 28. 13
ἄντιμον, v. μοῖτον
ἀντίχθων Πυθαγόρα, vii. 17
ἀνωμαλίαν, vii. 23 ; v. περὶ ἀν-
    αξίωμα, F. 28. 2, 4, 7, 8, 9, 12
Ἀρίσταρχον, vi. 2
ἀρραβών, v. 175
ἀσπάραγος, v. 104

βαρβαρικά, v. νόμιμα
βοῦς, v. 96
βοώτην, vii. 74

γαυσάπης, F. 14 a ; F. 14 b
γέργερα, v. 76
γερουσία, v. 156
γεύεται, vi. 84
γίγνεται, vi. 96

δαμάζειν, vi. 96
δεικνύω, vi. 61
δεπέσταν, v. 123
δεψῆσαι, vi. 96
Δία, vi. 4
διεζευγμένον ἀξίωμα, F. 28. 12
Διόσκορον, v. 66
Δίωνα, vi. 2
δόμα, v. 175
δόνειον, v. 175
δόσιν, v. 175
δυνατοί, v. θεοί
δωτίνη, v. 175

ἔδω, vi. 84
ἐκβολή, vii. 108
ἐλαία, v. 108
ἔνην καὶ νέαν, vi. 10
ἔντερον, v. τυφλὸν
Ἑρμῆς, F. 14 b
ἔρρειν, vii. 96
ἑσπέρα, vi. 6
ἑσπέριον, vii. 50
ἑσπέρον, vi. 6
ἐτυμολογίαν, v. 2
ἐτυμολογική, vii. 109 ; ἐτυμο-
    λογικήν, v. 1
ἐτυμολόγον, v. 29
ἔτυμον, vi. 83 : vii. 82 ; ἔτυμα,
    vi 40, 51, vii. 2, 45, 82

ἦρ, vi. 9

θεοὶ δυνατοί, v. 58
Θέτις, vii. 87
θριάμβῳ, vi. 68

ἴθι, vi. 96
ἰταλός, v. 96
ἴτε, vi. 96

675

INDEX